# AAT

AQ2016
AAT PROFESSIONAL DIPLOMA IN
ACCOUNTING LEVEL 4

## QUESTION BANK

Management Accounting: Decision and Control

2016 Edition

For assessments from September 2016

First edition June 2016

ISBN 9781 4727 4855 3

**British Library Cataloguing-in-Publication Data**
A catalogue record for this book is available from the
British Library

**Published by**

BPP Learning Media Ltd
BPP House, Aldine Place
142-144 Uxbridge Road
London W12 8AA

www.bpp.com/learningmedia

Printed in the United Kingdom by Martins of Berwick

Sea View Works
Spittal
Berwick-Upon-Tweed
TD15 1RS

Your learning materials, published by BPP Learning
Media Ltd, are printed on paper obtained from traceable
sustainable sources.

The contents of this book are intended as a guide and
not for professional advice. Although every effort has
been made to ensure that the contents of this book are
correct at the time of going to press, BPP Learning
Media makes no warranty that the information in this
book is accurate or complete and accepts no liability for
any loss or damage suffered by any person acting or
refraining from acting as a result of the material in this
book.

We are grateful to the AAT for permission to reproduce
the sample assessment(s). The answers to the sample
assessment(s) have been published by the AAT. All
other answers have been prepared by BPP Learning
Media Ltd.

# CONTENTS

# INTRODUCTION

This is BPP Learning Media's AAT Question Bank for *Management Accounting: Decision and Control*. It is part of a suite of ground-breaking resources produced by BPP Learning Media for AAT assessments.

This Question Bank has been written in conjunction with the BPP Course Book, and has been carefully designed to enable students to practise all of the learning outcomes and assessment criteria for the units that make up *Management Accounting: Decision and Control.* It is fully up to date as at April 2016 and reflects both the AAT's qualification specification and the sample assessment provided by the AAT.

This Question Bank contains these key features:

- Tasks corresponding to each chapter of the Course Book. Some tasks are designed for learning purposes, others are of assessment standard

- AAT's AQ2016 sample assessment and answers for *Management Accounting Decision and Control* and further BPP practice assessments

The emphasis in all tasks and assessments is on the practical application of the skills acquired.

**VAT**

You may find tasks throughout this Question Bank that need you to calculate or be aware of a rate of VAT. This is stated at 20% in these examples and questions.

# Approaching the assessment

When you sit the assessment it is very important that you follow the on screen instructions. This means you need to carefully read the instructions, both on the introduction screens and during specific tasks.

When you access the assessment you should be presented with an introductory screen with information similar to that shown below (taken from the introductory screen from one of the AAT's AQ2016 Sample Assessments for *Management Accounting: Decision and Control*).

---

We have provided this **sample assessment** to help you familiarise yourself with our e-assessment environment. It is designed to demonstrate as many as possible of the question types that you may find in a live assessment. It is not designed to be used on its own to determine whether you are ready for a live assessment.

At the end of this sample assessment you will receive an immediate assessment result. This will only take into account your responses to tasks 1 - 5 and 7 - 9, as these are the elements of the assessment that are computer marked. In the live assessment, your responses to tasks 6 and 10 will be human marked.

---

Assessment information:

You have **2 hours and 30 minutes** to complete this sample assessment.

This assessment contains **10 tasks** and you should attempt to complete **every** task.
Each task is independent. You will not need to refer to your answers to previous tasks.
Read every task carefully to make sure you understand what is required.

Where the date is relevant, it is given in the task data.
Both minus signs and brackets can be used to indicate negative numbers **unless** task instructions say otherwise.

You must use a full stop to indicate a decimal point. For example, write 100.57 NOT 100,57 or 100 57
You may use a comma to indicate a number in the thousands, but you don't have to. For example, 10000 and 10,000 are both acceptable.

---

The actual instructions will vary depending on the subject you are studying for. It is very important you read the instructions on the introductory screen and apply them in the assessment. You don't want to lose marks when you know the correct answer just because you have not entered it in the right format.

In general, the rules set out in the AAT Sample Assessments for the subject you are studying for will apply in the real assessment, but you should carefully read the information on this screen again in the real assessment, just to make sure. This screen may also confirm the VAT rate used if applicable.

A full stop is needed to indicate a decimal point. We would recommend using minus signs to indicate negative numbers and leaving out the comma signs to indicate thousands, as this results in a lower number of key strokes and less margin for error when working under time pressure. Having said that, you can use whatever is easiest for you as long as you operate within the rules set out for your particular assessment.

You have to show competence throughout the assessment and you should therefore complete all of the tasks. Don't leave questions unanswered.

In some assessments, written or complex tasks may be human marked. In this case you are given a blank space or table to enter your answer into. You are told in the assessments which tasks these are (note: there may be none if all answers are marked by the computer).

If these involve calculations, it is a good idea to decide in advance how you are going to lay out your answers to such tasks by practising answering them on a word document, and certainly you should try all such tasks in this Question Bank and in the AAT's environment using the sample assessment.

When asked to fill in tables, or gaps, never leave any blank even if you are unsure of the answer. Fill in your best estimate.

Note that for some assessments where there is a lot of scenario information or tables of data provided (eg tax tables), you may need to access these via 'pop-ups'. Instructions will be provided on how you can bring up the necessary data during the assessment.

Finally, take note of any task specific instructions once you are in the assessment. For example you may be asked to enter a date in a certain format or to enter a number to a certain number of decimal places.

# Grading

To achieve the qualification and to be awarded a grade, you must pass all the mandatory unit assessments, all optional unit assessments (where applicable) and the synoptic assessment.

The AAT Level 4 Professional Diploma in Accounting will be awarded a grade. This grade will be based on performance across the qualification. Unit assessments and synoptic assessments are not individually graded. These assessments are given a mark that is used in calculating the overall grade.

## How overall grade is determined

You will be awarded an overall qualification grade (Distinction, Merit, and Pass). If you do not achieve the qualification you will not receive a qualification certificate, and the grade will be shown as unclassified.

The marks of each assessment will be converted into a percentage mark and rounded up or down to the nearest whole number. This percentage mark is then weighted according to the weighting of the unit assessment or synoptic assessment within the qualification. The resulting weighted assessment percentages are combined to arrive at a percentage mark for the whole qualification.

| Grade definition | Percentage threshold |
|---|---|
| Distinction | 90–100% |
| Merit | 80–89% |
| Pass | 70–79% |
| Unclassified | 0–69% |
| | Or failure to pass one or more assessment/s |

## Re-sits

**The AAT Professional Diploma In Accounting is not subject to re-sit restrictions.**

You should only be entered for an assessment when you are well prepared and you expect to pass the assessment.

# AAT qualifications

The material in this book may support the following AAT qualifications:

AAT Professional Diploma in Accounting Level 4, AAT Professional Diploma in Accounting at SCQF Level 8 and Certificate: Accounting (Level 5 AATSA).

# Supplements

From time to time we may need to publish supplementary materials to one of our titles. This can be for a variety of reasons. From a small change in the AAT unit guidance to new legislation coming into effect between editions.

You should check our supplements page regularly for anything that may affect your learning materials. All supplements are available free of charge on our supplements page on our website at:

www.bpp.com/learning-media/about/students

# Improving material and removing errors

There is a constant need to update and enhance our study materials in line with both regulatory changes and new insights into the assessments.

From our team of authors BPP appoints a subject expert to update and improve these materials for each new edition.

Their updated draft is subsequently technically checked by another author and from time to time non-technically checked by a proof reader.

We are very keen to remove as many numerical errors and narrative typos as we can but given the volume of detailed information being changed in a short space of time we know that a few errors will sometimes get though our net.

We apologise in advance for any inconvenience that an error might cause. We continue to look for new ways to improve these study materials and would welcome your suggestions. If you have any comments about this book, please email nisarahmed@bpp.com or write to Nisar Ahmed, AAT Head of Programme, BPP Learning Media Ltd, BPP House, Aldine Place, London W12 8AA.

# Question bank

## Chapter 1 – Costing techniques

### Task 1.1

At a production level of 16,000 units the production cost incurred totals £54,400. At a production level of 22,000 units the same cost totals £68,200.

**This is a variable cost. True or false? Tick the correct box.**

True ☐

False ☐

### Task 1.2

The following details are available for four types of costs at two activity levels:

| Cost type | Cost at 1,000 units | Cost at 1,500 units |
|---|---|---|
| I | £7,000 | £10,500 |
| II | £11,000 | £12,500 |
| III | £12,000 | £12,000 |
| IV | £3,800 | £5,700 |

**Complete the table to classify each cost by behaviour:**

| Cost | Behaviour |
|---|---|
| Cost I | |
| Cost II | |
| Cost III | |
| Cost IV | |

## Task 1.3

A manufacturing business anticipates that its variable costs and fixed costs will be £32,000 and £25,000 respectively at a production level of 10,000 units.

**Complete the table to show the total production cost and the cost per unit at each of the activity levels.**

| Activity level – units | Total production cost £ | Cost per unit £ |
|---|---|---|
| 8,000 | | |
| 12,000 | | |
| 15,000 | | |

## Task 1.4

The costs of a supervisor at a manufacturing company are £20,000. One supervisor is required per 750 units produced.

**Complete the table to show the total supervisors cost and the supervisors cost per unit at each of the activity levels.**

| Activity level – units | Total supervisors cost £ | Supervisors cost per unit £ |
|---|---|---|
| 500 | | |
| 1,000 | | |
| 1,500 | | |

## Task 1.5

**Given below are a number of types of cost – classify each one according to its behaviour:**

| | | Cost behaviour |
|---|---|---|
| (a) | Maintenance department costs which are made up of £25,000 of salaries and an average of £500 cost per call out. | |
| (b) | Machinery depreciation based upon machine hours used. | |
| (c) | Salary costs of nursery school teachers, where one teacher is required for every six children in the nursery. | |
| (d) | Rent for a building that houses the factory, stores and maintenance departments. | |

## Task 1.6

A business produces one product which requires the following inputs:

| | |
|---|---|
| Direct materials | 6 kg @ £4.80 per kg |
| Direct labour | 4 hours @ £7.00 per hour |
| Building costs | £18,000 per quarter |
| Leased machines | £600 for every 500 units of production |
| Stores costs | £3,000 per quarter plus £3.00 per unit |

(a) **Complete the table to show the total cost of production and the cost per unit at each of the quarterly production levels.**

| Production level – units | Total cost of production £ | Cost per unit £ |
|---|---|---|
| 1,000 | | |
| 1,500 | | |
| 2,000 | | |

(b) **Explain why the cost per unit is different at each level of production.**

## Task 1.7

The costs of a factory maintenance department appear to be partially dependent upon the number of machine hours operated each month. The machine hours and the maintenance department costs for the last six months are given below:

| | Machine hours | Maintenance cost |
|---|---|---|
| | | £ |
| June | 14,200 | 285,000 |
| July | 14,800 | 293,000 |
| August | 15,200 | 300,000 |
| September | 14,500 | 290,000 |
| October | 15,000 | 298,000 |
| November | 14,700 | 292,000 |

**The variable cost per machine hour is £** [ ]

**The fixed costs of the maintenance department are £** [ ]

## Task 1.8

The activity levels and related production costs for the last six months of 20X8 for a business have been as follows:

|  | Activity level | Production cost |
| --- | --- | --- |
|  | Units | £ |
| July | 63,000 | 608,000 |
| August | 70,000 | 642,000 |
| September | 76,000 | 699,000 |
| October | 73,000 | 677,000 |
| November | 71,000 | 652,000 |
| December | 68,000 | 623,000 |

(a)  **The fixed element of the production costs is £** [           ]

    **The variable element of the production costs per unit is £** [           ]

(b)  **Complete the table to show the estimated production costs at each of the levels of production.**

| Level of production – units | Production cost – £ |
| --- | --- |
| 74,000 |  |
| 90,000 |  |

(c)  **Comment upon which of the two estimates of production costs calculated in (b) is likely to be most accurate and why.**

- - - - - - - - - - - - - - - - - - - - - - - - - - - - - - - - - - - - - - - - - - - - - - - - - - - - - - - - - - - - - - - - - - - - - - - - - - - - - - -

## Task 1.9

The costs of the factory maintenance department for DF Ltd appear to have a variable element dependent upon the number of units produced. The fixed element of the costs steps up by £50,000 when 45,000 or more units are produced. The variable cost per unit is constant.

| Production volume (units) | £ |
| --- | --- |
| 40,000 | 205,000 |
| 48,000 | 279,000 |

(a) The variable element of the production costs per unit is £ ⬚

(b) Complete the table to show the fixed costs at each of the levels of production.

| Level of production – units | Fixed cost – £ |
|---|---|
| 40,000 | |
| 48,000 | |

## Task 1.10

The costs of the factory maintenance department for JEB Ltd appear to have a variable element dependent upon the number of units produced. The fixed element of the costs steps up when 10,000 or more units are produced. At an activity level of 12,000 units, the fixed element of the cost is £15,000. The variable cost per unit is constant.

| Production volume (units) | £ |
|---|---|
| 8,000 | 58,000 |
| 13,000 | 93,000 |

(a) What would be the total cost for 9,000 units? £ ⬚

(b) What would be the total cost for 11,000 units? £ ⬚

## Task 1.11

The costs of the factory maintenance department for HM Ltd appear to have a variable element dependent upon the number of units produced. The fixed element of the costs steps up when 20,000 or more units are produced. The variable cost per unit is constant at £25.

| Production volume (units) | £ |
|---|---|
| 18,000 | 468,000 |
| 22,000 | 570,000 |

(a) What would be the total cost for 19,000 units? £ ⬚

(b) What would be the total cost for 21,000 units? £ ⬚

## Task 1.12

The budgeted and actual results for the month of June 20X1 are as follows.

|  |  | Budget |  | Actual |
|---|---|---|---|---|
| Production (units of X07) |  | 14,000 |  | 13,500 |
| Direct materials | 17,500 litres | £28,875 | 16,800 litres | £106,000 |
| Direct labour | 3,500 hours | £59,500 | 3,650 hours | £65,700 |
| Fixed overheads (absorbed on a unit basis) |  | £77,000 |  | £79,500 |
| Total |  | £165,375 |  | £251,200 |

**Complete the following sentences:**

(a) The standard quantity of labour per unit is [            ] minutes.

(b) The budgeted quantity of materials needed to produce 13,500 units of X07 is [            ] litres.

(c) The budgeted labour hours to produce 12,000 units of X07 is [            ] hours.

(d) The budgeted labour cost to produce 13,500 units of X07 is £ [            ].

(e) The budgeted overhead absorption rate per unit is £ [            ].

A company budgeted to produce 25,000 units with fixed production costs of £436,250. The actual volume of production was 27,000 units and the actual fixed costs were £475,230.

(f) The fixed production overheads were [          ▼] by £ [            ].

**Picklist:**
Over absorbed
Under absorbed

## Task 1.13

A company budgeted to produce 55,000 units with fixed production costs of £233,750. The actual volume of production was 57,000 units and the actual fixed costs were £241,000.

**Complete the following sentence.**

The fixed production overheads were [          ▼] by [            ].

**Picklist:**
Over absorbed
Under absorbed

## Task 1.14

The budgeted overheads of a manufacturing business have been allocated and apportioned to the two production cost centres as follows:

Cutting                                    £58,600
Finishing                                  £42,400

The two production cost centres are budgeted to produce 10,000 units in the next period.

You are also provided with the following further information:

|  | Cutting | Finishing |
|---|---|---|
| Direct labour hours | 4,000 | 24,000 |
| Machine hours | 12,000 | 2,000 |
| Direct labour cost | £24,500 | £168,000 |
| Direct materials cost | £180,000 | £25,000 |
| Prime cost | £204,500 | £193,000 |

**Complete the following table to calculate overhead absorption rates for each of the two production cost centres. Choose from the picklist when each absorption rate would be appropriate. Give your answers to TWO decimal places.**

| Absorption rate method | Cutting rate £ | Finishing rate £ | Most appropriate 1, 2 or 3 |
|---|---|---|---|
| Rate per unit |  |  | ▼ |
| Rate per direct labour hour |  |  | ▼ |
| Rate per machine hour |  |  | ▼ |

**Picklist:**

1    Most appropriate in a largely mechanised department where most of the overhead relates to machinery costs.

2    Most appropriate where all products are of similar size and require a similar input in terms of time and resources of the departments.

3    Most appropriate in labour intensive departments where most of the overhead relates to labour.

## Task 1.15

The budgeted overheads apportioned to a business's two production cost centres, C and D, together with the budgeted labour hours and machine hours, are given below:

|  | C | D |
| --- | --- | --- |
| Overheads | £125,000 | £180,000 |
| Direct labour hours | 12,000 | 80,000 |
| Machine hours | 100,000 | 10,000 |

Production cost centre C is a highly mechanised department with only a few machine operatives whereas production cost centre D is a highly labour intensive department.

**(a) Complete the table to calculate separate departmental overhead absorption rates for each production cost centre using an appropriate basis.**

| Department | Overhead absorption rate £ |
| --- | --- |
| C | |
| D | |

**(b)** Each unit of Product P spends the following hours in each production department:

|  | C | D |
| --- | --- | --- |
| Direct labour hours | 1 | 7 |
| Machine hours | 5 | 2 |

**The overhead to be included in the cost of each unit of product P is £** [        ]

## Task 1.16

The costs of the canteen department of a manufacturing business are estimated to be £20,000 for the following quarter. Both the packaging and assembly departments use the canteen. They have 20 and 30 employees respectively, but 50% of the assembly department work nights, when the canteen is not open. The packaging department employees do not work nights.

**Complete the table below to show how much canteen overhead will be apportioned to each of the packaging and assembly departments.**

| Overhead apportioned to packaging department | £ |
| --- | --- |
| Overhead apportioned to assembly department | £ |

## Task 1.17

In each of the following situations calculate any under- or over-absorption of overheads and state whether this would be a debit or a credit in the statement of profit or loss (income statement):

| | Under-absorption £ | Over-absorption £ | Debit/Credit |
|---|---|---|---|
| Budgeted production was 1,200 units and budgeted overheads were £5,400. Overheads are to be absorbed on a unit basis. The actual production was 1,000 units and the overheads incurred were £5,000. | | | |
| Budgeted production was 600 units to be produced in 1,800 labour hours. Budgeted overheads of £5,040 are to be absorbed on a direct labour hour basis. The actual production for the period was 700 units in 2,200 labour hours and the actual overheads were £5,100. | | | |
| Budgeted production was 40,000 units and the budgeted machine hours were 2 hours per unit. Budgeted overheads were £320,000 and were to be absorbed on a machine hour basis. The actual overheads incurred were £320,000 and the production was 42,000 units. The total machine hours were 82,000. | | | |

## Task 1.18

A business produces a single product in its factory which has two production departments, cutting and finishing. In the following quarter it is anticipated that 120,000 units of the product will be produced. The expected costs are:

| | | |
|---|---|---|
| Direct materials | | £12 per unit |
| Direct labour | | 2 hours cutting @ £7.40 per hour |
| | | 1 hour finishing @ £6.80 per hour |
| Variable overheads | cutting | £336,000 |
| | finishing | £132,000 |
| Fixed overheads | cutting | £144,000 |
| | finishing | £96,000 |

Overheads are absorbed on the basis of direct labour hours.

**The unit cost under absorption costing will be £** [ ]

**The unit cost under marginal costing will be £** [ ]

## Task 1.19

Given below are the budgeted production and sales figures for the single product that a business makes and sells for the months of July and August.

|  | July | August |
|---|---|---|
| Production | 24,000 units | 24,000 units |
| Sales | 22,000 units | 25,000 units |

There was inventory of 1,500 units of the product at the start of July.

The expected production costs for each of the two months are as follows:

| Direct materials | £6.80 per unit |
|---|---|
| Direct labour | £3.60 per unit |
| Variable production costs | £32,400 |
| Fixed production costs | £44,400 |

Overheads are absorbed on the basis of the budgeted production level and the product is sold for £16 per unit.

**(a)** **The absorption costing profit for July was £** [ ]

**The absorption costing profit for August was £** [ ]

**The marginal costing profit for July was £** [ ]

**The marginal costing profit for August was £** [ ]

**(b)** **Prepare a reconciliation explaining any difference in the two profit figures in each of the two months.**

## Task 1.20

You are given the budgeted data about the production of a business's single product for the following quarter:

| | |
|---|---|
| Opening inventory | 840 units |
| Production | 8,000 units |
| Sales | 8,200 units |
| Direct materials | £23.60 |
| Direct labour | 4 hours @ £5.80 per hour |
| Variable overheads | £88,000 |
| Fixed overheads | £51,200 |

Overheads are absorbed on the basis of units of production. The product has a selling price of £70 per unit.

**(a)** **The profit for the quarter under absorption costing is** £ [          ]

   **The profit for the quarter under marginal costing is** £ [          ]

**(b)** **Prepare a reconciliation explaining any difference in the profit using absorption costing and profit using marginal costing.**

......................................................................................................

# Chapter 2 – Statistical techniques

## Task 2.1

Given below are the production cost figures for the last ten months. **Calculate a three month moving average for these figures. Give your answer to the nearest whole £.**

|  | Production costs | Three month moving total | Three month moving average |
|---|---|---|---|
|  | £ | £ | £ |
| March | 104,500 |  |  |
| April | 110,300 |  |  |
| May | 112,800 |  |  |
| June | 109,400 |  |  |
| July | 117,600 |  |  |
| August | 116,000 |  |  |
| September | 119,200 |  |  |
| October | 122,300 |  |  |
| November | 120,500 |  |  |
| December | 119,300 |  |  |

## Task 2.2

A new restaurant has recently been opened which only trades for five days a week. The takings have been increasing rapidly over the first four weeks since opening, as given below.

**Complete the table to calculate the five day moving average and the daily seasonal variations in accordance with the additive model.**

| | | Actual | 5-day moving average – trend | Seasonal variation (actual – trend) |
|---|---|---|---|---|
| | | £ | £ | £ |
| Week 1 | Day 1 | 600 | | |
| | Day 2 | 700 | | |
| | Day 3 | 1,000 | | |
| | Day 4 | 1,200 | | |
| | Day 5 | 1,500 | | |
| Week 2 | Day 1 | 680 | | |
| | Day 2 | 750 | | |
| | Day 3 | 1,250 | | |
| | Day 4 | 1,400 | | |
| | Day 5 | 1,860 | | |
| Week 3 | Day 1 | 820 | | |
| | Day 2 | 1,030 | | |
| | Day 3 | 1,940 | | |
| | Day 4 | 2,100 | | |
| | Day 5 | 2,500 | | |
| Week 4 | Day 1 | 1,000 | | |
| | Day 2 | 1,320 | | |
| | Day 3 | 1,560 | | |
| | Day 4 | 2,290 | | |
| | Day 5 | 2,670 | | |

## Task 2.3

Given below are the quarterly sales figures for a small business.

**Complete the table to calculate the trend using a four month centred moving average and the seasonal variations using the additive model. Give your answers to the nearest whole £.**

|  |  | Actual | 4-quarter moving average | Centred moving average – trend | Seasonal variations |
|---|---|---|---|---|---|
|  |  | £ | £ | £ | £ |
| 20X5 | Quarter 3 | 50,600 |  |  |  |
|  | Quarter 4 | 52,800 |  |  |  |
| 20X6 | Quarter 1 | 55,600 |  |  |  |
|  | Quarter 2 | 48,600 |  |  |  |
|  | Quarter 3 | 51,200 |  |  |  |
|  | Quarter 4 | 53,900 |  |  |  |
| 20X7 | Quarter 1 | 58,000 |  |  |  |
|  | Quarter 2 | 49,800 |  |  |  |
|  | Quarter 3 | 53,000 |  |  |  |
|  | Quarter 4 | 54,600 |  |  |  |
| 20X8 | Quarter 1 | 60,100 |  |  |  |
|  | Quarter 2 | 50,700 |  |  |  |
|  | Quarter 3 | 54,200 |  |  |  |
|  | Quarter 4 | 55,200 |  |  |  |

## Task 2.4

A business uses time series analysis and has found that the predicted trend of sales for the next four quarters and historical seasonal variations are as follows:

|  | Predicted trend | Seasonal variation |
| --- | --- | --- |
|  | £ | £ |
| Quarter 1 | 418,500 | +21,500 |
| Quarter 2 | 420,400 | +30,400 |
| Quarter 3 | 422,500 | −16,700 |
| Quarter 4 | 423,800 | −35,200 |

**What are the predicted actual sales figures for these four quarters?**

|  | Predicted trend |
| --- | --- |
|  | £ |
| Quarter 1 |  |
| Quarter 2 |  |
| Quarter 3 |  |
| Quarter 4 |  |

## Task 2.5

Given below are the production cost figures for a business and the Retail Price Index for the last six months.

(a) **Complete the table to show the production cost figures in terms of January's prices. Give your answers to the nearest whole £.**

| | Actual costs | RPI | Workings | Costs at January prices |
|---|---|---|---|---|
| | £ | | | £ |
| January | 129,600 | 171.1 | | |
| February | 129,700 | 172.0 | | |
| March | 130,400 | 172.2 | | |
| April | 131,600 | 173.0 | | |
| May | 130,500 | 174.1 | | |
| June | 131,600 | 174.3 | | |

(b) **Complete the table to show the production cost figures in terms of June's prices. Give your answers to the nearest whole £.**

| | Actual costs | RPI | Workings | Costs at June prices |
|---|---|---|---|---|
| | £ | | | £ |
| January | 129,600 | 171.1 | | |
| February | 129,700 | 172.0 | | |
| March | 130,400 | 172.2 | | |
| April | 131,600 | 173.0 | | |
| May | 130,500 | 174.1 | | |
| June | 131,600 | 174.3 | | |

## Task 2.6

Given below are the quarterly sales figures for a business for the last two years. **Complete the table in order to calculate an index for these sales with quarter 1 20X7 as the base period. Give your answers to ONE decimal place.**

|  |  | Actual | Workings | Index |
|---|---|---|---|---|
|  |  | £ |  |  |
| 20X7 | Quarter 1 | 126,500 |  |  |
|  | Quarter 2 | 130,500 |  |  |
|  | Quarter 3 | 131,400 |  |  |
|  | Quarter 4 | 132,500 |  |  |
| 20X8 | Quarter 1 | 133,100 |  |  |
|  | Quarter 2 | 135,600 |  |  |
|  | Quarter 3 | 136,500 |  |  |
|  | Quarter 4 | 137,100 |  |  |

## Task 2.7

AB Ltd set the standard cost of material C at £3.50 per litre when an index of material prices stood at 115. The index now stands at 145.

**The updated standard cost for material C is £** [          ]

**Give your answer to TWO decimal places.**

## Task 2.8

The direct materials cost for quarter 1 and quarter 2 of next year have been estimated in terms of current prices at £657,000 and £692,500 respectively. The current price index for these materials is 126.4 and the price index is estimated as 128.4 for quarter 1 of next year and 131.9 for quarter 2.

**What are the forecast direct materials costs for quarters 1 and 2 of next year?**

Quarter 1 £ [          ]

Quarter 2 £ [          ]

**Give your answers to the nearest whole £.**

## Task 2.9

You have been given an equation and information to estimate the cost of a raw material for January and February 20X9.

The equation is Y = a + bX, where:

- X is the time period in months
- The value for X in November 20X8 is 29
- The value for X in December 20X8 is 30
- Y is the cost of the raw material
- The constant 'a' is 9 and constant 'b' is 0.1

**Complete the table to calculate the expected price of the raw material per kilogram for January and February 20X9. Give your answer to TWO decimal places.**

| January 20X9 | £ |
|---|---|
| February 20X9 | £ |

## Task 2.10

The total production cost varies linearly with the volume of production, and so can be described by the linear regression equation:

y = a + bx

where x is the volume of production.

**If the total production cost of 100 units is £2,500, and the total production cost of 1,000 units is £7,000, what are the values of a and b?**

a £ [                    ]

b £ [                    ]

**The total production cost for 750 units is £** [                    ]

## Task 2.11

The linear regression equation for production costs for a business is:

y = 138,000 + 6.4x

where x is the number of units.

**If production is expected to be 105,000 units in the next quarter the anticipated production costs are £** [                    ]

## Task 2.12

The linear regression equation for the power costs of a factory is given as follows:

$y = 80,000 + 0.5x$

where x is the number of machine hours used in a period.

The anticipated machine hours for April are 380,000 hours.

**The anticipated power costs for April are £** ⬜

## Task 2.13

The linear regression equation for the trend of sales in thousands of units per month based upon time series analysis of the figures for the last two years is:

$y = 3.1 + 0.9x$

**What is the estimated sales trend for each of the first three months of year 3?**

Month 1 ⬜ units

Month 2 ⬜ units

Month 3 ⬜ units

## Task 2.14

A time series analysis of sales volumes each quarter for the last three years, 20X6 to 20X8, has identified the trend equation as follows:

$y = 400 + 105x$

where y is the sales volume and x is the time period.

The seasonal variations for each quarter have been calculated as:

| | |
|---|---|
| Quarter 1 | −175 |
| Quarter 2 | +225 |
| Quarter 3 | +150 |
| Quarter 4 | −200 |

**Estimate the actual sales volume for each quarter of 20X9.**

Quarter 1 ⬜ units

Quarter 2 ⬜ units

Quarter 3 ⬜ units

Quarter 4 ⬜ units

## Task 2.15

You have been given an equation and information to estimate the cost of raw materials for the coming two months.

The equation is Y = a + bX, where

- X is the time period in months
- The value for X in May 20X8 is 25
- Y is the cost of raw materials
- The constant 'a' is 125 and constant 'b' is 2

The cost of raw materials is set on the first day of each month and is not changed during the month. The cost of the raw materials in May 20X8 was £175 per tonne.

(a) **Calculate the expected price of the raw material per tonne for June and July 20X8.**

| June cost per tonne (£) | |
|---|---|
| July cost per tonne (£) | |

(b) **Convert the raw materials prices per tonne for June and July to index numbers using May 20X8 as the base (correct to two decimal places).**

| June index | |
|---|---|
| July index | |

## Task 2.16

The relationship between distribution costs (y) and output of production and sales (x) can be described by the equation:

y = a + bx

You are given the following distribution costs at two different levels of output:

| Output (x) | Distribution costs (y) |
|---|---|
| 1,500 | 14,500 |
| 3,000 | 19,000 |

(a) **Calculate the values of a and b, using the two activity levels.**

| | £ |
|---|---|
| a | |
| b | |

**Question bank**

(b) Use the values of a and b in the equation to determine the distribution costs at the following activity levels.

| Output | £ |
|---|---|
| 2,000 units | |
| 4,000 units | |

(c) Complete the following sentence:

The value of distribution costs for [     ▼] units is most accurate.

**Picklist:**

2,000
4,000

........................................................................................................

## Task 2.17

The cost per kilogram for a raw material used in the production of product TNG for the last three months is shown below:

| Month | Actual price £ | Seasonally adjusted price £ |
|---|---|---|
| 1 | 985 | 1,040 |
| 2 | 1,223 | 1,015 |
| 3 | 1,150 | 990 |

(a) Complete the sentences below.

The trend in prices is [     ▼] of £ [          ] per month.

The seasonal variation for month 1 is [     ▼] of £ [          ].

**Picklist:**

A decrease
An increase

Production costs for product MIN2 are semi-variable. The company uses the regression equation y = a + bx to forecast costs where:

y = total costs

x = units

a = fixed element

b = variable element

BPP
LEARNING MEDIA

23

Data has been gathered on previous costs:

| Units (x) | Total cost (y) £ |
|-----------|------------------|
| 8,000     | 52,000           |
| 12,000    | 72,000           |
| 13,500    | 79,500           |

**(b)** **Using the data provided and the regression equation, calculate the values of a and b.**

| a = £ | |
|-------|--|
| b = £ | |

A labour rate index is used to forecast labour costs. The index base was set when the hourly rate was £12.

**(c)** **Complete the table below to forecast the hourly labour rate for each month to the nearest penny.**

| Month | Index number | Forecast hourly rate £ |
|-------|--------------|------------------------|
| March | 103.9        |                        |
| April | 105.2        |                        |
| May   | 105.7        |                        |

**(d)** **Based on your calculations in part (c), forecast the total labour cost for April assuming that 1,920 hours are worked.**

The forecast total labour cost for April is £ _____

........................................................................................................

# Chapter 3 – Standard costing

## Task 3.1

Write a brief memo to a new accounts assistant explaining what factors should be taken into account when setting the standard cost of labour for a product.

**MEMORANDUM**

To:         New Accounts Assistant

From:       Accountant

Date:       xx/xx/xx

Subject:    **Setting the standard cost of labour**

..................................................................................................

## Task 3.2

XYZ Ltd is planning to make 120,000 units per period of a new product. The following standards have been set.

|  |  | **Per unit** |
|---|---|---|
| Direct material A |  | 1.2 kgs at £11 per kg |
| Direct material B |  | 4.7 kgs at £6 per kg |
| Direct labour: | Operation 1 | 42 minutes |
|  | Operation 2 | 37 minutes |
|  | Operation 3 | 11 minutes |

Overheads are absorbed at the rate of £30 per labour hour. All direct operatives are paid at the rate of £8 per hour.

**What is the standard cost of one unit?**

£41.40 ☐

£53.40 ☐

£83.40 ☐

£98.40 ☐

..................................................................................................

## Task 3.3

The budgeted and actual results for the month of June 20X1 are as follows.

| | | Budget | | Actual |
|---|---|---|---|---|
| Production (units of XX6) | | 14,000 | | 13,500 |
| Direct materials | 17,500 L | £28,875 | 16,800 L | £106,000 |
| Direct labour | 3,500 hours | £59,500 | 3,650 hours | £65,700 |
| Fixed overheads (absorbed on a unit basis) | | £77,000 | | £79,500 |
| Total | | £165,375 | | £251,200 |

**Complete the standard cost card for the production of 1 unit of XX6.**

| 1 units of XX6 | Quantity | Cost per unit £ | Total £ |
|---|---|---|---|
| Materials | | | |
| Labour | | | |
| Fixed overheads | | | |
| Total | | | |

# Chapter 4 – Variance analysis

## Task 4.1

A business budgeted to produce 2,680 units of one of its products during the month of May. The product uses 5 kg of raw material with a standard cost of £4.00 per kg. During the month the actual production was 2,800 units using 14,400 kg of raw materials costing £60,480.

**Calculate the following variances:**

| | Variance £ | Adverse/Favourable |
|---|---|---|
| Total materials cost variance | | |
| Materials price variance | | |
| Materials usage variance | | |

## Task 4.2

A business has the following standard cost card for one unit of its product:

| | | |
|---|---|---|
| Direct materials | 4 kg @ £3 per kg | £12 |
| Direct labour | 3 hours @ £9 per hour | £27 |
| Fixed overheads | 3 hours @ £4 per hour | £12 |

The budgeted production level is 12,000 units.

The actual results for the period are:

| | |
|---|---|
| Production | 11,400 units |
| Materials 44,800 kgs | £150,480 |

**Calculate the following variances:**

| | Variance £ | Adverse/Favourable |
|---|---|---|
| Total materials cost variance | | |
| Materials price variance | | |
| Materials usage variance | | |

## Task 4.3

Production of product Z1 for the month of November in a manufacturing business was 12,100 units using 54,900 hours of direct labour costing £410,200. The standard cost card shows that the standard labour input for a unit of Z1 is 4.5 hours at a rate of £7.30 per hour.

**Calculate the following variances:**

| | Variance £ | Adverse/Favourable |
|---|---|---|
| Total labour cost variance | | |
| Labour rate variance | | |
| Labour efficiency variance | | |

## Task 4.4

Production of product X for the month of January was 10,680 units using 53,600 hours of direct labour costing £531,800. The standard cost card shows that the standard labour input for a unit of X is 5 hours at a rate of £10 per hour.

**Calculate the following variances:**

| | Variance £ | Adverse/Favourable |
|---|---|---|
| Total labour cost variance | | |
| Labour rate variance | | |
| Labour efficiency variance | | |

## Task 4.5

A business has the following standard cost card for one unit of its product:

| | | |
|---|---|---|
| Direct materials | 4 kg @ £3 per kg | £12 |
| Direct labour | 3 hours @ £9 per hour | £27 |
| Fixed overheads | 3 hours @ £4 per hour | £12 |

The budgeted production level is 12,000 units.

The actual results for the period are:

| | |
|---|---|
| Production | 11,400 units |
| Labour 34,700 hours | £316,400 |

**Calculate the following variances:**

|  | Variance £ | Adverse/Favourable |
|---|---|---|
| Total labour cost variance |  |  |
| Labour rate variance |  |  |
| Labour efficiency variance |  |  |

## Task 4.6

A business has budgeted to produce and sell 10,000 units of its single product. The standard cost per unit is as follows:

| Direct materials | £18 |
|---|---|
| Direct labour | £13 |
| Fixed production overhead | £7 |

During the period the actual results were:

| Production and sales | 11,500 units |
|---|---|
| Fixed production overheads | £75,000 |

**The fixed overhead expenditure variance is £** ☐

**The fixed overhead volume variance is £** ☐

## Task 4.7

A business has a single product into which fixed overheads are absorbed on the basis of labour hours. The standard cost card shows that fixed overheads are to be absorbed on the basis of 6 labour hours per unit at a rate of £7.60 per hour. The budgeted level of production is 50,000 units.

The actual results for the period were that fixed overheads were £2,200,000, the actual hours worked were 310,000 and the actual units produced were 52,000.

**Calculate the following variances:**

|  | Variance £ | Adverse/Favourable |
|---|---|---|
| Fixed overhead expenditure variance |  |  |
| Fixed overhead volume variance |  |  |
| Fixed overhead efficiency variance |  |  |
| Fixed overhead capacity variance |  |  |

## Task 4.8

A business incurred fixed overheads of £203,000 in the month of May. The fixed overheads are absorbed into units of production at the rate of £3.60 per direct labour hour. The actual production during the month was 13,200 units although the budget had been for 14,000 units. The standard labour cost for the production is 4 hours per unit at an hourly rate of £8.00. During the month 50,000 labour hours were worked at a total cost of £403,600.

**Calculate the following figures:**

**(a)  The budgeted fixed overhead for the month was £** [        ]

**(b)  The fixed overhead expenditure variance was £** [        ]

**(c)  The fixed overhead volume variance was £** [        ]

**(d)  The fixed overhead efficiency variance was £** [        ]

**(e)  The fixed overhead capacity variance was £** [        ]

## Task 4.9

The standard cost card for a business's product is shown below:

|  | £ |
|---|---|
| Direct materials 4.8 kg at £2.80 per kg | 13.44 |
| Direct labour 2.5 hours at £8.50 per hour | 21.25 |
| Fixed overheads 2.5 hours at £1.60 per hour | 4.00 |
|  | 38.69 |

The budgeted production was for 1,100 units in the month of July. The actual costs during the month of July for the production of 1,240 units were as follows:

|  | £ |
|---|---|
| Direct materials 5,800 kg | 17,100 |
| Direct labour 3,280 hours | 27,060 |
| Fixed overheads | 4,650 |

The following variances have been calculated:

| Materials price | £860 Adv |
|---|---|
| Materials usage | £426 Fav |
| Labour rate | £820 Fav |
| Labour efficiency | £1,530 Adv |
| Fixed overhead expenditure | £250 Adv |
| Fixed overhead efficiency | £288 Adv |
| Fixed overhead capacity | £848 Fav |

Calculate the budgeted cost of 1,240 units of production and insert the variances in the correct place in the following operating statement. Total the variances and reconcile the budgeted cost of actual production to the actual cost of actual production.

| | Favourable £ | Adverse £ | Total £ |
|---|---|---|---|
| **Budgeted cost of actual production** | | | |
| **Variances** | | | |
| Materials price | | | |
| Materials usage | | | |
| Labour rate | | | |
| Labour efficiency | | | |
| Fixed overhead expenditure | | | |
| Fixed overhead efficiency | | | |
| Fixed overhead capacity | _____ | _____ | _____ |
| **Total variances** | | | |
| **Actual cost of actual production** | | | |

## Task 4.10

A manufacturing company has provided you with the following data which relates to component RYX, for the period which has just ended.

| | Budget | Actual |
|---|---|---|
| Number of labour hours | 8,400 | 7,980 |
| Production units | 1,200 | 1,100 |
| Overhead cost (all fixed) | £22,260 | £25,536 |

Overheads are absorbed at a rate per standard labour hour.

**Which of the following is the overhead capacity variance?**

£5,131 Adverse ☐

£3,276 Adverse ☐

£742 Adverse ☐

£1,113 Adverse ☐

## Task 4.11

You are employed as part of the management accounting team in a large industrial company which operates a four-weekly system of management reporting. Your division makes a single product, the Omega, and, because of the nature of the production process, there is no work in progress at any time.

The group management accountant has completed the calculation of the material and labour standard costing variances for the current period to 1 April but has not had the time to complete any other variances. Details of the variances already calculated are reproduced in the working papers below, along with other standard costing data.

| Standard costing and budget data – four weeks ended 1 April | | | |
|---|---|---|---|
| | | Quantity | Unit price £ | Cost per unit £ |
| Material (kgs) | | 7 | 25.00 | 175 |
| Labour (hours) | | 40 | 7.50 | 300 |
| Fixed overheads (hours) | | 40 | 12.50 | 500 |
| | | | | 975 |
| | | Units | Standard unit cost | Standard cost of production |
| Budgeted production for the four weeks | | 4,100 | £975 | £3,997,500 |

### Working papers

### Actual production and expenditure for the four weeks ended 1 April

| | |
|---|---|
| Units produced | 3,850 |
| Cost of 30,000 kgs of materials consumed | £795,000 |
| Cost of 159,000 labour hours worked | £1,225,000 |
| Expenditure on fixed overheads | £2,195,000 |

### Calculate the following variances.

(a) The fixed overhead expenditure variance
(b) The fixed overhead volume variance
(c) The fixed overhead capacity variance
(d) The fixed overhead efficiency variance

## Task 4.12

The variable production overhead cost of product X is as follows:

2 hours at £1.50 = £3 per unit

During period 6, 400 units of product X were made. The labour force worked 760 hours. The variable overhead cost was £1,230.

**Calculate the following variances:**

| | Variance £ | Adverse/Favourable |
|---|---|---|
| Total variable production overhead total variance | | |
| Variable production overhead expenditure variance | | |
| Variable production overhead efficiency variance | | |

## Task 4.13

P Co, a manufacturing firm, operates a standard marginal costing system. It makes a single product, PG, using a single raw material.

Standard costs relating to PG have been calculated as follows.

| Standard cost schedule – PG | Per unit £ |
|---|---|
| Direct material, 100 kg at £5 per kg | 500 |
| Direct labour, 10 hours at £8 per hour | 80 |
| Variable production overhead, 10 hours at £2 per hour | 20 |
| | 600 |

The standard selling price of a PG is £900 and P Co plan to produce and sell 1,020 units a month.

During December 20X0, 1,000 units of PG were produced and sold. Relevant details of this production are as follows.

**Direct material**

90,000 kgs costing £720,000 were bought and used.

**Direct labour**

8,200 hours were worked during the month and total wages were £63,000.

**Variable production overhead**

The actual cost for the month was £25,000.

(a)   The variable production cost variance for December 20X0 is £ ⬚

(b)   (i)   The direct labour rate variance is £ ⬚

       (ii)  The direct labour efficiency variance is £ ⬚

(c)   (i)   The direct material price variance is £ ⬚

       (ii)  The direct material usage variance is £ ⬚

(d)   (i)   The variable production overhead expenditure variance is £ ⬚

       (ii)  The variable production overhead efficiency variance is £ ⬚

## Task 4.14

Bedworth Co has the following cost card for unit of product C.

| Direct materials | 5kg @ £2 per kg | £10 |
| Direct labour | 2 hours @ £8 per hour | £16 |
| Fixed overheads | 2 hours @ £4 per hour | £8 |

The budgeted level of production is 12,000 units. The actual results for the period are:

| Production | 11,400 units |
| Materials | 45,600 kg costing £136,800 |
| Labour | 11,400 hours costing £79,800 |
| Fixed overheads | £95,000 |

(a)   **Prepare a reconciliation of the budgeted material cost with the actual material cost using the material cost variances.**

| Standard cost of materials for actual production | | | |
|---|---|---|---|
| Variances | Favourable | Adverse | |
| Direct material price variance | | | |
| Direct material usage variance | | | |
| Total variance | | | |
| Actual cost of materials for actual production | | | |

(b) **Prepare a reconciliation of the budgeted labour cost with the actual labour cost using the labour cost variances.**

| Standard cost of labour for actual production | | | |
|---|---|---|---|
| Variances | Favourable | Adverse | |
| Direct labour rate variance | | | |
| Direct labour efficiency variance | | | |
| Total variance | | | |
| Actual cost of labour for actual production | | | |

(c) **Prepare a reconciliation of the budgeted fixed overhead cost with the actual fixed overhead cost using the fixed overhead cost variances.**

| Standard cost of fixed overhead for actual production | | | |
|---|---|---|---|
| Variances | Favourable | Adverse | |
| Fixed overhead expenditure variance | | | |
| Fixed overhead volume variance | | | |
| Total variance | | | |
| Actual cost of fixed overhead for actual production | | | |

## Task 4.15

You are given the following information about a manufacturing company.

| | |
|---|---|
| Budgeted overheads | £810,000 |
| Budgeted output | 27,000 units |
| Budgeted hours | 108,000 hours |
| Actual output | 29,000 units |
| Actual hours | 118,000 hours |
| Actual overheads | £834,500 |

**Calculate the fixed overhead capacity and efficiency variances from the information in the table above.**

## Task 4.16

A company purchases and uses 200,000 litres of material at a cost of £0.55 per litre. The budgeted production was 22,000 units which requires 220,000 litres of material at a total standard cost of £132,000. The actual production was 19,000 units.

**(a) Complete the following statement.**

The material usage variance is £ [          ] [                    ▼]

**Picklist:**

Adverse
Favourable

A company expects to produce 10,000 units of X using 6,000 hours of labour. The standard cost of labour is £15 per hour. The actual output was 12,000 units. 6,900 hours of labour were worked at a total cost of £105,850.

**(b) Complete the following statement.**

The total labour efficiency variance is £ [          ] [                    ▼]

**Picklist:**

Adverse
Favourable

## Task 4.17

Bert manufactures product RPB. Bert operates a standard cost system in which production overheads are fixed and absorbed on a unit basis.

The budgeted activity is for the production of 28,000 units at a total fixed production cost of £350,000. The actual volume of production was 30,000 units and the fixed overhead expenditure variance was £35,000 favourable.

**Complete the following sentences.**

**(a)** The fixed overhead volume variance is £ [          ] [                    ▼]

**Picklist:**

Adverse
Favourable

**(b)** The actual fixed production overheads incurred were £ [          ].

Ernie manufactures product RTF. The budgeted activity and actual results for the month are as follows.

| | Budget | Actual |
|---|---|---|
| Production units (RTF) | 64,000 | 67,000 |
| Direct labour costs | £5,760,000 | £5,896,000 |
| Fixed overheads | £3,840,000 | £3,950,000 |

Overheads are absorbed on a labour hour basis and the budget uses 480,000 labour hours. The actual labour hours used to produce 67,000 units totalled 536,000 labour hours.

**(c) Calculate the following variances.**

| Variance | Amount £ | Sign |
|---|---|---|
| Fixed overhead capacity | | ▼ |
| Fixed overhead efficiency | | ▼ |

**Picklist:**

Adverse
Favourable

## Task 4.18

The budgeted activity and actual results for the month of August 20X1 are as follows:

| | Budget | | Actual | |
|---|---|---|---|---|
| Production (KK1) | | 18,000 | | 15,000 |
| Direct materials | 9,000 kg | £60,750 | 7,800 kg | £55,770 |
| Direct labour | 5,400 hours | £47,250 | 4,230 hours | £38,070 |
| Fixed overheads | | £76,500 | | £71,300 |
| Total cost | | £184,500 | | £165,140 |

**Complete the following table.**

| Variance | Amount £ | Adverse/Favourable |
|---|---|---|
| Direct material usage variance | | ▼ |
| Direct material price variance | | ▼ |
| Total direct labour variance | | ▼ |

**Picklist:**

Adverse
Favourable

## Task 4.19

Albert manufactures product BRP. Albert operates a standard cost system in which production overheads are fixed and absorbed on a unit basis.

The budgeted activity and actual results for the month are as follows:

| | Budget | Actual |
|---|---|---|
| Production units (BRP) | 25,000 | 27,000 |
| Fixed overheads | £1,043,750 | £947,500 |

**(a) Calculate the following variances.**

| Variance | Amount £ | Sign |
|---|---|---|
| Fixed overhead expenditure | | ▼ |
| Fixed overhead volume | | ▼ |

**Picklist:**

Adverse
Favourable

Gordon manufactures product PHT. The budgeted activity and actual results for the month are as follows:

| | Budget | Actual |
|---|---|---|
| Production units (PHT) | 54,000 | 50,000 |
| Fixed overheads | £1,350,000 | £947,500 |

Overheads are absorbed on a labour hour basis and the budgeted production was 54,000 using 270,000 labour hours. The actual labour hours used to produce 50,000 units totalled 265,000 labour hours.

**(b) Calculate the following variance.**

| Variance | Amount £ | Sign |
|---|---|---|
| Fixed overhead capacity | | ▼ |
| Fixed overhead efficiency | | ▼ |

**Picklist:**

Adverse
Favourable

# Chapter 5 – Operating statements

## Task 5.1

You are employed as a management accountant in the head office of Travel Holdings plc. Travel Holdings owns a number of transport businesses. One of them is Travel Ferries Ltd. Travel Ferries operates ferries which carry passengers and vehicles across a large river. Each year, standard costs are used to develop the budget for Travel Ferries Ltd. The latest budgeted and actual operating results are reproduced below.

| Travel Ferries Ltd | | | | |
|---|---|---|---|---|
| **Budgeted and actual operating results for the year to 30 November 20X8** | | | | |
| **Operating data** | | *Budget* | | *Actual* |
| Number of ferry crossings | | 6,480 | | 5,760 |
| Operating hours of ferries | | 7,776 | | 7,488 |
| **Cost data** | | £ | | £ |
| Fuel | 1,244,160 litres | 497,664 | 1,232,800 litres | 567,088 |
| Labour | 93,312 hours | 699,840 | 89,856 hours | 696,384 |
| Fixed overheads | | 466,560 | | 472,440 |
| Cost of operations | | 1,664,064 | | 1,735,912 |

**Other accounting information**

- Fuel and labour are variable costs.
- Fixed overheads are absorbed on the basis of budgeted operating hours.

One of your duties is to prepare costing information and a standard costing reconciliation statement for the chief executive of Travel Holdings.

**(a) Calculate the following information.**

(1) The standard price of fuel per litre
(2) The standard litres of fuel for 5,760 ferry crossings
(3) The standard labour rate per hour
(4) The standard labour hours for 5,760 ferry crossings
(5) The standard fixed overhead cost per budgeted operating hour
(6) The standard operating hours for 5,760 crossings
(7) The standard fixed overhead cost absorbed by the actual 5,760 ferry crossings

**(b)** **Using the data provided in the operating results and your answers to part (a), calculate the following variances.**

    (1)   The material price variance for the fuel
    (2)   The material usage variance for the fuel
    (3)   The labour rate variance
    (4)   The labour efficiency variance
    (5)   The fixed overhead expenditure variance
    (6)   The fixed overhead volume variance
    (7)   The fixed overhead capacity variance
    (8)   The fixed overhead efficiency variance

**(c)** **Prepare a statement reconciling the actual cost of operations to the standard cost of operations for the year to 30 November 20X8.**

**Statement reconciling the actual cost of operations to the standard cost of operations for year ended 30 November 20X8**

| Number of ferry crossings | | |
|---|---|---|
| | £ | £ |
| Actual cost of operations | | |
| Cost variances | | |
| Material price for fuel | | |
| Material usage for fuel | | |
| Labour rate | | |
| Labour efficiency | | |
| Fixed overhead expenditure | | |
| Fixed overhead capacity | | |
| Fixed overhead efficiency | | |
| | | |
| Standard cost of operations | | |

## Task 5.2

The following budgetary control report has been provided together with the variances calculated below.

| | Budget | | Actual | |
|---|---|---|---|---|
| Production (units) | | 12,400 | | 13,600 |
| Direct materials | 37,200 kg | £130,200 | 37,400 kg | £112,200 |
| Direct labour | 24,800 hours | £223,200 | 28,560 hours | £285,600 |
| Fixed overheads | | £234,000 | | £221,000 |
| Total cost | | £587,400 | | £618,800 |

| Variance | Amount |
|---|---|
| Direct material price | £18,700 F |
| Direct materials usage | £11,900 F |
| Direct labour rate | £28,560 A |
| Direct labour efficiency | £12,240 |
| Fixed overhead expenditure | £13,000 |

The company normally prepares an operating statement under standard absorption costing principles but the financial director has asked you to prepare one under standard marginal costing principles.

(a) Select the fixed overhead volume variance from the Picklist, drag and drop the options from the Variances list into the correct spaces (Favourable or Adverse) and fill in the remaining spaces to complete the table.

| | | | |
|---|---|---|---|
| Budgeted variable cost for actual production | | | £ |
| Budgeted fixed cost | | | £ |
| Total budgeted cost for actual production | | | £ |
| **Variance** | **Favourable** | **Adverse** | |
| Direct materials price | | | |
| Direct materials usage | | | |
| Direct labour rate | | | |
| Direct labour efficiency | | | |
| Fixed overhead expenditure | | | |
| Fixed overhead volume | ▼ | ▼ | |
| Total variance | £ | £ | £ |
| Actual cost of actual production | | | £ |

Picklist for fixed overhead volume variance:

22,645.16
N/A

Drag and drop options for variances:

| £18,700 | £11,900 | £28,560 | £12,240 | £13,000 |
|---|---|---|---|---|

A company has a budgeted overhead absorption rate of £95 per unit and budgeted production of 27,000 units. The actual production was 25,000 units and the actual overheads incurred were £2,423,600.

(b) Complete the following statement.

The [ ▼ ] of overheads is £ [              ]

Picklist:

Over absorption
Under absorption

## Task 5.3

A budgetary control report has been provided for the manufacture of product PD98 and variances have been calculated.

| | Budget | | Actual | |
|---|---|---|---|---|
| Production (units) | | 450 | | 520 |
| Direct materials | 337.5 kg | £20,250 | 338 kg | £25,350 |
| Direct labour | 1,080 hours | £12,960 | 988 hours | £14,820 |
| Fixed overheads | | £28,080 | | £31,300 |
| Total cost | | £61,290 | | £71,470 |

| Variance | Amount |
|---|---|
| Direct materials price | £5,070 A |
| Direct materials usage | £3,120 |
| Fixed overhead expenditure | £3,220 |
| Fixed overhead capacity | £2,392 A |
| Fixed overhead efficiency | £6,760 F |
| Direct labour rate | £2,964 |
| Direct labour efficiency | £3,120 F |

**Complete the operating statement for the manufacture of PD98. Do not use brackets or minus signs for the variances.**

| Operating Statement – PD98 | | | £ |
|---|---|---|---|
| Budgeted/Standard cost for actual production | | | |
| **Variances** | **Adverse** | **Favourable** | |
| Direct material price | | | |
| Direct materials usage | | | |
| Direct labour rate | | | |
| Direct labour efficiency | | | |
| Fixed overhead expenditure | | | |
| Fixed overhead capacity | | | |
| Fixed overhead efficiency | | | |
| Total variance | 0 | 0 | |
| Actual cost of actual production | | | |

# Chapter 6 – Interpreting variances

## Task 6.1

State possible reasons for each of the following variances which are all independent of each other.

| Variance | Possible causes |
|---|---|
| Favourable materials price variance | |
| Favourable materials usage variance | |
| Adverse labour rate variance | |
| Adverse labour efficiency variance | |

## Task 6.2

What possible effect will the following scenarios have on the variances?

| Scenario | Possible effects |
|---|---|
| A business has had to use a less-skilled grade of labour in its production process. | |
| A factory had a machine breakdown which resulted in three days of production delays last month. | |

## Task 6.3

The standard direct materials cost for a business's product is:

6 kg @ £8.00 per kg = £48.00

During the month of October production was 7,400 units of the product and the actual materials cost was £397,400 for 45,100 kgs. The price of the materials has been unexpectedly increased to £8.50 per kg for the whole month.

The total materials price variance is £ [          ]

The non-controllable element of the materials price variance that has been caused by the price increase is £ [          ]

The controllable element of the materials price variance caused by other factors is

£ [          ]

## Task 6.4

A business's product has a standard direct material cost of £26.00 (4 kgs @ £6.50 per kg). During the month of March the total production of the product was 2,500 units using 10,600 kgs of materials at a total cost of £73,140. During the month the price was unexpectedly increased due to a shortage of the material to £7.00 per kg.

**The total materials price variance is £**

**The non-controllable variance due to price increase is £**

**The controllable variance due to other factors is £**

.....................................................................................................................

## Task 6.5

A business makes a product which uses a raw material which has a standard cost of £7.00 per kg. Each unit of the product requires 5 kgs of this material. The price of the materials for the last few years has been subjected to a time series analysis and the following seasonal variations have been seen to occur.

| | |
|---|---|
| Jan – Mar | –£0.42 |
| Apr – June | +£0.56 |
| July – Aug | +£0.77 |
| Sept – Dec | –£0.91 |

During March 18,000 units of the product were made and the price paid for the 92,000 kgs of material was £631,200.

**The total materials price variance is £**

**The non-controllable variance due to the season is £**

**The controllable variance due to other factors is £**

.....................................................................................................................

## Task 6.6

The standard cost of direct materials for a product is made up of 8 kgs of material at an average standard cost of £4.00 per kg. It has been noted over the years that the cost of the material fluctuates on a seasonal basis around the average standard cost as follows:

| | |
|---|---|
| Jan – Mar | +£0.48 |
| Apr – June | +£0.72 |
| July – Sept | –£0.64 |
| Oct – Dec | –£0.56 |

In the month of June the actual production was 5,000 units and 42,300 kgs of material were used at a cost of £194,580.

**The total materials price variance is £** [          ]

**The non-controllable variance caused by the seasonal price change is**

£ [          ]

**The controllable variance caused by other factors is £** [          ]

## Task 6.7

A business sets the standard cost of its materials at 5kg per unit at a price of £20 per kg, when the index for this particular materials price was 120. During January, 9,000 units were produced using 46,000 kg of material at a total cost of £946,000. In January, the index of the materials price stood at 130.

**The total materials price variance is £** [          ]

**The non-controllable variance caused by the index change is £** [          ]

**The controllable variance caused by other factors is £** [          ]

## Task 6.8

Keta operates a standard costing system and uses raw material C2X which is a global commodity. The standard price was set based upon a market price of £450 per litre when the material price index for C2X was 120.50. The following information has been gathered:

- The price index increased to 126.525 in June X3.
- The raw material price variance for June was £375,000 adverse.
- 12,500 litres of material C2X were purchased in June.

**Complete the statements below. In order to calculate your answers, you should split the raw material price variance into two components by calculating the part of the variance explained by the change in the price index and the part of the variance not explained by the changes in the price index.**

(a) The part of the variance explained by the increase in the price index is
£ [          ]

(b) The part of the variance not explained by the increase in the price index is
£ [          ]

(c) The percentage increase in the index is [          ] %

Hamma uses product Z4QX and has collected data from the last few months in order to forecast the cost per kilogram of Z4QX in the next period.

| | April X3 | May X3 | June X3 |
|---|---|---|---|
| Cost per kilogram of Z4QX (£) | 1,457.92 | 1,593.66 | 1,729.40 |

**(d) Complete the table below to forecast the expected price of product Z4QX in September and December X3.**

| | September X3 | December X3 |
|---|---|---|
| Cost per kilogram of Z4QX(£) | | |

A colleague has calculated the least squares regression line (the line of best fit) as **y = 24.69 + 2.14x**, where y is the cost per kilogram and x is the period. June X3 is period 41.

**(e) Complete the statement below.**

The forecast cost per kilogram, using the regression line, for September X3 is

£ [          ]

........................................................................................

## Task 6.9

A company purchases 3,700 kilograms of material at a cost of £10,915. The total material price variance is £1,665 adverse.

**Complete the following statement.**

The standard cost per kilogram is £ [          ]

........................................................................................

## Task 6.10

Delta manufactures 5,400 units of product QR1 using 11,880 labour hours. The budgeted production was 5,000 units using 11,250 labour hours at a cost of £163,125. The labour rate variance is £14,850 favourable.

**Complete the following sentence.**

The actual labour rate per hour is £ [          ] .

........................................................................................

## Task 6.11

You are employed as the assistant management accountant in the group accountant's office of Hampstead plc. Hampstead recently acquired Finchley Ltd, a small company making a specialist product called the Alpha. Standard marginal costing is used by all the companies within the group and, from 1 August 20X8, Finchley Ltd will also be required to use standard marginal costing in its management reports. Part of your job is to manage the implementation of standard marginal costing at Finchley Ltd.

John Wade, the managing director of Finchley, is not clear how the change will help him as a manager. He has always found Finchley's existing absorption costing system sufficient. By way of example, he shows you a summary of his management accounts for the three months to 31 May 20X8. These are reproduced below.

| Statement of budgeted and actual cost of Alpha production – 3 months ended 31 May 20X8 | | | | | |
|---|---|---|---|---|---|
| | **Actual** | | **Budget** | | **Variance** |
| Alpha production (units) | | 10,000 | | 12,000 | |
| | Inputs | £ | Inputs | £ | £ |
| Materials | 32,000 m | 377,600 | 36,000 m | 432,000 | 54,400 |
| Labour | 70,000 hrs | 422,800 | 72,000 hrs | 450,000 | 27,200 |
| Fixed overhead absorbed | | 330,000 | | 396,000 | 66,000 |
| Fixed overhead unabsorbed | | 75,000 | | 0 | (75,000) |
| | | 1,205,400 | | 1,278,000 | 72,600 |

John Wade is not convinced that standard marginal costing will help him to manage Finchley. 'My current system tells me all I need to know,' he said. 'As you can see, we are £72,600 below budget which is really excellent given that we lost production as a result of a serious machine breakdown.'

To help John Wade understand the benefits of standard marginal costing, you agree to prepare a statement for the three months ended 31 May 20X8 reconciling the standard cost of production to the actual cost of production.

(a) **Write a short memo to John Wade:**

Your memo should:

(i) **Use the budget data to determine the following.**

(1) The standard marginal cost per Alpha.

(2) The standard cost of actual Alpha production for the three months to 31 May 20X8.

(ii) **Calculate the following variances.**

    (1) Material price variance
    (2) Material usage variance
    (3) Labour rate variance
    (4) Labour efficiency variance
    (5) Fixed overhead expenditure variance

(iii) **Include a statement reconciling the actual cost of production to the standard cost of production.**

(iv) **Give TWO reasons why your variances might differ from those in his original management accounting statement, despite using the same basic data.**

(v) **Briefly discuss ONE further reason why your reconciliation statement provides improved management information.**

**MEMO**

To:     Managing Director
From:    Assistant Management Accountant
Date:    xx/xx/xx

Subject:   The use of standard marginal costing at Finchley Ltd

(i)   (1) Standard marginal cost of a unit of Alpha

    (2) Standard cost of producing 10,000 units of Alpha

(ii) Variance calculations

    (1) Material price variance
    (2) Material usage variance
    (3) Labour rate variance
    (4) Labour efficiency variance
    (5) Fixed overhead expenditure variance

(iii)

| Reconciliation statement | | | £ |
|---|---|---|---|
| **Standard cost of output** | | | |
| *Variances* | *Fav* | *Adv* | |
| | £ | £ | |
| Materials price | | | |
| Materials usage | | | |
| Labour rate | | | |
| Labour efficiency | | | |
| Fixed overhead expenditure | | | |
| **Actual cost of output** | | | |

## Task 6.12

Croxton Ltd makes a specialised chemical, X14, in barrels at its factory. The factory has two departments: the processing department and the finishing department. Because of the technology involved, Croxton apportions both budgeted and actual total factory fixed overheads between the two departments on the basis of budgeted machine hours.

The standard absorption cost per barrel of X14 in the processing department, and the budgeted production for the five weeks ended 31 May 20X8, are shown below.

| Processing department: standard cost per barrel of X14 | | | |
| --- | --- | --- | --- |
| Input | Quantity | Standard price/rate | Cost £ |
| Material | 10 litres | £60 per litre | 600 |
| Labour | 8 labour hrs | £8 per labour hr | 64 |
| Fixed overheads | 16 machine hrs | £20 per machine hr | 320 |
| **Standard absorption cost per barrel** | | | 984 |
| **Budgeted production 5 weeks ending 31 May 20X8** | | | 45 barrels |

You are employed by Croxton Ltd as an accounting technician. One of your duties is to prepare standard costing reconciliation statements. Croxton's finance director gives you the following information for the five weeks ended 31 May 20X8.

### Total factory budgeted and actual data

- Factory budgeted machine hours            1,152 machine hours
- Factory budgeted fixed overheads          £23,040
- Factory actual fixed overheads           £26,000
- Budgeted **and** actual factory fixed overheads are apportioned between the processing and finishing departments **on the basis of budgeted machine hours**.

### Processing department actual data

- Actual costs

  Materials at £58.50 per litre          £23,985
  Labour (328 hours)          £2,788
- Actual production output          40 barrels
- Actual machine hours worked          656 hours
- There was no work in progress at any stage

**(a)** **Calculate the following information for the processing department.**

    (i)    Actual litres of material used

    (ii)   Standard litres of material required for 40 barrels of X14

    (iii)  Average actual labour rate per hour

    (iv)  Standard labour hours required for 40 barrels of X14

    (v)   Budgeted number of machine hours

    (vi)  Budgeted fixed overheads

    (vii) Actual fixed overheads (based on its share of actual factory overhead)

    (viii) Standard machine hours for actual production

    (ix)  Standard absorption cost of actual production

    (x)   Actual absorption cost of actual production

**(b)** **Using data given and your answers to part (a), calculate the following variances for the processing department.**

    (i)    Material price variance

    (ii)   Material usage variance

    (iii)  Labour rate variance

    (iv)  Labour efficiency variance

    (v)   Fixed overhead expenditure variance

    (vi)  Fixed overhead volume variance

    (vii) Fixed overhead efficiency variance

    (viii) Fixed overhead capacity variance

**(c) Prepare a statement for the five weeks ended 31 May 20X8 reconciling the standard absorption cost of actual production with the actual absorption cost of actual production.**

| Reconciliation statement – five weeks ended 31 May 20X8 | | | |
|---|---|---|---|
| | | | £ |
| Standard absorption cost of actual production | | | |
| | £ | £ | |
| | (F) | (A) | |
| Variances | | | |
| Material price | | | |
| Material usage | | | |
| Labour rate | | | |
| Labour efficiency | | | |
| Fixed overhead expenditure | | | |
| Fixed overhead efficiency | | | |
| Fixed overhead capacity | | | |
| | | | |
| Actual absorption cost of actual production | | | |

**(d)** Judith Green is the production manager of the processing department. You show her the statement reconciling the actual and standard costs of actual production. Judith then gives you the following additional information.

- When the standard costs were agreed, a price index for the material used in making the X14 was 140, but during the five weeks ended 31 May it was 133.

- Actual production output was 40 barrels but Croxton had to make 41 barrels of X14 as one barrel had to be scrapped on completion. This was because the barrel was damaged. The scrapped barrel had no value.

- If labour hours worked exceed 320 hours per five weeks, overtime is incurred. The overtime premium is £8.00 per hour of overtime.

- There is just one customer for the X14. The customer purchased 40 barrels during the five weeks ended 31 May 20X8.

Judith believes there is no need to examine the variances any further, for a number of reasons.

- The material price variance clearly shows that the purchasing department is efficient.

- The labour rate, labour efficiency and material usage variances were entirely due to the one scrapped barrel.

- Fixed overheads are not controllable by the processing department.

**Write a memo to Judith Green. In your memo you should do the following.**

(i) **Use the material price index to identify a revised standard price for the materials used in X14.**

(ii) **Subdivide the material price variance calculated in task (b) (i) into that part due to the change in the price index and that part due to other reasons.**

(iii) **Briefly explain whether the material price variance calculated in task (b) (i) arose from efficiencies in the purchasing department.**

(iv) **Explain whether the one scrapped barrel might fully account for the following.**

   (1) **Material usage variance**
   (2) **Labour efficiency variance**
   (3) **Labour rate variance**

(v) **Give ONE reason why the fixed overheads might not be controllable by the processing department.**

| MEMO |
|---|
| **To:** Judith Green, production manager |
| **From:** Accounting technician |
| **Date:** 7 August 20X5 |
| **Subject:** **Croxton Ltd – analysis of variances for 5 weeks ended 31 May 20X8** |

## Task 6.13

(a) You are the assistant management accountant at the Bare Foot Hotel complex on the tropical island of St Nicolas. The hotel complex is a luxury development. All meals and entertainment are included in the price of the holiday and guests only have to pay for drinks.

The Bare Foot Hotel complex aims to create a relaxing atmosphere. Because of this, meals are available throughout the day and guests can eat as many times as they wish.

The draft performance report for the hotel for the seven days ended 27 November 20X8 is reproduced below.

| | Notes | Budget | | Actual | |
|---|---|---|---|---|---|
| **Bare Foot Hotel Complex** | | | | | |
| **Draft performance report for seven days ended 27 November 20X8** | | | | | |
| Guests | | 540 | | 648 | |
| | | £ | £ | £ | £ |
| Variable costs | | | | | |
| Meal costs | 1 | | 34,020 | | 49,896 |
| Catering staff costs | 2,3 | | 3,780 | | 5,280 |
| Total variable costs | | | 37,800 | | 55,176 |
| Fixed overhead costs | | | | | |
| Salaries of other staff | | 5,840 | | 6,000 | |
| Local taxes | | 4,500 | | 4,200 | |
| Light, heat and power | | 2,500 | | 2,600 | |
| Depreciation of buildings and equipment | | 5,000 | | 4,000 | |
| Entertainment | | 20,500 | | 21,000 | |
| Total fixed overheads | | | 38,340 | | 37,800 |
| Total cost of providing for guests | | | 76,140 | | 92,976 |

**Notes**

1  Budgeted cost of meals: number of guests × 3 meals per day × 7 days × £3 per meal

2  Budgeted cost of catering staff: each member of the catering staff is to prepare and serve 12 meals per hour. Cost = (number of guests × 3 meals per day × 7 days ÷ 12 meals per hour) × £4 per hour.

3  Actual hours worked by catering staff = 1,200 hours

**Other notes**

The amount of food per meal has been kept under strict portion control. Since preparing the draft performance report, however, it has been discovered that guests have eaten, on average, four meals per day.

You report to Alice Groves, the general manager of the hotel, who feels that the format of the draft performance report could be improved to provide her with more meaningful management information. She suggests that the budgeted and actual data given in the existing draft performance report is rearranged in the form of a standard costing report, using absorption costing.

(i)  **Use the budget data, the actual data and the notes to the performance report to calculate the following for the seven days ended 27 November 20X8.**

(1)  The actual number of meals served

(2)  The standard number of meals which should have been served for the actual number of guests

(3)  The actual hourly rate paid to catering staff

(4)  The standard hours allowed for catering staff to serve three meals per day for the actual number of guests

(5)  The standard fixed overhead per guest

(6)  The total standard cost for the actual number of guests

(ii)  **Use the data given in the task and your answers to part (a) (i) to calculate the following variances for the seven days ended 27 November 20X8.**

(1)  The material price variance for meals served

(2)  The material usage variance for meals served

(3)  The labour rate variance for catering staff

(4)  The labour efficiency variance for catering staff, based on a standard of three meals served per guest per day

(5)  The fixed overhead expenditure variance

(6)  The fixed overhead volume variance on the assumption that the fixed overhead absorption rate is based on the budgeted number of guests per seven days

(iii) **Prepare a statement reconciling the standard cost for the actual number of guests to the actual cost for the actual number of guests for the seven days ended 27 November 20X8.**

(b) On receiving your reconciliation statement, Alice Groves asks the following questions.

- How much of the labour efficiency variance is due to guests taking, on average, four meals per day rather than the three provided for in the budget and how much is due to other reasons?

- Would it be feasible to subdivide the fixed overhead volume variance into a capacity and efficiency variance?

**Write a memo to Alice Groves. Your memo should do the following.**

(i) **Divide the labour efficiency variance into that part due to guests taking more meals than planned and that part due to other efficiency reasons.**

(ii) **Explain the meaning of the fixed overhead capacity and efficiency variances.**

(iii) **Briefly discuss whether or not it is feasible to calculate the fixed overhead capacity and efficiency variances for the Bare Foot Hotel complex.**

---

**MEMO**

To:        Alice Groves, general manager

From:      Assistant management accountant

Date:      xx.xx.xx

Subject:   **Performance report** for seven days ended 27 November 20X8

**(i)   Subdivision of the catering labour efficiency variance**




**(ii)   The meaning of the fixed overhead capacity and efficiency variances**




**(iii)   Calculating the fixed overhead capacity and efficiency variances for the Bare Foot Hotel complex**

---

## Task 6.14

You have been provided with the following information for an organisation, which manufactures a product called Becks, for the month just ended.

| | Budget | | Actual | |
|---|---|---|---|---|
| Production (units) | | 20,000 | | 21,000 |
| Direct materials | 80,000 kg | £880,000 | 83,000 kg | £954,500 |

The finance director has asked you to write a note to help in the training of a junior accounting technician. The notes are to explain the calculation of the total direct material variance and how this variance can be split into a price variance and a usage variance.

**Prepare a note explaining the total direct material variance and how it can be split into a price variance and usage variance. Calculations should be used to illustrate the explanation.**

........................................................................

## Task 6.15

Dickenson plc manufactures a range of products for use in the motor racing industry. The company uses a standard absorption costing system with variances calculated quarterly.

It is midway through quarter 3 of the current financial year and a number of events have occurred which may impact on the quarter-end variances for a particular product, MTRF1.

The production director has asked for a report indicating the possible effects of the various events.

**Production notes for MTRF1**

- MTRF1 uses a specialist industry material – POL89.

- Recent advances in the production of POL89 have increased its availability which has led to a reduction in the price per litre by 18% in the last month. It is expected that the reduction in price will remain until at least the end of quarter 3.

- The standard price was set before the decrease in price occurred.

- The quality control officer has tested the latest batch of POL89 and reported that it is of a higher quality than expected.

- The company implemented a strict material usage policy at the beginning of quarter 3 to monitor levels of wastage. This was overseen by the quality control department with no additional payroll costs being incurred.

- Employees usually receive an annual pay rise at the beginning of quarter 3 and this was included in the standard cost. Due to the current economic climate this pay rise has been suspended indefinitely.

- The budgeted production for the quarter is 12,000 units.

- An order for 3,000 units was cancelled shortly after the beginning of quarter 3. The company has been unable to replace this order and the actual production for the quarter is now expected to be 9,000 units. The production machinery needed to be recalibrated to deal with the higher quality POL89. In addition, one of the machines was found to be defective and required a complete overhaul. These costs are to be included in fixed overheads at the end of the quarter.

**Complete the report for the Production Director on the possible impact of the above events on the POL89 price and usage variances, direct labour rate and efficiency variances and the fixed overhead expenditure and volume variances. The report should:**

- **Identify whether each variance is likely to be adverse or favourable at the end of the quarter**

- **Explain what each variance means**

- **Provide one possible reason why each variance is likely to be adverse or favourable at the end of the quarter**

- **Identify possible links between the variances**

**You are NOT required to make any calculations.**

| | | | |
|---|---|---|---|
| To: | Production Director | Subject: | Analysis of variances |
| From: | Accounts Technician | Date: | XX/XX/20XX |

**POL89 price variance**



**POL89 usage variance**



**Direct labour efficiency variance**

**Fixed overhead expenditure variance**

**Fixed overhead volume variance**

# Chapter 7 – Performance indicators

## Task 7.1

Suggest possible measures of productivity for each of the following types of organisation:

| Organisation | Possible productivity measures |
|---|---|
| Taxi firm | |
| Hospital | |
| Motorbike courier service | |
| Firm of accountants | |
| Retail store | |
| Maker of hand-made pottery | |

## Task 7.2

You are given the following information about a small manufacturing business for the year ending 31 March:

| | |
|---|---|
| Sales revenue | £1,447,600 |
| Cost of materials used | £736,500 |
| Cost of bought in services | £316,900 |
| Number of employees | 15 |

**The total value added is** £ _____

**The value added per employee is** £ _____

## Task 7.3

Given below is the summarised production information for a manufacturing organisation for the last month:

| | |
|---|---|
| Budgeted production in units | 15,000 |
| Actual production in units | 14,200 |
| Labour hours worked | 46,000 |
| Standard hours for each unit | 3 |

(a) **Complete the table to calculate the following performance indicators and briefly explain what each one means: Give your answers to TWO decimal places.**

|  | Calculation | Explanation |
|---|---|---|
| Efficiency ratio |  |  |
| Capacity ratio |  |  |
| Production volume ratio |  |  |

(b) **If the workforce had operated at 95% efficiency how many labour hours would have been saved last month? Give your answer to the nearest whole number.**

## Task 7.4

Given below is the statement of profit or loss (income statement) for a business for the year ending 31 March 20X9 and a statement of financial position at that date.

**Statement of profit or loss (income statement)**

|  | £ | £ |
|---|---|---|
| Revenue |  | 2,650,400 |
| Cost of sales |  |  |
| Opening inventory | 180,000 |  |
| Purchases | 1,654,400 |  |
|  | 1,834,400 |  |
| Less closing inventory | 191,200 |  |
|  |  | 1,643,200 |
| Gross profit |  | 1,007,200 |
| Less expenses |  |  |
| Selling and distribution costs | 328,400 |  |
| Administration expenses | 342,200 |  |
|  |  | 670,600 |
| Operating profit |  | 336,600 |
| Interest payable |  | 36,000 |
| Profit after interest |  | 300,600 |

## Statement of financial position

|  | £ | £ |
|---|---|---|
| Non-current assets |  | 1,920,400 |
| Current assets: |  |  |
| Inventory | 191,200 |  |
| Receivables | 399,400 |  |
| Bank | 16,800 |  |
|  | 607,400 |  |
| Payables | (190,300) |  |
| Net current assets |  | 417,100 |
|  |  | 2,337,500 |
| Less long term loan |  | 600,000 |
|  |  | 1,737,500 |
| Share capital |  | 1,000,000 |
| Other reserves |  | 150,000 |
| Retained earnings |  | 587,500 |
|  |  | 1,737,500 |

(a) Using the statement of profit or loss (income statement) and statement of financial position complete the table to calculate the performance indicators: Give your answer to TWO decimal places unless otherwise stated.

| | |
|---|---|
| Gross profit margin | |
| Operating profit margin | |
| Return on capital employed | |
| Asset turnover | |
| Non-current asset turnover | |
| Current ratio | |
| Quick ratio | |
| Receivables' collection period (to the nearest whole number) | |
| Inventory holding period in days (to the nearest whole number) | |
| Payables' payment period (to the nearest whole number) | |
| Interest cover | |
| Gearing ratio | |

(b) If the payables' payment period was increased to 60 days what effect would this have on the cash balance? Give your answer to the nearest whole £.

## Task 7.5

Given below is a summary of a business's performance for the last six months:

|  | July | Aug | Sept | Oct | Nov | Dec |
|---|---|---|---|---|---|---|
|  | £000 | £000 | £000 | £000 | £000 | £000 |
| Sales | 560 | 540 | 500 | 550 | 580 | 600 |
| Cost of sales | 370 | 356 | 330 | 374 | 400 | 415 |
| Expenses | 123 | 119 | 110 | 116 | 122 | 131 |
| Interest payable | – | – | – | 3 | 3 | 3 |
| Shareholders' funds | 440 | 445 | 458 | 468 | 480 | 490 |
| Loan | – | – | – | 50 | 50 | 50 |

(a) **For each month of the year complete the table to calculate the performance indicators. Give your answers to the nearest whole number (unless otherwise indicated):**

|  | July | Aug | Sept | Oct | Nov | Dec |
|---|---|---|---|---|---|---|
| Gross profit margin |  |  |  |  |  |  |
| Operating profit margin |  |  |  |  |  |  |
| % of expenses to sales |  |  |  |  |  |  |
| Return on capital employed (give answers to ONE decimal place) |  |  |  |  |  |  |
| Asset turnover (give answers to ONE decimal place) |  |  |  |  |  |  |

(b) **Comment on what the figures calculated in part (a) show about the performance of the business over the last six months.**

........................................................................................

## Task 7.6

A manufacturing business has three small divisions, North, South and Central. The figures for the last three months of 20X6 for each division are given below:

|  | North | South | Central |
|---|---|---|---|
|  | £ | £ | £ |
| **Financial details** |  |  |  |
| Sales | 870,000 | 560,000 | 640,000 |
| Opening inventory | 34,000 | 41,000 | 34,000 |

| | North | South | Central |
|---|---|---|---|
| | £ | £ | £ |
| Closing inventory | 32,000 | 29,000 | 38,000 |
| Purchases | 590,000 | 380,000 | 420,000 |
| Expenses | 121,000 | 106,000 | 138,000 |
| Share capital and reserves | 980,000 | 690,000 | 615,000 |
| Payables | 103,400 | 42,600 | 66,700 |
| Receivables | 100,100 | 107,300 | 87,600 |
| **Non-financial details** | | | |
| Factory floor area | 500 sq m | 400 sq m | 420 sq m |
| Factory employees | 18 | 12 | 15 |
| Hours worked | 8,500 | 5,800 | 7,000 |
| Units produced | 17,000 | 10,200 | 12,300 |

(a) **Complete the table to calculate the performance indicators for each division. Give your answer to ONE decimal place:**

| | North | South | Central |
|---|---|---|---|
| Gross profit margin | | | |
| Operating profit margin | | | |
| Return on capital employed | | | |
| Asset turnover | | | |
| Inventory holding in months (using average inventory) | | | |
| Receivables' collection period in months | | | |
| Payables' collection period in months | | | |
| Units produced per square metre of floor area | | | |
| Units produced per employee | | | |
| Units produced per hour | | | |

(b) **Use the performance indicators calculated in (a) to compare the performances of the three divisions for the three-month period.**

## Task 7.7

**(a)** A business operates on a gross profit margin of 48% and sales for the period were £380,000. **The gross profit is** £ [          ]

**(b)** A business operates on a gross profit margin of 34% and the gross profit made in the period was £425,000.

**The sales for the period were** £ [          ]

**(c)** A business had sales of £85,000 in a month and with a gross profit margin of 40% and an operating profit margin of 11.5%.

**The expenses for the month were** £ [          ]

**(d)** A business has a return on capital employed of 11.6% and made an operating profit for the period of £100,000.

**The capital employed is** £ [          ]

**(e)** A business has a net profit percentage of 8% and a return on capital employed of 10%.

**The asset turnover of the business is** [          ]

**(f)** A business has opening inventory and closing inventory of £158,000 and £182,000 and made purchases during the year totalling £560,000.

**Inventory turned over** [          ] **times during the year.**

**(g)** A business has a receivables' collection period of 48 days and the closing receivables figure is £96,000.

**The sales for the year are** £ [          ]

........................................................................................

# Task 7.8

Given below are the summarised statements of profit or loss (income statements) and statements of financial position of a business for the last two years.

**Summarised statements of profit or loss (income statements)**

|  | Y/e 31 Dec 20X8 | Y/e 31 Dec 20X7 |
|---|---|---|
|  | £000 | £000 |
| Revenue | 602 | 564 |
| Cost of sales | 329 | 325 |
| Gross profit | 273 | 239 |
| Expenses | 163 | 143 |
| Operating profit | 110 | 96 |
| Interest payable | 10 | 10 |
| Profit before tax | 100 | 86 |

**Summarised statements of financial position**

|  | 31 Dec 20X8 | | 31 Dec 20X7 | |
|---|---|---|---|---|
|  | £ | £ | £ | £ |
| Non-current assets |  | 709 |  | 632 |
| Current assets: |  |  |  |  |
| Inventory | 28 |  | 32 |  |
| Receivables | 66 |  | 68 |  |
| Cash | 2 |  | 3 |  |
|  | 96 |  | 103 |  |
| Payables | 55 |  | 45 |  |
| Net current assets |  | 41 |  | 58 |
|  |  | 750 |  | 690 |
| Long term loan |  | 150 |  | 150 |
|  |  | 600 |  | 540 |
| Share capital |  | 300 |  | 300 |
| Retained earnings |  | 300 |  | 240 |
|  |  | 600 |  | 540 |

(a) Complete the table for each of the two years to calculate the performance indicators, based on total capital employed when relevant.

|  | 31 Dec 20X8 | 31 Dec 20X7 |
|---|---|---|
| Gross profit margin |  |  |
| Operating profit margin |  |  |
| Return on capital employed |  |  |
| Asset turnover |  |  |
| Non-current asset turnover |  |  |
| Current ratio |  |  |
| Quick ratio |  |  |
| Receivables' collection period |  |  |
| Inventory holding in days |  |  |
| Payables' payment period |  |  |
| Interest cover |  |  |
| Gearing ratio |  |  |

(b) Comment upon the performance of the business for the last two years basing your comments on the performance indicators calculated in part (a).

## Task 7.9

Middle plc owns two subsidiaries, East Ltd and West Ltd, producing soft drinks. Both companies rent their premises and both use plant of similar size and technology. Middle plc requires the plant in the subsidiaries to be written off over ten years using straight-line depreciation and assuming zero residual values.

East Ltd was established five years ago but West Ltd has only been established for two years. Goods returned by customers generally arise from quality failures and are destroyed. Financial and other data relating to the two companies are reproduced below.

| Statements of profit or loss (Income statements) year to 30 November 20X8 | | | Statements of financial position extracts at 30 November 20X8 | | |
|---|---|---|---|---|---|
| | West Ltd £000 | East Ltd £000 | | West Ltd £000 | East Ltd £000 |
| Revenue | 18,000 | 17,600 | Plant | 16,000 | 10,000 |
| Less Returns | | | Depreciation to | 3,200 | 5,000 |
| | 90 | 176 | date | | |
| Net revenue | 17,910 | 17,424 | Non-current assets | 12,800 | 5,000 |
| Material | 2,000 | 2,640 | Current assets | 4,860 | 3,000 |
| Labour | 4,000 | 4,840 | Current liabilities | (2,320) | (1,500) |
| Production overheads* | 3,000 | 3,080 | Net assets | 15,340 | 6,500 |
| Gross profit | 8,910 | 6,864 | | | |
| Marketing | 2,342 | 1,454 | | | |
| Research & development | 1,650 | 1,010 | | | |
| Training | 950 | 450 | | | |
| Administration | 900 | 1,155 | | | |
| Operating profit | 3,068 | 2,795 | | | |

*Includes plant depreciation of £1,600,000 for West Ltd and £1,000,000 for East Ltd

| Other data (000's litres) | West Ltd | East Ltd |
|---|---|---|
| Gross sales | 20,000 | 22,000 |
| Returns | 100 | 220 |
| Net sales | 19,900 | 21,780 |
| Orders received in year | 20,173 | 22,854 |

You are employed by Middle plc as a member of a team monitoring the performance of subsidiaries within the group. Middle plc aims to provide its shareholders with the best possible return for their investment and to meet customers' expectations. It does this by comparing the performance of subsidiaries and using the more efficient ones for benchmarking.

Your team leader, Angela Wade, has asked you to prepare a report evaluating the performance of West Ltd and East Ltd. Your report should do the following.

(a) Calculate and explain the meaning of the following financial ratios for each company.

   (i)   The return on net assets
   (ii)  The net asset turnover
   (iii) The operating profit margin

(b) Calculate the percentage of faulty sales as a measure of the level of customer service for each company.

(c) Identify ONE other possible measure of the level of customer service which could be derived from the accounting data.

(d) Identify TWO limitations to your analysis in task (a), using the data in the accounts.

(a) Angela Wade

    From:     A Technician

    Date:     xx.xx.xx

    Subject:   West Ltd and East Ltd – Performance Report

    (i)    Return on net assets (RONA)

    (ii)   Net asset turnover

    (iii)  Operating profit margin

**(b) Measure of customer service: faulty sales**

**(c) Further measure of customer service**

**(d) Limitations of financial ratios**

## Task 7.10

You are employed by Micro Circuits Ltd as a financial analyst reporting to Angela Frear, the Director of Corporate Strategy. One of your responsibilities is to monitor the performance of subsidiaries within the group. Financial and other data relating to subsidiary A is reproduced below.

| Subsidiary A | | | | | | |
|---|---|---|---|---|---|---|
| **Statement of profit or loss (Income statement) year to 30 November 20X8** | | | **Extract from statement of financial position at 30 November 20X8** | | | |
| | £000 | £000 | | £000 | £000 | £000 |
| Revenue | | 4,000 | Non-current assets | Land and buildings | Plant and machinery | Total |
| less returns | | 100 | | | | |
| Net revenue[1] | | 3,900 | Cost | 2,000 | 2,500 | 4,500 |
| Material | 230 | | Additions | – | 1,800 | 1,800 |
| Labour | 400 | | | 2,000 | 4,300 | 6,300 |
| Production overheads[2] | 300 | | Accumulated dep'n | 160 | 1,700 | 1,860 |
| Cost of production | 930 | | | 1,840 | 2,600 | 4,440 |
| Opening finished inventory | 50 | | | | | |
| Closing finished inventory | (140) | | Raw material inventory | 15 | | |
| Cost of sales | | 840 | Finished goods inventory | 140 | | |
| Gross profit | | 3,060 | | 155 | | |
| Marketing | 500 | | Receivables | 325 | | |
| Customer support | 400 | | Cash and bank | 40 | | |
| Research and development | 750 | | Payables | (85) | | |
| Training | 140 | | | | | |
| Administration | 295 | 2,085 | | | | 435 |
| Operating profit | | 975 | Net assets | | | 4,875 |

## Other information

**Notes**

**(1) Analysis of revenue**

|  | £000 |  | £000 |
|---|---|---|---|
| Regular customers | 3,120 | New products | 1,560 |
| New customers | 780 | Existing products | 2,340 |
|  | 3,900 |  | 3,900 |

(2) Production overheads include £37,200 of reworked faulty production.

(3) Orders received in the year totalled £4,550,000.

**(a)** Angela Frear asks you to calculate the following performance indicators in preparation for a board meeting.

| Performance indicator | Workings | |
|---|---|---|
| Return on net assets | | |
| Net asset turnover | | |
| Operating profit margin | | |
| Average age of receivables in months | | |
| Average age of finished inventory in months | | |

**(b)** One of the issues to be discussed at the board meeting is the usefulness of performance indicators. Angela Frear has recently attended a conference on creating and enhancing value.

Three criticisms were made of financial performance indicators.

- They could give misleading signals.

- They could be manipulated.

- They focus on the short term and do not take account of other key, non-financial performance indicators.

At the conference, Angela was introduced to the idea of the balanced scorecard. The balanced scorecard looks at performance measurement from four perspectives.

---

**The financial perspective**

This is concerned with satisfying shareholders. Examples include the return on net assets and operating profit margin.

**The customer perspective**

This asks how customers view the business and is concerned with measures of customer satisfaction. Examples include speed of delivery and customer loyalty.

**The internal perspective**

This looks at the quality of the company's output in terms of technical excellence and customer needs. Examples would be striving towards total quality management and flexible production as well as unit cost.

**The innovation and learning perspective**

This is concerned with the continual improvement of existing products and the ability to develop new products as customers' needs change. An example would be the percentage of revenue attributable to new products.

---

**Angela Frear asks you to prepare briefing notes for the board meeting. Using the data from part (a) where necessary, your notes should do the following.**

(i)   Suggest ONE reason why the return on net assets calculated in (a) might be misleading.

(ii)  Identify ONE way of manipulating the operating profit margin.

(iii) Calculate the average delay in fulfilling orders.

(iv)  Identify ONE other possible measure of customer satisfaction other than the delay in fulfilling orders.

(v)   Calculate TWO indicators which may help to measure performance from an internal perspective.

(vi)  Calculate ONE performance indicator which would help to measure the innovation and learning perspective.

Briefing notes on the usefulness of performance indicators

Prepared for Angela Frear

Prepared by Financial Analyst

Dated: xx.xx.xx

(i)   **Return on net assets**

(ii)  **Operating profit margin**

(iii)  **Average delay in fulfilling orders**

(iv)  **Measures of customer satisfaction**

(v)  **Measuring performance from an internal perspective**

(vi)  **Measuring the innovation and learning perspective**

....................................................................................

## Task 7.11

(a)  Travel Bus Ltd is owned by Travel Holdings plc. It operates in the town of Camford. Camford is an old town with few parking facilities for motorists. Several years ago, the Town Council built a car park on the edge of the town and awarded Travel Bus the contract to carry motorists and their passengers between the car park and the centre of the town.

Originally, the Council charged motorists £4.00 per day for the use of the car park but, to encourage motorists not to take their cars into the town centre, parking has been free since 1 December 20X7.

The journey between the car park and the town centre is the only service operated by Travel Bus Ltd in Camford. A summary of the results for the first two years of operations, together with the net assets associated with the route and other operating data, is reproduced below.

| Statement of profit or loss (Income statement) year ended 30 November | | | Extract from statement of financial position at 30 November | | |
|---|---|---|---|---|---|
| | 20X7 £ | 20X8 £ | | 20X7 £ | 20X8 £ |
| Revenue | 432,000 | 633,600 | Buses | 240,000 | 240,000 |
| | | | Accumulated | | |
| Fuel | 129,600 | 185,328 | depreciation | 168,000 | 180,000 |
| Wages | 112,000 | 142,000 | Non-current assets | 72,000 | 60,000 |
| Other variable costs | 86,720 | 84,512 | Net current assets | 14,400 | 35,040 |
| Gross profit | 103,680 | 221,760 | | 86,400 | 95,040 |
| Bus road tax and insurance | 22,000 | 24,000 | | | |
| Depreciation of buses | 12,000 | 12,000 | | | |
| Maintenance of buses | 32,400 | 28,512 | | | |
| Fixed garaging costs | 29,840 | 32,140 | | | |
| Administration | 42,000 | 49,076 | | | |
| Operating profit/(loss) | (34,560) | 76,032 | | | |

| Other operating data | 20X7 | 20X8 |
|---|---|---|
| Fare per passenger journey | £0.80 | £1.00 |
| Miles per year | 324,000 | 356,400 |
| Miles per journey | 18.0 | 18.0 |
| Days per year | 360 | 360 |
| Wages per driver | £14,000 | £14,200 |

Throughout the two years, the drivers were paid a basic wage per week, no bonuses were paid and no overtime was incurred.

In two weeks there will be a meeting between officials of the Town Council and the chief executive of Travel Holdings to discuss the performance of Travel Bus for the year to 30 November 20X8. The previous year's performance indicators were as follows.

| | |
|---|---|
| Gross profit margin | 24% |
| Operating profit margin | –8% |
| Return on capital employed | –40% |
| Asset turnover | 5 times |
| Number of passengers in the year | 540,000 |
| Total cost per mile | £1.44 |
| Number of journeys per day | 50 |
| Maintenance cost per mile | £0.10 |
| Passengers per day | 1,500 |
| Passengers per journey | 30 |
| Number of drivers | 8 |

In preparation for the meeting, you have been asked to calculate the following performance indicators for the year to 30 November 20X8. Give your answers to the nearest whole number unless otherwise indicated.

|  |  | Performance indicator for year to 30 November 20X8 |
|---|---|---|
| (i) | Gross profit margin | |
| (ii) | Operating profit margin | |
| (iii) | Return on capital employed | |
| (iv) | Asset turnover (to the nearest dp) | |
| (v) | Number of passengers in the year | |
| (vi) | Total cost per mile (to the nearest two dps) | |
| (vii) | Number of journeys per day | |
| (viii) | Maintenance cost per mile (to the nearest two dps) | |
| (ix) | Passengers per day | |
| (x) | Passengers per journey | |
| (xi) | Number of drivers | |

**(b)** On receiving your performance indicators, the chief executive of Travel Holdings raises the following issues with you.

- The drivers are claiming that the improved profitability of Travel Bus reflects their increased productivity.

- The managers believe that the change in performance is due to improved motivation arising from the introduction of performance related pay for managers during the year to 30 November 20X8.

- The officials from the Town Council are concerned that Travel Bus is paying insufficient attention to satisfying passenger needs and safety.

The chief executive asks for your advice.

**Write a memo to the chief executive of Travel Holdings plc. Where relevant, you should make use of the data and answers to task a) to do the following.**

**(i) Briefly discuss whether or not increased productivity always leads to increased profitability.**

**(ii) Develop ONE possible measure of driver productivity and suggest whether or not the drivers' claim is valid.**

**(iii) Suggest ONE reason, other than improved motivation, why the profitability of Travel Bus might have improved.**

(iv) (1)  Suggest ONE existing performance indicator which might measure the satisfaction of passenger needs.

(2)  Suggest ONE other possible performance indicator of passenger needs which cannot be measured from the existing performance data collected by Travel Bus.

(v) (1)  Suggest ONE existing performance indicator which might measure the safety aspect of Travel Bus's operations.

(2)  Suggest ONE other possible performance indicator which cannot be measured from the existing performance data collected by Travel Bus.

### MEMO

To:       Chief executive

From:     Management accountant

Date:     xx.xx.xx

Subject:  **Performance of Travel Bus Ltd for the year to 30 November 20X8**

This memo addresses a number of issues concerning the productivity and profitability of Travel Bus Ltd.

(i)   Productivity and profitability

(ii)  Driver productivity

(iii) Reason for improved profitability

(iv)  Performance indicators to measure the satisfaction of passenger needs

(v)   Monitoring the safety aspect of Travel Bus's operations

## Task 7.12

TeesRus Ltd makes and packs tea bags. The company currently has 8 Pickmaster machines, which are coming to the end of their useful life. The company is considering replacing all 8 machines with either new Pickmaster machines or new Pickmaster 2 machines.

Each new Pickmaster machine costs £20,000 and requires 10 operators per day for the 100 days of the harvest. The machine will have a life of 10 years and a depreciation charge of £2,000 per year.

A new Pickmaster 2 machine requires only 1 operator per day for the 100 days. This machine costs £90,000 to purchase and will have a life of 10 years. The depreciation charge will be £9,000 per year.

Other budgeted information for 20X8 is as follows:

- The forecast harvest will last 100 days and produce 2.5 million kilograms of tea.

- The selling price of tea will be 45 pence per kilogram.

- Budgeted revenue is £1,125,000.

- Tea picker costs will be £150,000.

- Tea processor operators currently earn £6 per day.

- The tea pickers and tea processor operators are employed as and when needed on temporary contracts.

- Seed and fertiliser costs will be £75,000.

- Administration costs will be £150,000 if the Pickmaster machines are purchased.

- Administration costs will be £135,000 if the Pickmaster 2 machines are purchased.

- Distribution costs will be £350,000.

- The net assets at the end of the period will be £935,500 plus the budgeted operating profit.

- Disposing of the old machines will incur no profit, loss or any depreciation charge during 20X8.

(a) **Prepare TWO budgeted statements of profit or loss (income statements) and net asset workings assuming that the business purchases either 8 Pickmaster or 8 Pickmaster 2 machines.**

**Budgeted statements of profit or loss (income statements)**

|  | Pickmaster | Pickmaster 2 |
|---|---|---|
|  | £ | £ |
| Revenue |  |  |
| Cost of sales |  |  |
| Tea pickers |  |  |
| Tea processor operators |  |  |
| Depreciation |  |  |
| Seed and fertiliser costs |  |  |
| Total cost of sales |  |  |
| Gross profit |  |  |
| Administration costs |  |  |
| Distribution costs |  |  |
| Operating profit |  |  |

**Net assets at year end**

|  | Pickmaster | Pickmaster 2 |
|---|---|---|
|  | £ | £ |
| Budgeted net assets |  |  |
| Operating profit |  |  |
|  |  |  |

(b) **Complete the table to calculate the following indicators for each option:**

|  | Pickmaster | Pickmaster 2 |
|---|---|---|
| Gross profit margin |  |  |
| Operating profit margin |  |  |
| Return on net assets |  |  |

(c) **Prepare a report for the managing director to include the following:**

(i) **Comments on the indicators calculated in part (b) above.**

(ii) **Two other considerations.**

(iii) **A recommendation whether to purchase the Pickmaster or Pickmaster 2 machines.**

# REPORT

**To:**      Managing Director

**From:**    Accounting technician

**Date:**    December 20X7

**Subject:** Purchase of new machinery


**Performance indicators**




**Other considerations**




**Conclusion**


........................................................................................................

## Task 7.13

BeThere Airlines is reviewing its catering division and has provided the following information for the previous three months. The division has no administration or distribution costs. All costs are treated as costs of sales. All production has to be used in that day.

**Catering Division**

**Cost report for the three-month period**

| | September £ | October £ | November £ |
|---|---|---|---|
| Revenue | 690,000 | 697,200 | 672,000 |
| Cost of production | | | |
| Direct materials | 185,000 | 185,100 | 185,220 |
| Direct labour | 274,313 | 275,975 | 279,300 |
| Fixed production overheads | 82,000 | 82,000 | 82,000 |
| Total cost of sales | 541,313 | 543,075 | 546,520 |
| Profit | 148,687 | 154,125 | 125,480 |

**Catering Division statement of financial position**

| | | | |
|---|---|---|---|
| Non-current assets | | | |
| Land and buildings | 800,000 | 795,000 | 790,000 |
| Machinery | 480,000 | 460,000 | 420,000 |
| Current assets | | | |
| Inventory of raw materials | 231,000 | 251,500 | 307,800 |
| Amounts due from Airlines Division | 690,000 | 697,200 | 672,000 |
| Current liabilities | | | |
| Trade payables | 190,000 | 185,000 | 185,100 |
| **Net current assets** | 731,000 | 763,700 | 794,700 |
| Non-current liabilities | 800,000 | 800,000 | 800,000 |
| Net assets | 1,211,000 | 1,218,700 | 1,204,700 |

| | Units | Units | Units |
|---|---|---|---|
| Capacity (meals per month) | 125,000 | 125,000 | 125,000 |
| Meals ordered by Flights Division | 115,000 | 117,000 | 112,000 |
| Budgeted meals | 115,000 | 117,000 | 112,000 |
| Meals produced | 115,500 | 116,200 | 117,600 |

(a) **Calculate the following performance indicators for each month, expressing each answer to two decimal places:**

(i) Profit margin
(ii) Direct material cost as a percentage of revenue
(iii) Direct labour cost as a percentage of revenue
(iv) Return on capital employed (ROCE)
(v) Meals produced as a percentage of orders
(vi) Meals produced as a percentage of capacity

(b) **Draft a brief report to the managing director commenting on the performance of the division in November.** You should base your report on your calculations above.

---

**REPORT**

To:         Managing Director

From:      Accounting Technician

Subject:   Performance of the Catering Division

Date:      7 December 20X6

---

(c) The operations director is now reviewing various alternatives to determine whether it is possible to reduce monthly costs.

She is considering whether to invest in a new machine which:

- Will mechanise part of the process and reduce the labour cost per meal from the current rate of £2.375 to £1.50

- Could either be purchased for £3 million or rented for £50,000 per month

- Is expected to have a life of 10 years and a scrap value of £900,000.

If the company purchases the machine, the division's net assets as at the end of November will increase by £1 million plus the profit for the period.

If the company rents the machine, the division's net assets will only increase by the profit for the period.

The operations director's performance is measured on ROCE, which she would like to see improved.

(i) **Prepare a forecast statement of profit or loss (income statement) and net asset calculation (a full statement of financial position is not required) for both options (renting and purchasing) for one month.**

**Note: Assume that the number of meals produced and sold will be 120,000 per month at a cost of £6 per meal. The material cost will remain as standard at £2 per meal, and monthly overheads will stay at £82,000 before any additional costs of the new machine. Ignore the time value of money.**

(ii) **Calculate the profit margin and the ROCE for both options.**

(iii) **What action would you recommend to the operations director?**

## Task 7.14

A company makes two products, S1 and S2. The following information is available for the year.

|  | S1 | S2 |
|---|---|---|
| Sales volume (units) | 50,000 | 100,000 |
|  | £ | £ |
| Sales price per unit | 20 | 16 |
| Total sales revenue | 1,000,000 | 1,600,000 |
| Material costs | 300,000 | 600,000 |
| Labour costs | 300,000 | 600,000 |
| Fixed production costs | 250,000 | 250,000 |
| Total cost of sales | 850,000 | 1,450,000 |
| Gross profit | 150,000 | 150,000 |
|  |  |  |
| Material cost per unit | £6.00 | £6.00 |
| Labour cost per unit | £6.00 | £6.00 |
| Fixed production cost per unit | £5.00 | £2.50 |
| Gross profit margin | 15.00% | 9.38% |

**Explain why the gross profit margin is different between S1 and S2 by considering the following:**

(a) Sales price and sales volume
(b) Material cost
(c) Fixed production cost

## Task 7.15

You have been provided with the following information for two scenarios involving a company which operates an absorption costing system.

|  | Scenario 1 | Scenario 2 |
|---|---|---|
| Sales volume (units) | 120,000 | 150,000 |
|  | £ | £ |
| Revenue | 1,680,000 | 1,800,000 |
| Gross profit | 600,000 | 450,000 |
| Profit from operations | 275,000 | 200,000 |
| Net assets | 2,298,400 | 2,100,340 |
| Inventory | 147,950 | 167,500 |

(a) **Calculate the following performance indicators for Scenario 1 and 2. Give your answers to TWO decimal places.**

|  | Scenario 1 | Scenario 2 |
|---|---|---|
| Return on net assets |  |  |
| Inventory holding period in days |  |  |
| Sales price per unit |  |  |
| Full production cost per unit |  |  |

(b) **Complete the table below for Scenario 3.**

|  | Scenario 3 |
|---|---|
| Net assets (£) | £175,000 |
| Return on net assets (%) | 13 |
| Profit margin (%) | 14 |
| Gearing (%) | 32.75 |
| Profit (to the nearest £) |  |
| Sales revenue (to the nearest £) |  |

(c) **Fill in the boxes with the appropriate options to show how to calculate the gearing. If there is more than one correct answer either answer will achieve full marks.**

$$\frac{\boxed{\phantom{XXXXXXXXXXXX}}}{\boxed{\phantom{XXXXXXXXXXXX}}} \times \boxed{\phantom{XXXXXXXXXXXX}}$$

**Options:**

| | | |
|---|---|---|
| Total Debt | Profit | 365 |
| Net Assets | Total Equity | 100 |
| Total Debt plus Total Equity | Total Debt less Total Equity | % |

## Task 7.16

The following information, shown in the Income Statement below, has been supplied for two different companies. The sales volume of Company A is 900,000 units and for Company B is 1,400,000 units.

| Income statement | Company A | Company B |
|---|---|---|
| | £000 | £000 |
| Total sales revenue | 37,800 | 49,000 |
| **Production costs** | | |
| Material cost | 6,300 | 8,400 |
| Labour cost | 16,200 | 16,800 |
| Fixed production cost | 3,150 | 4,200 |
| Total cost of sales | 25,650 | 29,400 |
| **Gross profit** | **12,150** | **19,600** |

| Income statement | Company A | Company B |
|---|---|---|
| | £000 | £000 |
| Selling and distribution costs | 900 | 1,680 |
| Administration costs | 1,980 | 2,940 |
| Advertising costs | 1,260 | 3,220 |
| **Profit** | **8,010** | **11,760** |
| | | |
| Additional information | | |
| Net assets | 89,000 | 60,000 |

(a) **Complete the table below by calculating the performance indicators for Company A and Company B. If rounding is required, show your answer to two decimal places.**

| | Company A | Company B |
|---|---|---|
| Selling price per unit | | |
| Labour cost per unit | | |
| Fixed production cost per unit | | |
| Selling and distribution costs as a % of revenue | | |
| Gross profit margin % | | |
| Profit margin % | | |
| Return on net assets % | | |

You have been requested to calculate control ratios for a company. The following has been provided to assist you in making the calculations.

**Labour efficiency ratio**

Standard hours for actual production/actual hours worked expressed as a percentage

**Capacity ratio**

Actual hours worked/Budgeted hours expressed as a percentage

**Activity ratio**

Actual output/Budgeted output expressed as a percentage

Data is available for two years:

|  | Year 1 | Year 2 |
|---|---|---|
| Budgeted production (units) | 42,000 | 48,000 |
| Standard hours per unit | 0.8 hours | 0.8 hours |
| Actual hours worked | 30,920 | 38,720 |
| Actual production (units) | 37,200 | 51,000 |

(b) **Calculate the labour efficiency ratio for each year. Round your answers to two decimal places.**

| Ratio | Year 1 % | Year 2 % |
|---|---|---|
| Labour efficiency ratio |  |  |

# Chapter 8 – Cost management

## Task 8.1

A company is considering the purchase of a small sole trader's business for a cost of £84,000 on 30 June 20X5. The estimated cash inflows from the purchased business are:

|  | £ |
|---|---|
| 30 June 20X6 | 26,000 |
| 30 June 20X7 | 30,000 |
| 30 June 20X8 | 21,000 |
| 30 June 20X9 | 14,000 |

Thereafter the purchased business will be closed down and its operations merged with the other operations of the company.

The company has a cost of capital of 7% and analyses potential investments using the net present value method.

The discount factors at 7% are as follows:

| Year | Discount factor |
|---|---|
| 0 | 1.000 |
| 1 | 0.935 |
| 2 | 0.873 |
| 3 | 0.816 |
| 4 | 0.763 |

**The net present value of the investment is £**

## Task 8.2

The managers of a business are considering investing in a new factory. It has been estimated that the cost now would total £355,000. The anticipated profit for the factory for each of the next five years are as follows:

|  | Profit<br>£ |
|---|---|
| Year 1 | 47,000 |
| Year 2 | 55,000 |
| Year 3 | 68,000 |
| Year 4 | 53,000 |
| Year 5 | 22,000 |

The profit figures given are after charging depreciation of £60,000 in each year. The business has a cost of capital of 12%.

The discount factors at 12% are as follows:

| Year | Discount factor |
|------|-----------------|
| 0 | 1.000 |
| 1 | 0.893 |
| 2 | 0.797 |
| 3 | 0.712 |
| 4 | 0.635 |
| 5 | 0.567 |

**The net present value of the potential investment is £** [            ]

## Task 8.3

**What is life cycle costing?**

## Task 8.4

(a) **Explain the five stages of the product life cycle and how costs and income will alter in each of the five stages.**

(b) **How does knowledge of the product life cycle affect forecasting of future sales?**

## Task 8.5

A company is developing a new product. There are currently several other companies manufacturing similar products which sell for a price of £50 each. The company wishes to make a margin of 20%.

**The target cost of the new product is £** [            ]

## Task 8.6

A company can sell 10,000 units in the next year, giving total sales of £250,000. The company wants to make a profit margin of 70%.

**The target cost per unit is £** [            ]

## Task 8.7

Alpha Limited is considering designing a new product, product BPT, and will use target costing to arrive at the target cost of the product. You have been given the following information.

- The price at which the product will be sold has not yet been decided.

- It has been estimated that if the price is set at £40 the demand will be 500,000 units, and if the price is set at £50 the demand will be 430,000 units.

- The costs of production include fixed production costs of £8,500,000 which will give a production capacity of 500,000 units.

- In order to produce above this level the fixed costs will step up by £1,500,000.

- The required profit margin is 30%.

- The variable cost per unit is £13 for the production volume of 430,000 units.

- For production volume of 500,000 units the variable cost will be £12 per unit.

**(a) Complete the table for both levels of demand.**

|  | Sales price £40 | Sales price £50 |
|---|---|---|
| The target total production cost per unit |  |  |
| The target fixed production cost per unit |  |  |
| The target fixed production cost |  |  |

**(b) Complete the following sentence.**

Alpha should set the price at [　　　　　　▼] in order to achieve the target profit margin.

**Picklist:**

£40
£50

..........................................................................................

## Task 8.8

A company manufactures and sells an electronic product and is preparing information for the next period.

The marketing department has estimated that if the price is set at £70 the demand will be 10,000 units and if the price is set at £90 the demand will be 6,000 units.

The cost information below has been provided by the finance department.

|  | Option 1 | Option 2 |
|---|---|---|
| Sales price | £70 | £90 |
| Sales volume | 10,000 | 6,000 |
| Costs |  |  |
| Variable materials cost | £20 | £20 |
| Variable labour cost | £10 | £10 |
| Fixed production cost per unit | £24 | £40 |
| Total cost | £54 | £70 |

The production manager says that the capacity of the factory is 8,000 units.

**(a) Calculate the profit achieved if the price is set at £90 and the demand is 6,000 units.**

The profit achieved is £ [          ] .

**(b) Calculate the profit achieved if the price is set at £70 and the demand is 10,000 units but the factory can only produce 8,000 units.**

The profit achieved is £ [          ] .

An overseas supplier has offered to manufacture 4,000 units at a price of £45.

**(c) Calculate the profit achieved if the price is set at £70 with demand of 10,000 units, manufacturing 6,000 units and purchasing 4,000 units from the overseas supplier.**

The profit achieved is £ [          ] .

Company Alpha is developing a new product and expects the target cost to be £50 and will set the sales price to achieve a profit margin of 20%.

**(d) Complete the following sentence.**

The sales price per unit will need to be £ [          ] to achieve a profit margin of 20%.

Company Beta sells a product with a mark up of 30% on cost. The cost of the product is £80.

**(e) Complete the following sentence.**

The sales price to achieve a mark up of 30% is £ [          ] .

## Task 8.9

Beta Limited will be replacing some machines in the next year and needs to decide whether to purchase or lease the machines.

(a) Calculate the discounted lifecycle cost of purchasing the machines based upon the following:

- Purchase price of £400,000

- Annual running costs of £50,000 in year 1 increasing by 5% for year 2 and another 5% for year 3 and then remaining constant for the next two years

- The running costs are paid annually in arrears

- A residual value of £35,000 at the end of the five years

If there are nil cashflows for any years you MUST enter 0 in the appropriate box. Net cash outflows must be shown as positive figures and net cash inflows as negative figures (use minus signs).

Round to the nearest whole £.

| Year | 0 | 1 | 2 | 3 | 4 | 5 |
|---|---|---|---|---|---|---|
| Cash flow (£) | | | | | | |
| Discounted factor | 1 | 0.952 | 0.907 | 0.864 | 0.823 | 0.784 |
| Present value (£) | | | | | | |
| Net present cost (£) | | | | | | |

(b) Calculate the discounted lifecycle cost of leasing the machines for five years based upon annual costs of £140,000 paid annually in advance.

If there are nil cashflows for any years you MUST enter 0 in the appropriate box. Net cash outflows must be shown as positive figures and net cash inflows as negative figures (use minus signs).

Round to the nearest whole £.

| Year | 0 | 1 | 2 | 3 | 4 | 5 |
|---|---|---|---|---|---|---|
| Cash flow (£) | | | | (140,000) | | |
| Discounted factor | 1 | 0.952 | 0.907 | 0.864 | 0.823 | 0.784 |
| Present value (£) | | | | | | |
| Net present cost (£) | | | | | | |

**(c)  Complete the following sentence.**

Based on the calculations it is best to [ _____ ▼ ] as this saves

£ [ _____ ] .

**Picklist:**

Lease
Purchase

..........................................................................................................

# Chapter 9 – Activity based costing (ABC)

## Task 9.1

Charleroi Aircon Ltd design and install industrial air-conditioning systems. The company is based in Birmingham.

Charleroi's usual pricing policy is to use direct costs (equipment and installation labour) plus a mark-up of 50% to establish the selling price for an air-conditioning installation.

The company is about to tender for two contracts, quotation HMG/012 and quotation CFG/013.

The company is in the process of designing an Activity Based Costing system and the following information has been obtained about the two jobs.

| Estimates related to contracts HMG/012 and CFG/013 | | |
|---|---|---|
| Contract number: | HMG/012 | CFG/013 |
| Equipment: cost | £175,000 | £120,000 |
| number of items purchased | 650 | 410 |
| Direct labour: hours | 10,000 | 6,000 |
| hourly rate | £13 | £11 |
| Design hours | 1,280 | 620 |
| Distance from Birmingham office (miles round-trip) | 320 | 90 |
| Engineer site visits required | 30 | 10 |

The following overhead information is also available in relation to ABC costs.

| ABC details for overhead activities connected with air conditioning installation contracts | | | |
|---|---|---|---|
| Activity | Budgeted cost pool | Cost driver | Cost driver units pa |
| | £pa | | |
| Design department | 675,000 | Design hours | 25,000 |
| Site engineers | 370,000 | Miles travelled | 185,000 |
| Purchasing department | 105,000 | Items purchased | 15,000 |
| Payroll department | 75,000 | Direct hours | 300,000 |
| Site management | 750,000 | Direct hours | 300,000 |
| Post-installation inspection | 80,000 | Items purchased | 20,000 |

(a) **Usual pricing policy**

The price of job HMG/012 based upon direct costs plus 50% mark-up is

£ [          ]

The price of job CFG/013 based upon direct costs plus 50% mark-up is

£ [          ]

(b) **Complete the tables to show the activity-based overhead costs for each of jobs HMG/012 and CFG/013.**

| Activity | Budgeted cost pool | Cost driver | Cost driver units pa | Cost per unit of cost driver |
|---|---|---|---|---|
| | £ | | | £ |
| Design department | | | | |
| Site engineers | | | | |
| Purchasing department | | | | |
| Payroll dept | | | | |
| Site management | | | | |
| Post-installation inspection | | | | |

| Cost pool | Total cost HMG/012 | Total cost CFG/013 |
|---|---|---|
| | £ | £ |
| Design department | | |
| Site engineers | | |
| Purchasing department | | |
| Payroll dept | | |
| Site management | | |
| Post-installation inspection | | |
| **Total cost** | | |

## Task 9.2

You are employed as a financial analyst at Drampton plc, a computer retailer. Drampton plc has recently taken over Little Ltd, a small company making personal computers and servers. Little appears to make all of its profits from servers. Drampton's finance director tells you that Little's fixed overheads are currently charged to production using standard labour hours and gives you their standard cost of making PCs and servers. These are shown below.

**Little Ltd: Standard cost per computer**

| Model | Server | PC |
|---|---|---|
| Annual budgeted volume | 5 | 5,000 |
| **Unit standard cost** | | |
| | £ | £ |
| Material and labour | 50,000 | 500 |
| Fixed overhead | 4,000 | 40 |
| Standard cost per unit | 54,000 | 540 |

The finance director asks for your help and suggests you reclassify the fixed overheads between the two models using activity-based costing. You are given the following information.

- **Budgeted total annual fixed overheads**

|  | £ |
|---|---|
| Set-up costs | 10,000 |
| Rent and power (production area) | 120,000 |
| Rent (stores area) | 50,000 |
| Salaries of store issue staff | 40,000 |
| Total | 220,000 |

Every time Little makes a server, it has to stop making PCs and rearrange the factory layout. The cost of this is shown as set-up costs. If the factory did not make any servers these costs would be eliminated.

- **Cost drivers**

| | Server | PC | Total |
|---|---|---|---|
| Number of set-ups | 5 | 0 | 5 |
| Number of weeks of production | 10 | 40 | 50 |
| Floor area of stores (square metres) | 400 | 400 | 800 |
| Number of issues of inventory | 2,000 | 8,000 | 10,000 |

Complete the table to show how to reallocate Little's budgeted total fixed annual overheads between server and PC production on an Activity Based Costing basis.

|  | Server allocated overheads £ | PC allocated overheads £ |
|---|---|---|
| Set-up costs |  |  |
| Rent and power (production area) |  |  |
| Rent (stores area) |  |  |
| Salaries of stores issue staff |  |  |
| Total overheads |  |  |

## Task 9.3

You are the management accountant at a manufacturing company which makes two products, the Plastic and the Metal. Standard costing information for direct material and labour costs are given for the two products below.

| Product | Plastic | Metal |
|---|---|---|
| Budgeted production units | 5,000 | 1,000 |
| **Unit standard cost** |  |  |
|  | £ | £ |
| Material | 10 | 25 |
| Labour | 2 | 4 |

The company has the following budgeted overheads.

|  | £ |
|---|---|
| Power for machinery | 110,000 |
| Rent of factory | 120,000 |
| Canteen costs | 40,000 |
| Total | 270,000 |

The cost drivers for these costs are given below, for the different products.

### Cost drivers

|  | Plastic | Metal | Total |
|---|---|---|---|
| Machine hours | 2,500 | 3,000 | 5,500 |
| Floor space (square metres) | 1,000 | 200 | 1,200 |
| Number of employees | 200 | 50 | 250 |

**Complete the table to show how to reallocate the budgeted total overheads between the two products on an Activity Based Costing basis.**

| | Plastic allocated overheads £ | Metal allocated overheads £ |
|---|---|---|
| Power for machinery | | |
| Rent of factory | | |
| Canteen costs | | |
| Total overheads | | |

# Chapter 10 – Decision making techniques

## Task 10.1

A business sells a single product and has budgeted sales of 115,000 units for the next period. The selling price per unit is £28 and the variable costs of production are £17. The fixed costs of the business are £1,100,000.

**The breakeven point in units is** ☐ **units**

**The margin of safety in units is** ☐ **units**

**The margin of safety as a percentage of budgeted sales is** ☐

## Task 10.2

The following information relates to one period for Product D which is manufactured by Mild Ltd.

Expected sales revenue = £160,000

Selling price per unit = £16 per unit

Variable cost = £8 per unit

Fixed costs = £40,000

**The breakeven point both in terms of units and sales revenue is:**

| Breakeven point in units | | Breakeven point in sales revenue | |
|---|---|---|---|
| 5,000 units | ☐ | £40,000 | ☐ |
| 5,000 units | ☐ | £80,000 | ☐ |
| 10,000 units | ☐ | £40,000 | ☐ |
| 10,000 units | ☐ | £80,000 | ☐ |

## Task 10.3

The following information relates to one period for Product V which is manufactured by Hay-on-Wye Ltd.

Selling price per unit = £80

Variable cost per unit = £25

Budgeted fixed costs = £110,000

Budgeted sales = 2,500 units

**The margin of safety, in terms of both units and sales revenue is:**

Units

500 ☐

2,000 ☐

1,900 ☐

500 ☐

Sales revenue

£12,500 ☐

£160,000 ☐

£152,000 ☐

£40,000 ☐

## Task 10.4

A business sells a single product at a selling price of £83 and the variable costs of production and sales are £65 per unit. The fixed costs of the business are £540,000.

**The number of units of the product that the business must sell in order to make a target profit of £300,000 is** ⬚ **units.**

## Task 10.5

A business sells its single product for £40. The variable costs of this product total £28. The fixed costs of the business are £518,000.

**The sales revenue required in order to make a target profit of £250,000 is**
£ ⬚

## Task 10.6

Three products are produced by a business. There is a shortage of the material which is used to make each product, with only 3,000 kg available in the coming period.

| | Product | | |
|---|---|---|---|
| | A | B | C |
| Direct materials @ £4 per kg | £8 | £4 | £16 |
| Direct labour @ £10 per hour | £20 | £5 | £15 |
| Selling price | £40 | £25 | £47 |
| Maximum sales demand | 1,000 units | 800 units | 600 units |

**Complete the table to determine the production plan which will maximise contribution.**

| Product | Units |
|---|---|
| | |
| | |
| | |

## Task 10.7

A business produces three products. Production and sales details are given below:

| | Product | | |
|---|---|---|---|
| | R | S | T |
| Direct materials @ £5 per kg | £20 | £25 | £15 |
| Direct labour @ £7 per hour | £14 | £21 | £21 |
| Selling price | £45 | £60 | £55 |
| Machine hours per unit | 4 | 3 | 2 |
| Maximum sales demand | 20,000 units | 25,000 units | 8,000 units |

During the next period the supply of materials is limited to 250,000 kgs, the labour hours available are 100,000 and the machine hours available are 180,000.

Complete the table to determine the production plan which will maximise contribution.

| Product | Units |
|---|---|
|  |  |
|  |  |
|  |  |

The contribution that will be earned under this production plan is £ [               ]

---

## Task 10.8

An organisation makes two products, X and Y. The following information is available for the next month.

|  | Product X £ per unit | Product Y £ per unit |
|---|---|---|
| Selling prices | 100 | 135 |
| **Variable costs** |  |  |
| Material cost (£5 per kilogram) | 30 | 40 |
| Labour cost | 25 | 38 |
| Total variable costs | 55 | 78 |
| **Fixed costs** |  |  |
| Fixed production costs | 12 | 15 |
| Fixed administration costs | 8 | 8 |
| Total fixed costs | 20 | 23 |
| Profit per unit | 25 | 34 |
| Monthly demand | 3,500 | 4,250 |

The materials are in short supply in the coming month and only 45,000 kilograms of material will be available.

(a) Complete the following table, rounding to the nearest penny.

|  | Product X | Product Y |
|---|---|---|
| The contribution per unit is |  |  |
| The contribution per kilogram of materials |  |  |

(b) The optimal production order for products X, and Y is [               ▼]

Picklist:

Product X then Product Y
Product Y then Product X

**(c)  Complete the table below for the optimal production mix**

|  | Product X | Product Y |
|---|---|---|
| Production in units |  |  |

**(d)  Complete the table below for the total contribution for each product.**

|  | Product X | Product Y |
|---|---|---|
| Total contribution |  |  |

## Task 10.9

Alpha makes two products, Tig and Tag. The following information is available for the next month.

|  | Product Tig | Product Tag |
|---|---|---|
|  | £ per unit | £ per unit |
| Selling price | 4,000 | 4,950 |
| Variable costs |  |  |
| Material cost (£400 per kilogram) | 2,400 | 3,000 |
| Labour cost | 400 | 600 |
| Total variable cost | 2,800 | 3,600 |
| Fixed costs |  |  |
| Production cost | 450 | 450 |
| Administration cost | 300 | 300 |
| Total fixed costs | 750 | 750 |
| Profit per unit | 450 | 600 |
|  |  |  |
| Monthly demand | 200 units | 300 units |

The materials are in short supply in the coming month and only 3,000 kilograms of material will be available from the existing supplier.

**(a)  Complete the table below.**

|  | Product Tig | Product Tag |
|---|---|---|
| The contribution per unit is |  |  |
| The contribution per kilogram of materials is |  |  |

**(b)** **Complete the following statement.**

The optimal production order for products Tig and Tag is [ ▼ ]

**Picklist:**

Tag then Tig
Tig then Tag

**(c)** **Complete the table below for the optimal production mix.**

|  | Product Tig | Product Tag |
|---|---|---|
| Production in units |  |  |

**(d)** **Complete the table below for the total contribution for each product.**

|  | Product Tig £ | Product Tag £ |
|---|---|---|
| Total contribution |  |  |

Alpha has been approached by another materials supplier who can supply up to 500 kilograms of material at a cost per kilogram of £500. This is a premium of £100 above the normal cost per kilogram.

**(e)** **Complete the table below.**

| Should Alpha purchase the additional material? | Give a reason |
|---|---|
| [ ▼ ] | [ ▼ ] |

**Picklist:**

No
Yes

**Picklist:**

The additional cost per kilogram is greater than the contribution per kilogram
The additional cost per kilogram is greater than the contribution per unit
The additional cost per kilogram is less than the contribution per kilogram
The additional cost per kilogram is less than the contribution per unit

# Answer bank

**Answer bank**

# Chapter 1

## Task 1.1

True ☐

False ☑

|  | 16,000 units | 22,000 units |
|---|---|---|
| Total cost | £54,400 | £68,200 |
| Cost per unit | £3.40 | £3.10 |

Therefore this is not a variable cost – if it were a true variable cost then the cost per unit would be the same at each activity level.

........................................................................................

## Task 1.2

| Cost | Behaviour |
|---|---|
| Cost I | Variable |
| Cost II | Semi-variable or stepped |
| Cost III | Fixed |
| Cost IV | Variable |

**Workings**

Cost I: £7,000 ÷ 1,000 units = £7 per unit

£10,500 ÷ 1,500 units = £7 per unit

Costs increase in direct proportion to output, therefore cost is variable.

Cost II: £11,000 ÷ 1,000 units = £11 per unit

£12,500 ÷ 1,500 units = £8.33 per unit

Costs increase but not in direct proportion to output, therefore cost is semi-variable or stepped.

Cost III: Cost remains the same regardless of level of output, therefore cost is fixed.

Cost IV: £3,800 ÷ 1,000 units = £3.8 per unit

£5,700 ÷ 1,500 units = £3.8 per unit

Costs increase in direct proportion to output, therefore cost is variable.

........................................................................................

## Task 1.3

| Activity level – units | Total production cost £ | Cost per unit £ |
|---|---|---|
| 8,000 | 50,600 | 6.325 |
| 12,000 | 63,400 | 5.283 |
| 15,000 | 73,000 | 4.867 |

**Workings**

| | 8,000 units £ | 12,000 units £ | 15,000 units £ |
|---|---|---|---|
| Variable costs | | | |
| £32,000/10,000 × 8,000 | 25,600 | | |
| £32,000/10,000 × 12,000 | | 38,400 | |
| £32,000/10,000 × 15,000 | | | 48,000 |
| Fixed costs | 25,000 | 25,000 | 25,000 |
| | 50,600 | 63,400 | 73,000 |
| Cost per unit | £6.325 | £5.283 | £4.867 |

## Task 1.4

| Activity level – units | Total supervisors cost £ | Supervisors cost per unit £ |
|---|---|---|
| 500 | 20,000 | 40 |
| 1,000 | 40,000 | 40 |
| 1,500 | 40,000 | 26.67 |

**Workings**

| | 500 units £ | 1,000 units £ | 1,500 units £ |
|---|---|---|---|
| Number of supervisors required | | | |
| 500/750 = 0.67, round up to 1 @ £20,000 | 20,000 | | |
| 1,000/750 = 1.33, round up to 2 @ £20,000 | | 40,000 | |
| 1,500/750 = 2 @ £20,000 | | | 40,000 |
| Cost per unit | £40 | £40 | £26.67 |

# Task 1.5

| | | Cost behaviour |
|---|---|---|
| (a) | Maintenance department costs which are made up of £25,000 of salaries and an average of £500 cost per call out | Semi-variable |
| (b) | Machinery depreciation based upon machine hours used | Variable |
| (c) | Salary costs of nursery school teachers where one teacher is required for every six children in the nursery | Stepped fixed |
| (d) | Rent for a building that houses the factory, stores and maintenance departments | Fixed |

# Task 1.6

**(a)**

| Production level – units | Total cost of production £ | Cost per unit £ |
|---|---|---|
| 1,000 | 82,000 | 82.00 |
| 1,500 | 112,500 | 75.00 |
| 2,000 | 143,000 | 71.50 |

**Workings**

| | 1,000 units £ | 1,500 units £ | 2,000 units £ |
|---|---|---|---|
| Direct materials 6kgs × £4.80 × units | 28,800 | 43,200 | 57,600 |
| Direct labour 4 hours × £7.00 × units | 28,000 | 42,000 | 56,000 |
| Building costs – fixed | 18,000 | 18,000 | 18,000 |
| Leased machines | 1,200 | 1,800 | 2,400 |
| Stores costs £3,000 + £3.00 × units | 6,000 | 7,500 | 9,000 |
| | 82,000 | 112,500 | 143,000 |
| Cost per unit | £82.00 | £75.00 | £71.50 |

**(b)** The cost per unit is decreasing as production quantities increase. This is due to the fact that not all of the costs are variable. The buildings costs are fixed and part of the stores costs are also fixed. For these elements of total cost, as the production quantity increases, the cost per unit decreases. This in turn reduces the total overall unit cost as the quantity increases.

## Task 1.7

The variable cost per machine hour is £15.00

The fixed costs of the maintenance department are £72,000

**Workings**

Variable costs

|  | Machine hours | Cost £ |
|---|---|---|
| June (lowest) | 14,200 | 285,000 |
| August (highest) | 15,200 | 300,000 |
| Increase | 1,000 | 15,000 |
|  |  |  |
| Variable cost = £15,000/1,000 hours |  |  |
|    = £15 per hour |  |  |
|  |  |  |
| Fixed costs: |  |  |
| June |  |  |
| Variable element £15 × 14,200 hours |  | 213,000 |
| Fixed element (bal fig) |  | 72,000 |
| Total cost |  | 285,000 |

## Task 1.8

(a) The fixed element of the production cost is £167,000

    The variable element of the production cost per unit is £7

**Workings**

|  | Activity level | Cost |
|---|---|---|
|  |  | £ |
| July (lowest) | 63,000 | 608,000 |
| September (highest) | 76,000 | 699,000 |
| Increase | 13,000 | 91,000 |
|  |  |  |
| Variable element    = £91,000/13,000 |  |  |
|  |  |  |
|    = £7 per unit |  |  |
| Fixed costs: |  |  |
| July |  |  |
| Variable element £7 × 63,000 units |  | 441,000 |
| Fixed element (bal fig) |  | 167,000 |
| Total cost |  | 608,000 |

**(b)**

| Level of production – units | Production cost £ |
|---|---|
| 74,000 | 685,000 |
| 90,000 | 797,000 |

**Workings**

(i)    Production level of 74,000 units:

|  | £ |
|---|---|
| Variable cost £7 × 74,000 | 518,000 |
| Fixed cost | 167,000 |
| Total cost | 685,000 |

(ii)    Production level of 90,000 units:

|  | £ |
|---|---|
| Variable cost £7 × 90,000 | 630,000 |
| Fixed cost | 167,000 |
| Total cost | 797,000 |

(c) The estimate for the 74,000 units of production is likely to be more accurate than the estimate for 90,000 units. Estimating the costs at 74,000 units is an example of interpolation, in that the estimate is being made for a production level that is within the range of production levels used to estimate the variable and fixed costs. 90,000 units of production is significantly higher than the levels of production used in estimating fixed and variable costs and therefore it is possible that the costs would behave differently at this level of production. This is an example of extrapolation.

## Task 1.9

(a) The variable element of the production cost per unit is £3

(b)

| Level of production – units | Fixed cost – £ |
|---|---|
| 40,000 | 85,000 |
| 48,000 | 135,000 |

### Workings

| | Activity level | Cost – £ |
|---|---|---|
| High | 48,000 | 279,000 – 50,000 = 229,000 |
| Low | 40,000 | 205,000 |
| Increase | 8,000 | 24,000 |
| | | |
| Variable element = £24,000/8,000 | | |
| = £3 per unit | | |
| Fixed element | | |
| At 40,000 units: | | |
| Variable element £3 × 40,000 units | | 120,000 |
| Fixed element (bal fig) | | 85,000 |
| Total cost | | 205,000 |

| | Activity level | Cost – £ |
|---|---|---|
| Fixed element: | | |
| At 48,000 units: | | |
| Variable element £3 × 48,000 units | | 144,000 |
| Fixed element (bal fig) | | 135,000 |
| Total cost | | 279,000 |

## Task 1.10

(a)    Cost of 9,000 units = £64,000

(b)    Cost of 11,000 units = £81,000

**Workings**

Variable cost per unit = $\dfrac{£93,000 - £15,000}{13,000}$ = £6 per unit

Fixed element for activity level up to 9,999 units = £58,000 – (8,000 × £6) = £10,000

Cost at 9,000 units = £10,000 + (9,000 × £6) = £64,000

Cost at 11,000 units = £15,000 + (11,000 × £6) = £81,000

## Task 1.11

(a)    £493,000

(b)    £545,000

We have been told that the variable element is £25 per unit so we can find the fixed element from this at each activity level:

Fixed element at 18,000 units = £468,000 – (18,000 × £25) = £18,000

Fixed element at 22,000 units = £570,000 – (22,000 × £25) = £20,000

Therefore:

Cost at 19,000 units = £18,000 + (19,000 × £25) = £493,000

Cost at 21,000 units = £20,000 + (21,000 × £25) = £545,000

## Task 1.12

**(a)** The standard quantity of labour per unit is [ 15 ] minutes.

**(b)** The budgeted quantity of materials needed to produce 13,500 units of X07 is [ 16,875 ] litres.

**(c)** The budgeted labour hours to produce 12,000 units of X07 is [ 3,000 ] hours.

**(d)** The budgeted labour cost to produce 13,500 units of X07 is £ [ 57,375 ].

**(e)** The budgeted overhead absorption rate per unit is £ [ 5.50 ].

**(f)** The fixed production overheads were [ under absorbed ▼ ] by £ [ 4,080 ].

**Workings**

**(a)** 3,500 direct labour hours / 14,000 units = 0.25 hours (15 minutes).

**(b)** Budgeted quantity per unit = 17,500 litres / 14,000 units = 1.25 litres

13,500 units × 1.25 litres = 16,875 litres

**(c)** Budgeted labour hours per unit = 0.25 hours (see part (a))

12,000 units × 0.25 hours = 3,000 hours

**(d)** Budgeted labour cost per unit = £59,500 / 14,000 units = £4.25

13,500 units × £4.25 hours = £57,375

**(e)** Budgeted OAR = £77,000 / 14,000 units = £5.50 per unit

**(f)** Budgeted OAR = £436,250 / 25,000 units = £17.45 per unit

Overheads absorbed = 27,000 units × £17.45 = £471,150

| | |
|---|---|
| Actual fixed costs | £475,230 |
| Under absorbed | £4,080 |

## Task 1.13

The fixed production overheads were [ over absorbed ] by [ 1250 ] .

**Workings**

Budgeted overhead absorption rate per unit: $\dfrac{£233,750}{55,000}$ = £4.25

Overhead absorbed = actual production at the standard rate: 57,000 units × £4.25 = £242,250.

Actual fixed costs incurred: £241,000.

£242,250 – £241,000 = £1,250.

••••••••••••••••••••••••••••••••••••••••••••••••••••••••••••••••••••••••••••••••••

## Task 1.14

| Absorption rate method | Cutting rate £ | Finishing rate £ | Most appropriate 1, 2 or 3 |
|---|---|---|---|
| Rate per unit | 5.86 | 4.24 | 2 - most appropriate where all products are of similar size and require a similar input in terms of time and resources of the departments |
| Rate per direct labour hour | 14.65 | 1.77 | 3 - most appropriate in labour intensive departments where most of the overhead relates to labour |
| Rate per machine hour | 4.88 | 21.20 | 1 - most appropriate in a largely mechanised department where most of the overhead relates to machinery costs |

**Workings**

| | Cutting | Finishing |
|---|---|---|
| Rate per unit | $\dfrac{58,600}{10,000}$ | $\dfrac{42,400}{10,000}$ |
| | = £5.86 per unit | = £4.24 per unit |

BPP
LEARNING MEDIA

| | Cutting | Finishing |
|---|---|---|
| Rate per direct labour hour | $\dfrac{58,600}{4,000}$ | $\dfrac{42,400}{24,000}$ |
| | = £14.65 per labour hour | = £1.77 per labour hour |
| Rate per machine hour | $\dfrac{58,600}{12,000}$ | $\dfrac{42,400}{2,000}$ |
| | = £4.88 per machine hour | £21.20 per machine hour |

## Task 1.15

(a)

| Department | Overhead absorption rate |
|---|---|
| C | £1.25 per machine hour |
| D | £2.25 per direct labour hour |

**Workings**

$C = \dfrac{£125,000}{100,000}$

= £1.25 per machine hour

as C is a highly mechanised department most of the overhead will relate to the machinery therefore machine hours have been used to absorb the overhead.

$D = \dfrac{£180,000}{80,000}$

= £2.25 per direct labour hour

as D is a highly labour intensive department then most of the overhead will relate to the hours that are worked by the labour force therefore labour hours are used to absorb the overhead.

(b) The overhead to be included in the cost of product P is £22.00

**Workings**

Product P – department C overhead    £1.25 × 5    = £ 6.25

department D overhead    £2.25 × 7    = £15.75
£22.00

## Task 1.16

| Overhead apportioned to packaging department | £11,429 |
|---|---|
| Overhead apportioned to assembly department | £8,571 |

**Workings**

Number of employees who use canteen = 20 + 50% × 30 = 35 employees

Cost per employee = £20,000/35 = £571.43 per employee

Therefore cost apportioned to packaging department = 20 × £571.43 = £11,429

Cost apportioned to assembly department = 15 × £571.43 = £8,571

## Task 1.17

| | Under-absorption £ | Over-absorption £ | Debit/Credit |
|---|---|---|---|
| Budgeted production was 1,200 units and budgeted overheads were £5,400. Overheads are to be absorbed on a unit basis. The actual production was 1,000 units and the overheads incurred were £5,000. | 500 | | Debit |
| Budgeted production was 600 units to be produced in 1,800 labour hours. Budgeted overheads of £5,040 are to be absorbed on a direct labour hour basis. The actual production for the period was 700 units in 2,200 labour hours and the actual overheads were £5,100. | | 1,060 | Credit |
| Budgeted production was 40,000 units and the budgeted machine hours were 2 hours per unit. Budgeted overheads were £320,000 and were to be absorbed on a machine hour basis. The actual overheads incurred were £320,000 and the production was 42,000 units. The total machine hours were 82,000. | | 8,000 | Credit |

## Workings

**(a)** Overhead absorption rate = $\dfrac{£5,400}{1,200}$

= £4.50 per unit

Overhead incurred = £5,000

Overhead absorbed

1,000 units × £4.50 = £4,500

Under-absorbed overhead = £500 – a further expense in the statement of profit or loss (income statement)

**(b)** Overhead absorption rate = $\dfrac{£5,040}{1,800}$

= £2.80 per direct labour hour

Overhead incurred = £5,100

Overhead absorbed

2,200 hours × £2.80 = £6,160

Over-absorbed overhead = £1,060 – a credit to the statement of profit or loss (income statement)

**(c)** Overhead absorption rate = $\dfrac{£320,000}{80,000}$

= £4.00 per machine hour

Overhead incurred = £320,000

Overhead absorbed

82,000 × £4.00 = £328,000

Over-absorbed overhead = £8,000 – a credit to the statement of profit or loss (income statement)

# Task 1.18

The unit cost under absorption costing will be £39.50

The unit cost under marginal costing will be £37.50

**Workings**

**(a) Absorption costing**

|  | £ |
|---|---|
| Direct materials | 12.00 |
| Direct labour – Cutting (2 × £7.40) | 14.80 |
| Finishing | 6.80 |
| Variable overheads: |  |
| Cutting (2 × £1.40) | 2.80 |
| Finishing (1 × £1.10) | 1.10 |
| Fixed overheads: |  |
| Cutting (2 × £0.60) | 1.20 |
| Finishing (1 × £0.80) | 0.80 |
|  | 39.50 |

**(b) Marginal costing**

|  | £ |
|---|---|
| Direct materials | 12.00 |
| Direct labour – Cutting (2 × £7.40) | 14.80 |
| Finishing | 6.80 |
| Variable overheads: |  |
| Cutting (2 × £1.40) | 2.80 |
| Finishing (1 × £1.10) | 1.10 |
|  | 37.50 |

**Workings: Hourly absorption rates**

|  | Rate per hour £ |
|---|---|
| Variable overheads: |  |
| Cutting (£336,000/240,000) | 1.40 |
| Finishing (£132,000/120,000) | 1.10 |
| Fixed overheads: |  |
| Cutting (£144,000/240,000) | 0.60 |
| Finishing (£96,000/120,000) | 0.80 |

# Task 1.19

(a) The absorption costing profit for July was £52,800

The absorption costing profit for August was £60,000

The marginal costing profit for July was £49,100

The marginal costing profit for August was £61,850

## Workings

### Cost per unit – absorption costing

| | £ |
|---|---|
| Direct materials | 6.80 |
| Direct labour | 3.60 |
| Variable costs (£32,400/24,000) | 1.35 |
| Fixed costs (£44,400/24,000) | 1.85 |
| | 13.60 |

### Cost per unit – marginal costing

| | £ |
|---|---|
| Direct materials | 6.80 |
| Direct labour | 3.60 |
| Variable costs (£32,400/24,000) | 1.35 |
| | 11.75 |

### Absorption costing – statement of profit loss (income statement)

| | | July | | August | |
|---|---|---|---|---|---|
| | | £ | £ | £ | £ |
| Sales | (22,000 × £16) | | 352,000 | | |
| | (25,000 × £16) | | | | 400,000 |
| Less cost of sales | | | | | |
| Opening inventory | (1,500 × £13.60) | 20,400 | | | |
| | (3,500 × £13.60) | | | 47,600 | |
| Production | (24,000 × £13.60) | 326,400 | | 326,400 | |
| | | 346,800 | | 374,000 | |
| Less closing inventory | | | | | |
| | (3,500 × £13.60) | (47,600) | | | |
| | (2,500 × £13.60) | | | (34,000) | |
| | | | 299,200 | | 340,000 |
| Profit | | | 52,800 | | 60,000 |

### Marginal costing – statement of profit or loss (income statement)

| | | July | | August | |
|---|---|---|---|---|---|
| | | £ | £ | £ | £ |
| Sales | (22,000 × £16) | | 352,000 | | |
| | (25,000 × £16) | | | | 400,000 |
| Less: cost of sales | | | | | |
| Opening inventory | (1,500 × £11.75) | 17,625 | | | |
| | (3,500 × £11.75) | | | 41,125 | |
| Production | (24,000 × £11.75) | 282,000 | | 282,000 | |
| | | 299,625 | | 323,125 | |
| Less: closing inventory | | | | | |
| | (3,500 × £11.75) | (41,125) | | | |
| | (2,500 × £11.75) | | | (29,375) | |
| | | | 258,500 | | 293,750 |
| Contribution | | | 93,500 | | 106,250 |
| Fixed costs | | | (44,400) | | (44,400) |
| | | | 49,100 | | 61,850 |

**(b)** Reconciliation of profit figures

|  | July £ | August £ |
|---|---|---|
| Absorption cost profit | 52,800 | 60,000 |
| Increase in inventory  (3,500 – 1,500) | | |
| × fixed c.p.u.    2,000 × £1.85 | (3,700) | |
| Decrease in inventory  (3,500 – 2,500) | | |
| × fixed c.p.u.    1,000 × £1.85 | | 1,850 |
| Marginal cost profit | 49,100 | 61,850 |

## Task 1.20

**(a)** The profit for the quarter under absorption costing is £47,560

The profit for the quarter under marginal costing £48,840

**Workings**

**Unit cost – absorption costing**

|  | £ |
|---|---|
| Direct materials | 23.60 |
| Direct labour (4 × £5.80) | 23.20 |
| Variable overheads (£88,000/8,000) | 11.00 |
| Fixed overheads (£51,200/8,000) | 6.40 |
|  | 64.20 |

**Unit cost – marginal costing**

|  | £ |
|---|---|
| Direct materials | 23.60 |
| Direct labour (4 × £5.80) | 23.20 |
| Variable overheads (£88,000/8,000) | 11.00 |
|  | 57.80 |

**Absorption costing – statement of profit or loss (income statement)**

|  | £ | £ |
|---|---|---|
| Sales (8,200 × £70) | | 574,000 |
| Less cost of sales | | |
| Opening inventory  (840 × £64.20) | 53,928 | |
| Production cost (8,000 × £64.20) | 513,600 | |
|  | 567,528 | |
| Less closing inventory (640 × £64.20) | (41,088) | |
|  | | 526,440 |
| Profit | | 47,560 |

### Marginal costing – statement of profit or loss (income statement)

|  | £ | £ |
|---|---:|---:|
| Sales (8,200 × £70) | | 574,000 |
| Less cost of sales | | |
| Opening inventory (840 × £57.80) | 48,552 | |
| Production cost (8,000 × £57.80) | 462,400 | |
| | 510,952 | |
| Less closing inventory (640 × £57.80) | (36,992) | |
| | | 473,960 |
| Contribution | | 100,040 |
| Less fixed costs | | (51,200) |
| Profit | | 48,840 |

**(b)**

|  | £ |
|---|---:|
| Absorption costing profit | 47,560 |
| Decrease in inventory × fixed cost per unit (200 × £6.40) | 1,280 |
| Marginal costing profit | 48,840 |

# Chapter 2

## Task 2.1

| | Production costs | Three month moving total | Three month moving average |
|---|---|---|---|
| | £ | £ | £ |
| March | 104,500 | | |
| April | 110,300 | 327,600 | 109,200 |
| May | 112,800 | 332,500 | 110,833 |
| June | 109,400 | 339,800 | 113,267 |
| July | 117,600 | 343,000 | 114,333 |
| August | 116,000 | 352,800 | 117,600 |
| September | 119,200 | 357,500 | 119,167 |
| October | 122,300 | 362,000 | 120,667 |
| November | 120,500 | 362,100 | 120,700 |
| December | 119,300 | | |

## Task 2.2

| | | Actual | 5-day moving average trend | Seasonal variation (actual – trend) |
|---|---|---|---|---|
| | | £ | £ | £ |
| Week 1 | Day 1 | 600 | | |
| | Day 2 | 700 | | |
| | Day 3 | 1,000 | 1,000 | – |
| | Day 4 | 1,200 | 1,016 | +184 |
| | Day 5 | 1,500 | 1,026 | +474 |
| Week 2 | Day 1 | 680 | 1,076 | −396 |
| | Day 2 | 750 | 1,116 | −366 |
| | Day 3 | 1,250 | 1,188 | + 62 |
| | Day 4 | 1,400 | 1,216 | +184 |
| | Day 5 | 1,860 | 1,272 | +588 |

| | | Actual | 5-day moving average trend | Seasonal variation (actual – trend) |
|---|---|---|---|---|
| Week 3 | Day 1 | 820 | 1,410 | –590 |
| | Day 2 | 1,030 | 1,550 | –520 |
| | Day 3 | 1,940 | 1,678 | +262 |
| | Day 4 | 2,100 | 1,714 | +386 |
| | Day 5 | 2,500 | 1,772 | +728 |
| Week 4 | Day 1 | 1,000 | 1,696 | –696 |
| | Day 2 | 1,320 | 1,734 | –414 |
| | Day 3 | 1,560 | 1,768 | –208 |
| | Day 4 | 2,290 | | |
| | Day 5 | 2,670 | | |

## Task 2.3

| | | Actual | 4-quarter moving average | Centred moving average – trend | Seasonal variations |
|---|---|---|---|---|---|
| | | £ | £ | £ | £ |
| 20X5 | Quarter 3 | 50,600 | | | |
| | | | | | |
| | Quarter 4 | 52,800 | | | |
| | | | 51,900 | | |
| 20X6 | Quarter 1 | 55,600 | | 51,975 | +3,625 |
| | | | 52,050 | | |
| | Quarter 2 | 48,600 | | 52,188 | –3,588 |
| | | | 52,325 | | |
| | Quarter 3 | 51,200 | | 52,625 | –1,425 |
| | | | 52,925 | | |
| | Quarter 4 | 53,900 | | 53,075 | +825 |
| | | | 53,225 | | |
| 20X7 | Quarter 1 | 58,000 | | 53,450 | +4,550 |
| | | | 53,675 | | |
| | Quarter 2 | 49,800 | | 53,763 | –3,963 |
| | | | 53,850 | | |

| | | Actual | 4-quarter moving average | Centred moving average – trend | Seasonal variations |
|---|---|---|---|---|---|
| | Quarter 3 | 53,000 | | 54,113 | –1,113 |
| | | | 54,375 | | |
| | Quarter 4 | 54,600 | | 54,488 | +112 |
| | | | 54,600 | | |
| 20X8 | Quarter 1 | 60,100 | | 54,750 | +5,350 |
| | | | 54,900 | | |
| | Quarter 2 | 50,700 | | 54,975 | –4,275 |
| | | | 55,050 | | |
| | Quarter 3 | 54,200 | | | |
| | | | | | |
| | Quarter 4 | 55,200 | | | |

## Task 2.4

Predicted sales

| | | £ |
|---|---|---|
| Quarter 1 | £418,500 + £21,500 | 440,000 |
| Quarter 2 | £420,400 + £30,400 | 450,800 |
| Quarter 3 | £422,500 – £16,700 | 405,800 |
| Quarter 4 | £423,800 – £35,200 | 388,600 |

## Task 2.5

(a)

| | Actual costs | RPI | Workings | Costs at January prices |
|---|---|---|---|---|
| | £ | | | £ |
| January | 129,600 | 171.1 | 129,600 | 129,600 |
| February | 129,700 | 172.0 | 129,700 × 171.1/172.0 | 129,021 |
| March | 130,400 | 172.2 | 130,400 × 171.1/172.2 | 129,567 |
| April | 131,600 | 173.0 | 131,600 × 171.1/173.0 | 130,155 |
| May | 130,500 | 174.1 | 130,500 × 171.1/174.1 | 128,251 |
| June | 131,600 | 174.3 | 131,600 × 171.1/174.3 | 129,184 |

**(b)**

| | Actual costs | RPI | Workings | Costs at June prices |
|---|---|---|---|---|
| | £ | | | £ |
| January | 129,600 | 171.1 | 129,600 × 174.3/171.1 | 132,024 |
| February | 129,700 | 172.0 | 129,700 × 174.3/172.0 | 131,434 |
| March | 130,400 | 172.2 | 130,400 × 174.3/172.2 | 131,990 |
| April | 131,600 | 173.0 | 131,600 × 174.3/173.0 | 132,589 |
| May | 130,500 | 174.1 | 130,500 × 174.3/174.1 | 130,650 |
| June | 131,600 | 174.3 | 131,600 × 174.3/174.3 | 131,600 |

## Task 2.6

| | | Sales | | Index |
|---|---|---|---|---|
| | | £ | | |
| 20X7 | Quarter 1 | 126,500 | | 100.0 |
| | Quarter 2 | 130,500 | 130,500/126,500 × 100 | 103.2 |
| | Quarter 3 | 131,400 | 131,400/126,500 × 100 | 103.9 |
| | Quarter 4 | 132,500 | 132,500/126,500 × 100 | 104.7 |
| 20X8 | Quarter 1 | 133,100 | 133,100/126,500 × 100 | 105.2 |
| | Quarter 2 | 135,600 | 135,600/126,500 × 100 | 107.2 |
| | Quarter 3 | 136,500 | 136,500/126,500 × 100 | 107.9 |
| | Quarter 4 | 137,100 | 137,100/126,500 × 100 | 108.4 |

## Task 2.7

The updated standard cost for material C is £4.41

**Workings**

£3.50 × 145/115 = £4.41

## Task 2.8

Quarter 1 £667,396

Quarter 2 £722,633

**Workings**

Quarter 1    £657,000 × 128.4/126.4  =  £667,396

Quarter 2    £692,500 × 131.9/126.4  =  £722,633

....................................................................................................

## Task 2.9

| January 20X9 | £12.10 |
|---|---|
| February 20X9 | £12.20 |

**Workings**

In January:

a = 9

b = 0.1

X = 31

Therefore Y = 9 + (0.1 × 31) = £12.10 per kilogram

In February:

a = 9

b = 0.1

X = 32

Therefore Y = 9 + (0.1 × 32) = £12.20 per kilogram

....................................................................................................

## Task 2.10

a is £2,000

b is £5

If production is 750 units, the cost of production is £5,750.

**Workings**

100 units          £2,500

1,000 units        £7,000

**Answer bank**

Subtract the highest less the lowest activities to find the variable cost which is b in the equation:

1,000 – 100 = 900 units with additional cost of £(7,000 – 2,500) = £4,500, ie £4,500/900 per unit = £5 per unit

b = £5

Therefore, to find the fixed cost element, consider 100 units:

Fixed costs = Total costs – Variable costs

= £2,500 – 5 × 100

= £2,000

so a = £2,000

## Task 2.11

If production is expected to be 105,000 units in the next quarter the anticipated production costs are £810,000

**Workings**

Production costs = 138,000 + (6.4 × 105,000)

= £810,000

## Task 2.12

The anticipated power costs for April are £270,000.

**Workings**

Power costs 80,000 + (380,000 × 0.5) = £270,000

## Task 2.13

| | |
|---|---|
| Month 1 | 25,600 units |
| Month 2 | 26,500 units |
| Month 3 | 27,400 units |

**Workings**

Month 1: sales trend $= 3.1 + (0.9 \times 25)$ (month 25)

$\qquad\qquad\qquad = 25,600$ units

Month 2: sales trend $= 3.1 + (0.9 \times 26)$

$\qquad\qquad\qquad = 26,500$ units

Month 3: sales trend $= 3.1 + (0.9 \times 27)$

$\qquad\qquad\qquad = 27,400$ units

············································································

## Task 2.14

| | |
|---|---|
| Quarter 1 | 1,590 units |
| Quarter 2 | 2,095 units |
| Quarter 3 | 2,125 units |
| Quarter 4 | 1,880 units |

**Workings**

| | Trend | | Seasonal variation | | Estimate of actual |
|---|---|---|---|---|---|
| Quarter 1 | $400 + (105 \times 13)$* | = | 1,765 – 175 | = | 1,590 |
| Quarter 2 | $400 + (105 \times 14)$ | = | 1,870 + 225 | = | 2,095 |
| Quarter 3 | $400 + (105 \times 15)$ | = | 1,975 + 150 | = | 2,125 |
| Quarter 4 | $400 + (105 \times 16)$ | = | 2,080 – 200 | = | 1,880 |

*$x = 13$.
Q 1 20X6 – Q4 20X8 = 12 quarters
Therefore, Q1 20X6 – Q1 20X9 = 13
Q1 20X6 – Q2 20X9 = 14
Q1 20X6 – Q3 20X9 = 15
Q1 20X6 – Q4 20X9 = 16

············································································

Answer bank

## Task 2.15

**(a)**

| June cost per tonne (£) | 177 |
|---|---|
| July cost per tonne (£) | 179 |

**Workings**

$Y = a + bX$

    For June, X = 26, therefore Y = 125 + (2 × 26) = £177 per tonne

    For July = X = 27, therefore Y = 125 + (2 × 27) = £179 per tonne

**(b)**

| June index | 101.14 |
|---|---|
| July index | 102.29 |

**Workings**

As May is the base,   May = 100 when price was £175 per tonne

Therefore,       June = 177/175 × 100 = 101.14

             July = 179/175 × 100 = 102.29

## Task 2.16

**(a)**

|  | £ |
|---|---|
| a | 10,000 |
| b | 3 |

**Workings**

Substituting the outputs and corresponding distribution costs into the equation gives:

£14,500 = a + 1,500 b

£19,000 = a + 3,000 b

Subtracting the two equations gives:

£4,500 = 1,500 b

b = £3 per unit

Substituting this into the first equation gives:

£14,500 = a + 1,500 × £3

a = £10,000

**(b)**

| Output | £ |
|---|---|
| 2,000 units (£10,000 + £3 × 2,000) | 16,000 |
| 4,000 units (£10,000 + £3 × 4,000) | 22,000 |

**(c)** The value of distribution costs for **2,000** units is most accurate.

**Tutorial note** – this is because this is within the range of the activities (1,500 – 3,000) which were used to determine a and b in the equation (interpolation). 4,000 units is an activity outside the range (and so requires extrapolation).

## Task 2.17

**(a)** The trend in prices is [ a decrease ] of £ [ 25 ] per month.

The seasonal variation for month 1 is [ a decrease ] of £ [ 55 ].

**Workings**

£1,040 – **£25** = £1,015    £1,015 – **£25** = £990

£1,040 – £985 = £55

**(b)**

| a = £ | 12,000 |
|---|---|
| b = £ | 5 |

**Workings**

1: 52,000 = a + (b × 8,000)

2: 72,000 = a + (b × 12,000)

3: 79,500 = a + (b × 13,500)

Equation 2 less Equation 1 gives:

20,000 = (b × 4,000)

b = £5

Substitute b in equation 3

79,500 = a + (5 × 13,500)

79,500 = a + 67,500

a = £12,000

Alternatively you could have used the high-low method to calculate a and b.

**(c)**

| Month | Index number | Forecast hourly rate £ |
|---|---|---|
| March | 103.9 | 12.47 |
| April | 105.2 | 12.62 |
| May | 105.7 | 12.68 |

**Workings**

Index base 100 = £12

$$\left(\frac{103.9}{100}\right) \times £12 = £12.47$$

$$\left(\frac{105.2}{100}\right) \times £12 = £12.62$$

$$\left(\frac{105.7}{100}\right) \times £12 = £12.68$$

**(d)** The forecast total hour cost for April is £ | 24,230.40 |

**Workings**

1,920 × £12.62 = £24,230.40

# Chapter 3

## Task 3.1

**MEMORANDUM**

To:             New Accounts Assistant

From:           Accountant

Date:           xx/xx/xx

Subject:        **Setting the standard cost of labour**

The standard cost of the direct labour for a product will be made up of:

*   The amount of time being spent on each unit of the product
*   The hourly wage rate for the employees working on the product

Factors that should be taken into account when setting the standard for the amount of labour time include:

*   The level of skill or training of the labour used on the product
*   Any anticipated changes in the grade of labour used on the product
*   Any anticipated changes in work methods or productivity levels
*   The effect on productivity of any bonus scheme to be introduced

The hourly rate for the direct labour used on the product can be found from the payroll records. However consideration should be given to:

*   Anticipated pay rises
*   Any anticipated changes in the grade of labour to be used
*   The effect of any bonus scheme on the labour rate
*   Whether any overtime is anticipated and should be built into the hourly rate

## Task 3.2

The correct answer is £98.40

|  | £ | £ |
|---|---|---|
| *Materials* | | |
| A   1.2 kg × £11 = | 13.20 | |
| B   4.7 kg × £6 = | 28.20 | |
| | | 41.40 |
| *Labour* | | |
| 1.5 hours × £8 | | 12.00 |
| *Prime cost* | | 53.40 |
| *Overheads* | | |
| 1.5 hours × £30 | | 45.00 |
| Standard cost per unit | | 98.40 |

# Task 3.3

| 1 unit of XX6 | Quantity | Cost per unit £ | Total £ |
|---|---|---|---|
| Materials | 1.25 | 1.65 | 2.06 |
| Labour | 0.25 | 17.00 | 4.25 |
| Fixed overheads | 1 | 5.50 | 5.50 |
| Total | | | 11.81 |

**Workings**

Standard materials quantity per unit of XX6: $\dfrac{17,500}{14,000}$ = 1.25 litres

Standard labour quantity per unit of XX6: $\dfrac{3,500}{14,000}$ = 0.25 hours

Standard fixed overhead units: Fixed overheads absorbed on a unit basis = 1

Standard materials cost per litre: $\dfrac{£28,875}{17,500}$ = £1.65

Standard labour rate per hour: $\dfrac{£59,500}{3,500}$ = £17.00

Fixed overheads cost per unit: $\dfrac{£77,000}{14,000}$ = £5.50

Materials total cost per unit of XX6: $\dfrac{£28,875}{14,000}$ = £2.06

Labour total cost per unit of XX6: $\dfrac{£59,500}{14,000}$ = £4.25

Fixed overheads total cost per unit of XX6: $\dfrac{£77,000}{14,000}$ = £5.50

## Chapter 4

### Task 4.1

|  | Variance £ | Adverse/Favourable |
|---|---|---|
| Total materials cost variance | 4,480 | Adverse |
| Materials price variance | 2,880 | Adverse |
| Materials usage variance | 1,600 | Adverse |

**Workings**

(i)  Total materials cost variance

|  | £ |
|---|---|
| Standard cost of actual production 2,800 units × 5 kg × £4.00 | 56,000 |
| Actual cost | 60,480 |
| Total cost variance | 4,480 (A) |

(ii)  Materials price variance

|  | £ |
|---|---|
| 14,400 kg should have cost  (× £4.00) | 57,600 |
| But did cost | 60,480 |
| Price variance | 2,880 (A) |

(iii)  Materials usage variance

|  |  |
|---|---|
| 2,800 units should have used × 5 kg | 14,000 kg |
| But did use | 14,400 kg |
|  | 400 kg |
| At standard cost | × £4.00 |
| Usage variance | £1,600 (A) |

## Task 4.2

|  | Variance £ | Adverse/Favourable |
|---|---|---|
| Total materials cost variance | 13,680 | Adverse |
| Materials price variance | 16,080 | Adverse |
| Materials usage variance | 2,400 | Favourable |

**Workings**

(i)   Total materials cost variance

|  | £ |
|---|---|
| Standard cost for actual production 11,400 units × 4 kg × £3 | 136,800 |
| Actual cost | 150,480 |
| Total cost variance | 13,680 (A) |

(ii)  Materials price variance

|  | £ |
|---|---|
| 44,800 kg should have cost (× £3) | 134,400 |
| But did cost | 150,480 |
| Price variance | 16,080 (A) |

(iii) Materials usage variance

|  | £ |
|---|---|
| 11,400 units should have used (× 4 kg) | 45,600 |
| But did use | 44,800 |
|  | 800 (F) |
| At standard cost | × £3 |
| Usage variance | 2,400 (F) |

........................................................................................

## Task 4.3

|  | Variance £ | Adverse/Favourable |
|---|---|---|
| Total labour cost variance | 12,715 | Adverse |
| Labour rate variance | 9,430 | Adverse |
| Labour efficiency variance | 3,285 | Adverse |

**Workings**

(i)   Total labour cost variance

|  | £ |
|---|---|
| Standard cost for actual production 12,100 units × 4.5 hours × £7.30 | 397,485 |
| Actual cost | 410,200 |
| Total cost variance | 12,715 (A) |

(ii)   Labour rate variance

|                                              |             | £          |
|----------------------------------------------|-------------|------------|
| 54,900 hours should have cost (× £7.30)      |             | 400,770    |
| But did cost                                 |             | 410,200    |
| Rate variance                                |             | 9,430 (A)  |

(iii)  Labour efficiency variance

|                                             |                |
|---------------------------------------------|----------------|
| 12,100 units should have taken (× 4.5 hours)| 54,450 hrs     |
| But did take                                | 54,900 hrs     |
|                                             | 450 hrs (A)    |
| At standard rate                            | × £7.30        |
| Efficiency variance                         | £3,285 (A)     |

## Task 4.4

|                             | Variance<br>£ | Adverse/Favourable |
|-----------------------------|---------------|--------------------|
| Total labour cost variance  | 2,200         | Favourable         |
| Labour rate variance        | 4,200         | Favourable         |
| Labour efficiency variance  | 2,000         | Adverse            |

**Workings**

(i)   Total labour cost variance

|                                                                      | £          |
|----------------------------------------------------------------------|------------|
| Standard cost for actual production 10,680 units × 5 hours × £10      | 534,000    |
| Actual cost                                                          | 531,800    |
| Total cost variance                                                  | 2,200 (F)  |

(ii)  Labour rate variance

|                                        | £          |
|----------------------------------------|------------|
| 53,600 hours should have cost (× £10)   | 536,000    |
| But did cost                            | 531,800    |
| Rate variance                           | 4,200 (F)  |

(iii) Labour efficiency variance

|                                          |                |
|------------------------------------------|----------------|
| 10,680 units should have taken (× 5 hours)| 53,400 hrs     |
| But did take                             | 53,600 hrs     |
|                                          | 200 hrs (A)    |
| At standard rate                         | × £10          |
| Efficiency variance                      | £2,000 (A)     |

Answer bank

# Task 4.5

| | Variance £ | Adverse/Favourable |
|---|---|---|
| Total labour cost variance | 8,600 | Adverse |
| Labour rate variance | 4,100 | Adverse |
| Labour efficiency variance | 4,500 | Adverse |

## Workings

(i)   Total labour cost variance

| | £ |
|---|---|
| Standard cost for actual production 11,400 × 3 hours × £9 | 307,800 |
| Actual cost | 316,400 |
| Total variance | 8,600 (A) |

(ii)   Labour rate variance

| | £ |
|---|---|
| 34,700 hours should have cost  (× £9) | 312,300 |
| But did cost | 316,400 |
| Rate variance | 4,100 (A) |

(iii)   Labour efficiency variance

| | |
|---|---|
| 11,400 units should have taken  (× 3 hours) | 34,200 hrs |
| But did take | 34,700 hrs |
| | 500 hrs (A) |
| At standard rate × £9 | × £9 |
| Efficiency variance | £4,500 (A) |

# Task 4.6

The fixed overhead expenditure variance is £5,000 Adverse

The fixed overhead volume variance is £10,500 Favourable

## Workings

(i)   Fixed overhead expenditure variance

| | £ |
|---|---|
| Budgeted overhead £7 × 10,000 units | 70,000 |
| Actual overhead | 75,000 |
| Expenditure variance | 5,000 (A) |

(ii)   Fixed overhead volume variance

| | £ |
|---|---|
| Actual production @ standard OAR 11,500 × £7 | 80,500 |
| Budgeted production @ standard OAR 10,000 × £7 | 70,000 |
| Volume variance | 10,500 (F) |

BPP LEARNING MEDIA

# Task 4.7

|  | Variance<br>£ | Adverse/Favourable |
|---|---|---|
| Fixed overhead expenditure variance | 80,000 | Favourable |
| Fixed overhead volume variance | 91,200 | Favourable |
| Fixed overhead efficiency variance | 15,200 | Favourable |
| Fixed overhead capacity variance | 76,000 | Favourable |

**Workings**

Fixed overhead expenditure variance

|  | £ |
|---|---|
| Budgeted fixed overhead 50,000 units × 6 hours × £7.60 | 2,280,000 |
| Actual fixed overhead | 2,200,000 |
| Expenditure variance | 80,000 (F) |

Fixed overhead volume variance

|  | £ |
|---|---|
| Standard hours for actual production @ standard OAR<br>52,000 units × 6 hours × £7.60 | 2,371,200 |
| Standard hours for budgeted production @ standard OAR<br>50,000 units × 6 hours × £7.60 | 2,280,000 |
| Volume variance | 91,200 (F) |

Fixed overhead efficiency variance

|  | £ |
|---|---|
| Standard hours for actual production @ standard OAR<br>52,000 × 6 hours × £7.60 | 2,371,200 |
| Actual hours @ standard OAR 310,000 × £7.60 | 2,356,000 |
| Efficiency variance | 15,200 (F) |

Fixed overhead capacity variance

|  | £ |
|---|---|
| Actual hours @ standard OAR 310,000 × £7.60 | 2,356,000 |
| Budgeted hours @ standard OAR 50,000 × 6 × £7.60 | 2,280,000 |
| Capacity variance | 76,000 (F) |

## Task 4.8

**(a)** The budgeted fixed overhead for the month was £201,600
**(b)** The fixed overhead expenditure variance was £1,400 Adverse
**(c)** The fixed overhead volume variance was £11,520 Adverse
**(d)** The fixed overhead efficiency variance was £10,080 Favourable
**(e)** The fixed overhead capacity variance was £21,600 Adverse

### Workings

(i)

|  | £ |
|---|---|
| Budgeted fixed overhead | |
| 14,000 units × 4 hours × £3.60 | 201,600 |

(ii)  Fixed overhead expenditure variance

|  | £ |
|---|---|
| Budgeted fixed overhead | 201,600 |
| Actual fixed overhead | 203,000 |
| Expenditure variance | 1,400 (A) |

(iii)  Fixed overhead volume variance

|  | £ |
|---|---|
| Standard hours for actual production @ standard OAR | |
| 13,200 units × 4 hours × £3.60 | 190,080 |
| Standard hours for budgeted production @ standard OAR | |
| 14,000 units × 4 hours × £3.60 | 201,600 |
| Volume variance | 11,520 (A) |

(iv)  Fixed overhead efficiency variance

|  | £ |
|---|---|
| Standard hours for actual production @ standard OAR | |
| 13,200 × 4 hours × £3.60 | 190,080 |
| Actual hours @ standard OAR 50,000 × £3.60 | 180,000 |
| Efficiency variance | 10,080 (F) |

(v)  Fixed overhead capacity variance

|  | £ |
|---|---|
| Actual hours @ standard OAR 50,000 × £3.60 | 180,000 |
| Budgeted hours @ standard OAR 14,000 × 4 × £3.60 | 201,600 |
| Capacity variance | 21,600 (A) |

## Task 4.9

| | Favourable £ | Adverse £ | Total £ |
|---|---|---|---|
| Budgeted cost of actual production 1,240 × £38.69 | | | 47,976 |
| **Variances** | | | |
| Materials price | | 860 | |
| Materials usage | 426 | | |
| Labour rate | 820 | | |
| Labour efficiency | | 1,530 | |
| Fixed overhead expenditure | | 250 | |
| Fixed overhead efficiency | | 288 | |
| Fixed overhead capacity | 848 | | |
| Total variances | 2094 | 2928 | 834 |
| Actual cost of actual production (17,100 + 27,060 + 4,650) | | | 48,810 |

## Task 4.10

The correct answer is £1,113 Adverse

Budgeted fixed overhead absorption rate = £22,260 ÷ 8,400 hours = £2.65 per labour hour

| | |
|---|---|
| Budgeted hours of work | 8,400 hrs |
| Actual hours of work | 7,980 hrs |
| | 420 hrs (A) |
| × standard rate per hour | × £2.65 |
| **Fixed production overhead capacity variance** | £1,113 (A) |

## Task 4.11

(a)

| | |
|---|---|
| Budgeted fixed overhead expenditure (4,100 × 40 × £12.50) | 2,050,000 |
| Actual fixed overhead expenditure | 2,195,000 |
| Fixed overhead **expenditure variance** | 145,000 (A) |

(b)

| | £ |
|---|---|
| Actual production at standard rate (3,850 × 40 × £12.50) | 1,925,000 |
| Budgeted production at standard rate (4,100 × 40 × £12.50) | 2,050,000 |
| Fixed overhead **volume variance** | 125,000 (A) |

(c)

| | |
|---|---|
| Budgeted hours (4,100 × 40) | 164,000 hrs |
| Actual hours | 159,000 hrs |
| Fixed overhead capacity variance in hours | 5,000 hrs (A) |
| × standard rate per hour | × £12.50 |
| Fixed overhead **capacity variance** | £62,500 (A) |

(d)

| | |
|---|---|
| 3,850 units should have taken (× 40 hrs) | 154,000 hrs |
| but did take | 159,000 hrs |
| Fixed overhead efficiency variance in hours | 5,000 hrs (A) |
| × standard rate per hour | × £12.50 |
| Fixed overhead **efficiency variance** | £62,500 (A) |

## Task 4.12

| | Variance £ | Adverse/Favourable |
|---|---|---|
| Total variable production overhead variance | 30 | Adverse |
| Variable production overhead efficiency variance | 60 | Favourable |
| Variable production overhead expenditure variance | 90 | Adverse |

### Workings

**Tutorial note**: Since this question relates to variable production costs, the total variance is based on actual units of production. (If the overhead had been a variable selling cost, the variance would be based on sales volumes.)

Total variable production overhead variance

| | £ |
|---|---|
| 400 units of product X should cost (× £3) | 1,200 |
| but did cost | 1,230 |
| Variable production overhead total variance | 30 (A) |

Variable overhead expenditure variance

|  | £ |
|---|---|
| 760 hours of variable production overhead should cost ( × £1.50) | 1,140 |
| but did cost | 1,230 |
| Variable production overhead expenditure variance | 90 (A) |

Variable overhead efficiency variance

|  |  |
|---|---|
| 400 units of product X should take (× 2hrs) | 800 hrs |
| but did take | 760 hrs |
| Variable production overhead efficiency variance in hours | 40 hrs (F) |
| × standard rate per hour | × £1.50 |
| Variable production overhead efficiency variance in £ | £60 (F) |

···········································································

# Task 4.13

**(a)** The variable production cost variance is £208,000 Adverse

**Workings**

This is simply a 'total' variance.

|  | £ |
|---|---|
| 1,000 units should have cost (× £600) | 600,000 |
| but did cost (£720,000 + £63,000 + £25,000) | 808,000 |
| Variable production cost variance | 208,000 (A) |

**(b)** (i) The direct labour rate variance is £2,600 Favourable

**Workings**

|  | £ |
|---|---|
| 8,200 hours should cost (× £8) | 65,600 |
| but did cost | 63,000 |
| Direct labour rate variance | 2,600 (F) |

(ii) The direct labour efficiency variance is £14,400 Favourable

**Workings**

|  |  |
|---|---|
| 1,000 units should take (× 10 hours) | 10,000 hrs |
| but did take | 8,200 hrs |
| Direct labour efficiency variance in hrs | 1,800 hrs (F) |
| × standard rate per hour | × £8 |
| Direct labour efficiency variance in £ | £14,400 (F) |

**(c)** (i) The direct material price variance is £270,000 Adverse

**Workings**

|  | £ |
|---|---|
| 90,000 kg should cost (× £5) | 450,000 |
| but did cost | 720,000 |
| Direct material price variance | 270,000 (A) |

(ii) The direct material usage variance is £50,000 Favourable

**Workings**

| | |
|---|---:|
| 1,000 units should use (× 100 kg) | 100,000 kg |
| but did use | 90,000 kg |
| Direct material usage variance in kgs | 10,000 kg (F) |
| × standard cost per kg | × £5 |
| Direct material usage variance in £ | £50,000 (F) |

**(d)** (i) The variable production overhead expenditure variance is £8,600 Adverse

**Workings**

| | £ |
|---|---:|
| 8,200 hours incurring o/hd should cost (× £2) | 16,400 |
| but did cost | 25,000 |
| Variable production overhead expenditure variance | 8,600 (A) |

(ii) The variable production overhead efficiency variance is £3,600 Favourable

**Workings**

| | |
|---|---:|
| Efficiency variance in hrs (from (b)(ii)) | 1,800 hrs (F) |
| × standard rate per hour | × £2 |
| Variable production overhead efficiency variance | £3,600 (F) |

# Task 4.14

**(a)**

| Standard cost of materials for actual production | | | £114,000 |
|---|---|---|---:|
| Variances | Favourable | Adverse | |
| Direct material price variance | | £45,600 | |
| Direct material usage variance | £22,800 | | |
| Total variance | | | £22,800 |
| Actual cost of materials for actual production | | | £136,800 |

**Workings**

Standard cost for actual units produced = 11,400 units × 5kg × £2 = £114,000

| Materials price variance | £ |
|---|---:|
| 45,600 kg should have cost (× £2) | 91,200 |
| But did cost | 136,800 |
| Price variance | 45,600 (A) |

Materials usage variance

| | |
|---|---|
| 11,400 units should have used (× 5 kg) | 57,000 kg |
| But did use | 45,600 |
| | 11,400 (F) |
| At standard price per kg | × £2 |
| Usage variance | 22,800 (F) |

**(b)**

| | Favourable | Adverse | |
|---|---|---|---|
| Standard cost of labour for actual production | | | £182,400 |
| Variances | Favourable | Adverse | |
| Direct labour rate variance | £11,400 | | |
| Direct labour efficiency variance | £91,200 | | |
| Total variance | | | £(102,600) |
| Actual cost of labour for actual production | | | £79,800 |

**Workings**

Standard cost for actual units produced = 11,400 units × 2hrs × £8 = £182,400

| | £ |
|---|---|
| Labour rate variance | |
| 11,400 hrs should have cost (× £8) | 91,200 |
| But did cost | 79,800 |
| Rate variance | 11,400 (F) |

| | |
|---|---|
| Labour efficiency variance | |
| 11,400 units should have taken (× 2 hours) | 22,800 hrs |
| But did take | 11,400 hrs |
| | 11,400 (F) |
| At standard cost | × £8 |
| Usage variance | 91,200 (F) |

**(c)**

| | Favourable | Adverse | |
|---|---|---|---|
| Standard cost of fixed overhead for actual production | | | 91,200 |
| Variances | Favourable | Adverse | |
| Fixed overhead expenditure variance | 1,000 | | |
| Fixed overhead volume variance | | 4,800 | |
| Total variance | | | 3,800 |
| Actual cost of fixed overhead for actual production | | | 95,000 |

**Workings**

Standard cost for actual units produced = 11,400 units × 2hrs × £4 = £91,200

| | £ |
|---|---|
| Budgeted fixed overhead expenditure (12,000 × 2 × £4) | 96,000 |
| Actual fixed overhead expenditure | 95,000 |
| Fixed overhead **expenditure variance** | 1,000 (F) |

|  | £ |
|---|---|
| Standard hours for actual production @ standard OAR | |
| 11,400 units × 2 hours × £4 | 91,200 |
| Standard hours for budgeted production @ standard OAR | |
| 12,000 units × 2 hours × £4 | 96,000 |
| Volume variance | 4,800 (A) |

## Task 4.15

Capacity variance:

OAR = Budgeted overheads £810,000 ÷ budgeted hours 108,000 = £7.50 per hour

|  | Hours |
|---|---|
| Budgeted hours of work | 108,000 |
| Actual hours of work | 118,000 |
| Fixed overhead capacity variance | 10,000 (F) |
| × standard fixed overhead absorption rate per hour | × £7.50 |
| Fixed overhead capacity variance in £ | £75,000 (F) |

Efficiency variance:

Actual production 29,000 units × 4 (expected number of hours per unit) = 116,000 hours

|  | Hours |
|---|---|
| Actual units should take | 116,000 |
| But did take | 118,000 |
| Fixed overhead efficiency variance in hours | 2,000 (A) |
| × standard fixed overhead absorption rate per hour | × £7.50 |
| Fixed overhead efficiency variance in £ | £15,000 (A) |

## Task 4.16

(a) The material usage variance is £ | 6,000 | Adverse. ▼

| 19,000 units should use (× 10 litres per unit) | 190,000 litres |
|---|---|
| but did use | 200,000 litres |
| Material usage variance in litres | 10,000 litres (A) |
| × standard cost per litre (£132,000/220,000 litres) | × £0.60 |
| Material usage variance in £ | £6,000 (A) |

(b) The total labour efficiency variance is £ | 4,500 | Favourable. ▼

**Workings**

Labour efficiency variance

| | |
|---|---|
| 12,000 units should have taken (× 0.6 hours) | 7,200 hrs |
| But did take | 6,900 hrs |
| | 300 hrs (F) |
| At standard rate | × £15.00 |
| Efficiency variance | £4,500 (F) |

## Task 4.17

**(a)** The fixed overhead volume variance is £ 25,000  Favourable. 

| | £ |
|---|---|
| Actual production @ standard OAR 30,000 × £12.50 | 375,000 |
| Budgeted production @ standard OAR 28,000 × £12.50 | 350,000 |
| Volume variance | 25,000 (F) |

**(b)** The actual fixed production overheads incurred were £ 315,000 .

| | £ |
|---|---|
| Budgeted overhead | 350,000 |
| Actual overhead (Balancing figure) | 315,000 |
| Expenditure variance | 35,000 (F) |

**(c)**

| Variance | Amount £ | Sign |
|---|---|---|
| Fixed overhead capacity | 448,000 | Favourable.  |
| Fixed overhead efficiency | 268,000 | Adverse.  |

**Workings**

Fixed overhead capacity variance

| | £ |
|---|---|
| Actual hours @ standard OAR 536,000 × £8.00* | 4,288,000 |
| Budgeted hours @ standard OAR 480,000 × £8.00 | 3,840,000 |
| Capacity variance | 448,000 (F) |

*£3,840,000 ÷ 480,000 hours = £8.00

Fixed overhead efficiency variance

|  | £ |
|---|---|
| Standard hours for actual production @ standard OAR 67,000 × 7.5 hours* × £8.00 | 4,020,000 |
| Actual hours @ standard OAR 536,000 × £8.00 | 4,288,000 |
| Efficiency variance | 268,000 (A) |

*480,000 hours ÷ 64,000 units = 7.5 hours

## Task 4.18

| Variance | Amount £ | Adverse / Favourable |
|---|---|---|
| Direct material usage variance | 2,025 | Adverse |
| Direct material price variance | 3,120 | Adverse |
| Total direct labour variance | 1,305 | Favourable |

**Workings**

**Direct material usage variance**

Budgeted direct material per unit of KK1: $\dfrac{9,000\,\text{kg}}{18,000\,\text{units}} = 0.5\text{kg}$

Budgeted direct material price per kg: $\dfrac{£60,750}{9,000} = £6.75$

| | |
|---|---|
| 15,000 units should have used ( × 0.5kg ) | 7,500 kg |
| But did use | 7,800 kg |
| Variance in kg | 300 kg Adverse |
| × standard cost per kg | × £6.75 |
| Variance in £ | £2,025 Adverse |

**Direct material price variance**

| | £ |
|---|---|
| 7,800 kg should have cost (× £6.75) | 52,650 |
| But did cost | 55,770 |
| Direct material price variance | 3,120 Adverse |

**Total direct labour variance**

Standard hours per unit $\dfrac{5,400 \text{ hrs}}{18,000 \text{ units}}$ = 0.3 hours per unit

Standard labour cost per hour $\dfrac{47,250}{5,400 \text{ hrs}}$ = £8.75 per hr

Therefore one unit should cost 0.3 hours × £8.75 = £2.625

|  | £ |
|---|---|
| Actual production should have cost 15,000 units × £2.625 | 39,375 |
| But did cost | 38,070 |
| Variance | 1,305 Favourable |

## Task 4.19

**(a)**

| Variance | Amount £ | Sign |
|---|---|---|
| Fixed overhead expenditure | 96,250 | Favourable |
| Fixed overhead volume | 83,500 | Favourable |

**Workings**

Fixed overhead expenditure variance: (£1,043,750 – £947,500) = £96,250 Favourable

Fixed overhead expenditure budgeted absorption rate: $\dfrac{£1,043,750}{25,000}$ = £41.75 per unit

Fixed overhead volume variance: (27,000 units – 25,000 units) × £41.75 = £83,500 Favourable

**(b)**

| Variance | Amount £ | Sign |
|---|---|---|
| Fixed overhead capacity | 25,000 | Adverse |
| Fixed overhead efficiency | 75,000 | Adverse |

**Workings**

Budgeted labour hours per unit: $\dfrac{270,000 \text{ hrs}}{54,000 \text{ units}}$ = 5 hours per unit

Fixed overhead budgeted overhead absorption rate: $\dfrac{£1,350,000}{270,000}$ = £5 per hr

### Fixed overhead capacity variance

| | |
|---|---:|
| Budgeted hours of work | 270,000 hours |
| Actual hours of work | 265,000 hours |
| Fixed overhead capacity variance in hours | 5,000 hours Adverse |
| × standard fixed o/h absorption rate | × £5 |
| Fixed overhead capacity variance in £ | £25,000 Adverse |

### Fixed overhead efficiency variance

| | |
|---|---:|
| Actual units should take ( 50,000 × 5 hrs) | 250,000 hrs |
| But did take | 265,000 hrs |
| Variance in hours | 15,000 hrs Adverse |
| × standard fixed o/h absorption rate | × £5 |
| Fixed overhead efficiency variance | £75,000 Adverse |

# Chapter 5

## Task 5.1

**(a)** (1) Standard price of fuel = £497,664/1,244,160 litres = £0.40 per litre

(2) Standard litres of fuel per crossing = 1,244,160/6,480 = 192 litres

Standard litres of fuel for 5,760 crossings = 192 × 5,760 = 1,105,920 litres

(3) Standard labour rate per hr = £699,840/93,312 hrs = £7.50 per hour

(4) Standard labour hours per crossing = 93,312/6,480 = 14.4 hours

Standard labour hours for 5,760 crossings = 14.4 × 5,760 = 82,944 hours

(5) Standard fixed overhead cost per budgeted operating hour = £466,560/7,776 = £60 per hour

(6) Standard operating hours per crossing = 7,776/6,480 = 1.2 hours

Standard operating hours for 5,760 crossings = 1.2 × 5,760 = 6,912 hours

(7) Standard fixed overhead cost absorbed by 5,760 crossings = 6,912 hours (6) × £60 per hour (from (5)) = £414,720

**(b)** (1)

| | £ |
|---|---|
| 1,232,800 litres should cost (× £0.40 (a)(i)(1)) | 493,120 |
| but did cost | 567,088 |
| **Material price variance for fuel** | 73,968 (A) |

(2)

| | £ |
|---|---|
| 5,760 crossings should have used ((a)(i)(2)) | 1,105,920 litres |
| but did use | 1,232,800 litres |
| Usage variance in litres | 126,880 litres (A) |
| × standard price per litre ((a)(i)(1)) | × £0.40 |
| **Material usage variance for fuel** | £50,752 (A) |

(3)

| | £ |
|---|---|
| 89,856 hours should have cost (× £7.50 (a)(i)(3)) | 673,920 |
| but did cost | 696,384 |
| **Labour rate variance** | 22,464 (A) |

(4)

| | |
|---|---|
| 5,760 crossing should have used ((a)(i)(4)) | 82,944 hours |
| but did take | 89,856 hours |
| Efficiency variance in hours | 6,912 hours (A) |
| × standard rate per hours ((a)(i)(3)) | × £7.50 |
| **Labour efficiency variance** | £51,840 (A) |

(5)

| | £ |
|---|---|
| Budgeted fixed overhead expenditure | 466,560 |
| Actual fixed overhead expenditure | 472,440 |
| **Fixed overhead expenditure variance** | 5,880 (A) |

(6)

| | £ |
|---|---|
| Actual number of crossings (5,760) at standard rate ((a)(i)(7)) | 414,720 |
| Budgeted number of crossings at standard rate | 466,560 |
| **Fixed overhead volume variance** | 51,840 (A) |

(7)

| | |
|---|---|
| Budgeted operating hours | 7,776 |
| Actual operating hours | 7,488 |
| Capacity variance in hours | 288 (A) |
| × std fixed o/hd cost per operating hours ((a)(i)(5)) | × £60 |
| **Fixed overhead capacity variance** | £17,280 (A) |

(8)

| | |
|---|---|
| 5,760 crossing should take ((a)(i)(6)) | 6,912 operating hours |
| But did take | 7,488 operating hours |
| Efficiency variance in operating hours | 576 operating hours (A) |
| × std fixed o/hd cost per op hr ((a)(i)(5)) | × £60 |
| **Fixed overhead efficiency variance** | £34,560 (A) |

**(c)** **Statement reconciling the actual cost of operations to the standard cost of operations for year ended 30 November 20X8**

| Number of ferry crossings | | 5,760 |
|---|---|---|
| | £ | £ |
| Actual cost of operations | | 1,735,912 |
| **Cost variances** | *Adverse* | |
| Material price for fuel | 73,968 | |
| Material usage for fuel | 50,752 | |
| Labour rate | 22,464 | |
| Labour efficiency | 51,840 | |
| Fixed overhead expenditure | 5,880 | |
| Fixed overhead capacity | 17,280 | |
| Fixed overhead efficiency | 34,560 | |
| | | 256,744 (A) |
| Standard cost of operations | | 1,479,168* |

* Check. 5,760/6,480 × £1,664,064 = £1,479,168

154

# Task 5.2

## (a)

| | Favourable | Adverse | |
|---|---|---|---|
| **Budgeted variable cost for actual production** | | | £387,600 |
| **Budgeted fixed cost** | | | £234,000 |
| **Total budgeted cost for actual production** | | | £621,600 |
| **Variance** | **Favourable** | **Adverse** | |
| Direct materials price | £18,700 | | |
| Direct materials usage | £11,900 | | |
| Direct labour rate | | £28,560 | |
| Direct labour efficiency | | £12,240 | |
| Fixed overhead expenditure | £13,000 | | |
| Fixed overhead volume | N/A ▼ | N/A ▼ | |
| Total variance | £43,600 | £40,800 | £–2,800 |
| Actual cost of actual production | | | £618,800 |

### Workings

Budgeted variable cost per unit = (£130,200 + £223,200)/12,400 units = £28.50

Budgeted variable cost for actual production = £13,600 units × £28.50 = £387,600

Total budgeted cost for actual production = £387,600 + £234,000 (fixed costs)

= £621,600

Direct labour efficiency variance

| | |
|---|---|
| 13,600 units should have taken (× 2 hours) | 27,200 hrs |
| But did take | 28,560 hrs |
| | 1,360 hrs (A) |
| At standard rate | × £9.00 |
| Efficiency variance | £12,240 (A) |

Fixed overhead expenditure variance = Actual £13,000 lower than budgeted, so favourable.

**(b)**

The | under absorption ▼ | of overheads is £ | 48,600 |

|  | £ |
|---|---|
| Overheads absorbed 25,000 × £95 | 2,375,000 |
| Actual overheads | 2,423,600 |
| Under absorbed | 48,600 |

## Task 5.3

| Operating statement – PD98 |  |  | £ |
|---|---|---|---|
| Budgeted/Standard cost for actual production |  |  | 70,824 |
| **Variances** | **Adverse** | **Favourable** |  |
| Direct materials price | 5,070 |  |  |
| Direct materials usage |  | 3,120 |  |
| Direct labour rate | 2,964 |  |  |
| Direct labour efficiency |  | 3,120 |  |
| Fixed overhead expenditure | 3,220 |  |  |
| Fixed overhead capacity | 2,392 |  |  |
| Fixed overhead efficiency |  | 6,760 |  |
| Total variance | 13,646 | 13,000 | 646 |
| Actual cost of actual production |  |  | 71,470 |

### Workings

Budgeted/Standard cost for actual production, $\left(\dfrac{£61,290}{450}\right) \times 520 = £70,824$

Direct materials price variance: given in the question.

Direct materials usage variance:

520 units should use $\left(\dfrac{337.5\,kg}{450} = 0.75\,kg\right) = 390\,kg$

But did use                                                                338 kg

Variance in kg                                                         52 kg Favourable

Therefore the variance in the question is favourable.

Direct labour rate variance:

$$\frac{£12,960}{1,080} = £12 \text{ hr}$$

Actual hours should cost (£12 × 988)                    £11,856

But did cost                                                              £14,820

                                                                              £2,964 Adverse

Therefore the £2,964 variance, as provided in the question is Adverse.

Direct labour efficiency variance: given in the question.

Fixed overhead expenditure variance: £3,220 figure given in question. Variance is Adverse as the £31,300 Actual figure is higher than the £28,080 Budget figure.

Fixed overhead capacity variance: given in the question.

Fixed overhead efficiency variance: given in the question.

## Chapter 6

### Task 6.1

| Variance | Possible causes |
|---|---|
| Favourable materials price variance | • Negotiation of a better price from a supplier<br>• Negotiation of a trade or bulk purchase discount from a supplier<br>• Purchase of a lower grade of materials |
| Favourable materials usage variance | • Use of a higher grade of material which led to less wastage<br>• Use of more skilled labour leading to less wastage than normal<br>• New machinery which provides greater efficiency |
| Adverse labour rate variance | • Unexpected increase in labour costs<br>• Use of a higher grade of labour than anticipated<br>• Unexpectedly high levels of overtime |
| Adverse labour efficiency variance | • Use of a less skilled grade of labour<br>• Use of a lower grade of material which takes longer to work on<br>• More idle time than budgeted for<br>• Poor supervision of the workforce<br>• Problems with machinery |

# Task 6.2

| Scenario | Possible effects |
|---|---|
| A business has had to use a less-skilled grade of labour in its production process | • Favourable labour rate variance<br><br>• Adverse labour efficiency variance<br><br>• Adverse materials usage variance |
| A factory had a machine breakdown which resulted in three days of production delays last month | • Adverse labour efficiency variance<br><br>• Adverse fixed overhead expenditure variance (due to additional costs of mending the machine)<br><br>• Adverse fixed overhead volume variance<br><br>• Adverse fixed overhead efficiency variance<br><br>• Adverse fixed overhead capacity variance |

# Task 6.3

The total materials price variance is £36,600 Adverse

The non-controllable element of the materials price variance that has been caused by the price increase is £22,550 Adverse

The controllable element of the materials price variance caused by other factors is £14,050 Adverse

**Workings**

Total materials price variance

|  | £ |
|---|---|
| Standard cost for actual quantity 45,100 × £8 | 360,800 |
| Actual cost | 397,400 |
|  | 36,600 (A) |

Non-controllable variance caused by price increase

|  | £ |
|---|---|
| Standard cost for actual quantity 45,100 × £8 | 360,800 |
| Adjusted cost for actual quantity 45,100 × £8.50 | 383,350 |
|  | 22,550 (A) |

Controllable variance caused by other factors

|  | £ |
|---|---|
| Adjusted cost for actual quantity 45,100 × £8.50 | 383,350 |
| Actual cost | 397,400 |
|  | 14,050 (A) |

# Task 6.4

The total materials price variance is £4,240 Adverse

The non-controllable variance due to price increase is £5,300 Adverse

The controllable variance due to other factors is £1,060 Favourable

**Workings**

Total materials price variance

|  | £ |
|---|---|
| Standard cost of actual quantity 10,600 × £6.50 | 68,900 |
| Actual cost | 73,140 |
|  | 4,240 (A) |

Non-controllable variance due to price increase

|  | £ |
|---|---|
| Standard cost of actual quantity 10,600 × £6.50 | 68,900 |
| Price adjusted cost of actual quantity 10,600 × £7.00 | 74,200 |
|  | 5,300 (A) |

Controllable variance due to other factors

|  | £ |
|---|---|
| Price adjusted cost of actual quantity 10,600 × £7.00 | 74,200 |
| Actual cost | 73,140 |
|  | 1,060 (F) |

.....................................................................................

# Task 6.5

The total materials price variance is £12,800 Favourable

The non-controllable variance due to the season is £38,640 Favourable

The controllable variance due to other factors is £25,840 Adverse

**Workings**

Total materials price variance

|  | £ |
|---|---|
| Standard cost of actual quantity 92,000 × £7.00 | 644,000 |
| Actual cost | 631,200 |
|  | 12,800 (F) |

Non-controllable variance due to season

|  | £ |
|---|---|
| Standard cost of actual quantity 92,000 × £7.00 | 644,000 |
| Seasonally adjusted price 92,000 × (£7.00 – £0.42) | 605,360 |
|  | 38,640 (F) |

Controllable variance due to other factors

| | £ |
|---|---|
| Seasonally adjusted price 92,000 × (£7.00 – £0.42) | 605,360 |
| Actual cost | 631,200 |
| | 25,840 (A) |

## Task 6.6

The total materials price variance is £25,380 Adverse

The non-controllable variance caused by the seasonal price change is £30,456 Adverse

The controllable variance caused by other factors is £5,076 Favourable

**Workings**

Total materials cost variance

| | £ |
|---|---|
| Standard cost of actual quantity 42,300 × £4.00 | 169,200 |
| Actual cost | 194,580 |
| | 25,380 (A) |

Non-controllable variance due to season

| | £ |
|---|---|
| Standard cost of actual quantity 42,300 × £4.00 | 169,200 |
| Seasonally adjusted cost 42,300 × (£4.00 + £0.72) | 199,656 |
| | 30,456 (A) |

Controllable variance due to other factors

| | £ |
|---|---|
| Seasonally adjusted cost 42,300 × (£4.00 + £0.72) | 199,656 |
| Actual cost | 194,580 |
| | 5,076 (F) |

## Task 6.7

The total materials price variance is £26,000 Adverse

The non-controllable variance caused by the index change is £76,667 Adverse

The controllable variance caused by other factors is £50,667 Favourable

**Workings**

Total materials cost variance

| | £ |
|---|---|
| Standard cost of actual quantity 46,000 × £20 | 920,000 |
| Actual cost | 946,000 |
| | 26,000 (A) |

Non-controllable variance due to index change

|  | £ |
|---|---|
| Standard cost of actual quantity 46,000 × £20 | 920,000 |
| Index adjusted cost 46,000 × £20 × 130/120 | 996,667 |
|  | 76,667 (A) |

Controllable variance due to other factors

|  | £ |
|---|---|
| Index adjusted cost 46,000 × £20 × 130/120 | 996,667 |
| Actual cost | 946,000 |
|  | 50,667 (F) |

## Task 6.8

**(a)** The part of the variance explained by the increase in the price index is

£ | 281,250 |

|  | £ |
|---|---|
| 12,500 litres × £450 (original standard rate) | 5,625,000 |
| 12,500 litres × £472.50 (£450 × 126.525/120.50) | 5,906,250 |
|  | 281,250 (A) |

**(b)** The part of the variance not explained by the increase in the price index is

£ | 93,750 |

£375,000 – £281,250 = £93,750

**(c)** The percentage increase in the index is | 5 | %

(126.525 – 120.50) / 120.50 = 0.05 (5%)

**(d)**

|  | September X3 | December X3 |
|---|---|---|
| Cost per kilogram of Z4QX(£) | 2,136.62 | 2,543.84 |

Difference between April X3 and May X3 = £135.74

Difference between May X3 and June X3 = £135.74

September X3 cost = £1,729.40 (June X3) + (£135.74 × 3) = £2,136.62

December X3 cost = £2,136.62 (September X3) + (£135.74 × 3) = £2,543.84

**(e)** The forecast cost per kilogram, using the regression line, for September X3 is

£ ☐ 118.85

June X3 is period 41. Therefore September X3 = period 44

y = 24.69 + 2.14x        where y = cost per kilogram      x = the period

y = 24.69 + (2.14 × 44)

y = 118.85

## Task 6.9

The standard cost per kilogram is £ ☐ 2.50 ☐.

£10,915 – £1,665 = £9,250 standard cost

Standard cost per kilogram = £9,250 / 3,700 kilograms = £2.50

## Task 6.10

The actual labour rate per hour is £ ☐ 13.25 ☐.

**Workings**

Standard labour rate per hour: $\dfrac{£163,125}{11,250}$ = £14.50 hr

Actual production at standard labour rate: 11,880 × £14.50 = £172,260

Adjust for the variance: £172,260 – £14,850 = £157,410

Calculate actual rate based on actual hours: $\dfrac{£157,410}{11,880}$ = £13.25 hr

## Task 6.11

**MEMO**

To:            Managing Director
From:         Assistant Management Accountant
Date:         xx/xx/xx
Subject:     The use of standard marginal costing at Finchley Ltd

As discussed at our earlier meetings, because all companies within the Hampstead Group use standard marginal costing, Finchley Ltd will need to adopt the system from 1 August 20X8. This report is intended to demonstrate and describe the use of standard marginal costing in your company.

(i) (1) **Standard marginal cost of a unit of Alpha**

|  | £ |
|---|---|
| Material (36,000m ÷ 12,000) 3m × (£432,000 ÷ 36,000) £12 per m | 36.00 |
| Labour (72,000 hrs ÷ 12,000) 6 hrs × (£450,000 ÷ 72,000) £6.25 per hr | 37.50 |
|  | 73.50 |

(2) **Standard cost of producing 10,000 units of Alpha**

|  | £ |
|---|---|
| Material (£36 × 10,000) | 360,000 |
| Labour (£37.50 × 10,000) | 375,000 |
| Standard marginal cost | 735,000 |
| Fixed overheads | 396,000 |
| Total cost | 1,131,000 |

(ii) (1)

|  | £ |
|---|---|
| 32,000 m should have cost (× £12) | 384,000 |
| but did cost | 377,600 |
| **Material price variance** | 6,400 (F) |

(2)

|  |  |
|---|---|
| 10,000 units should have used (× 3 m) | 30,000 m |
| but did use | 32,000 m |
| Material usage variance in metres | 2,000 m (A) |
| × standard cost per metre | × £12 |
| **Material usage variance in £** | £24,000 (A) |

(3)

|  | £ |
|---|---|
| 70,000 hrs should have cost (× £6.25) | 437,500 |
| but did cost | 422,800 |
| **Labour rate variance** | 14,700 (F) |

(4)

|  |  |
|---|---|
| 10,000 units should have taken (× 6 hrs) | 60,000 hrs |
| but did take | 70,000 hrs |
| Efficiency variance in hours | 10,000 hrs (A) |
| × standard rate per hour | × £6.25 |
| **Labour efficiency variance in £** | £62,500 (A) |

(5)

|  | £ |
|---|---|
| Budgeted fixed overhead expenditure | 396,000 |
| Actual fixed overhead expenditure (£330,000 + £75,000) | 405,000 |
| **Fixed overhead expenditure variance** | 9,000 (A) |

(iii) Set out below is a statement reconciling the standard cost of production for the three months ended 31 May 2008 with the actual cost of production for that period.

| | Fav | Adv | £ |
|---|---|---|---|
| **Standard cost of output** ((see (a)(i)(2)) | | | 1,131,000 |
| *Variances* | *Fav* | *Adv* | |
| | *£* | *£* | |
| Material price | 6,400 | | |
| Material usage | | 24,000 | |
| Labour rate | 14,700 | | |
| Labour efficiency | | 62,500 | |
| Fixed overhead expenditure | | 9,000 | |
| | 21,100 | 95,500 | 74,400 (A) |
| **Actual cost of output** | | | 1,205,400 |

(iv) The total labour variance in the statement above (£47,800 (A)) differs from that in your absorption costing management report for the three months ended 31 May 20X8 because the original report compares the actual cost of producing 10,000 units and the budgeted cost of producing 12,000 units. It therefore fails to compare like with like. The report above, however, compares actual costs of producing 10,000 units and what costs should have been given the actual output of 10,000 units. The total material variances in the two reports also differ for this reason. There is very little point comparing a budgeted cost with an actual cost if the production level upon which the budgeted cost was based is not achieved.

The fixed overhead expenditure variance in the statement above also differs from the fixed overhead variance reported in the absorption costing statement. This is because the absorption costing statement compares overhead absorbed whereas the marginal costing statement compares overhead expenditure.

(v) There are other reasons why the reconciliation statement provides improved management information. (**Note.** Only ONE is actually required)

(1) It separates total variances into their components and so you will be able to determine whether, for example, the total material variance is the responsibility of the purchasing manager (price variance) or the production manager (usage variance).

(2) It avoids the use of under-or over-absorbed overhead, which is simply a bookkeeping exercise and does not reflect higher or lower cash spending.

(3) It allows management by exception.

(4) The original statement conveys the wrong message (that the overall variance was favourable).

I hope this information has proved useful. If I can be of further assistance or you have any questions, please do not hesitate to contact me.

# Task 6.12

**(a)** (i) **Actual litres of material used** = actual total cost of materials/actual cost per litre = £23,985/£58.50 = 410 litres

(ii) **Standard litres of material required for 40 barrels of X14** = standard litres per barrel × 40 = 10 litres × 40 = 400 litres

(iii) **Average actual labour rate per hour** = actual total cost of labour/actual number of hours = £2,788/328 hours = £8.50

(iv) **Standard labour hours required for 40 barrels of X14** = standard labour hours per barrel × 40 = 8 hours × 40 = 320 hours

(v) **Budgeted number of machine hours** = budgeted production × budgeted number of hours per barrel = 45 barrels × 16 = 720 hours

(vi) **Budgeted fixed overheads** = standard fixed overhead per barrel × budgeted production = £320 × 45 = £14,400

or = budgeted number of machine hours for processing department × standard rate per machine hour = 720 hours × £20 = £14,400

or = (budgeted machine hours for processing department/factory budgeted machine hours) × factory budgeted fixed overheads = (720 hours/1,152 hours) × £23,040 = £14,400)

(vii) **Actual fixed overheads** (for the processing department) = (budgeted machine hours for processing department/factory budgeted machine hours) × factory actual fixed overheads = (720 hours/1,152 hours) × £26,000 = £16,250

(viii) **Standard machine hours for actual production** = actual production output × standard machine hours per barrel = 40 barrels × 16 machine hours = 640 standard machine hours

(ix) **Standard absorption cost of actual production** = standard absorption cost per barrel × actual production = £984 × 40 barrels = £39,360

(x) **Actual absorption cost of actual production** = actual cost of material + labour + fixed overheads = £(23,985 + 2,788 + 16,250(a)(vii)) = £43,023

**(b)** (i) **Material price variance**

|  | £ |  |
|---|---:|---|
| 410 litres (from (a)(i)) should have cost (× £60) | 24,600 | |
| but did cost | 23,985 | |
|  | 615 | (F) |

(ii) **Material usage variance**

|  |  |  |
|---|---:|---|
| 40 barrels should have used (× 10 litres) (from (a)(ii)) | 400 | litres |
| but did use (from (a)(i)) | 410 | litres |
| Variance in litres | 10 | litres (A) |
| × standard cost per litre | × £60 | |
|  | £600 | (A) |

(iii) **Labour rate variance**

|  | £ |  |
|---|---|---|
| 328 hours should have cost (× £8) | 2,624 | |
| but did cost | 2,788 | |
| | 164 | (A) |

(iv) **Labour efficiency variance**

| | | |
|---|---|---|
| 40 barrels should have taken (× 8 hours) (from (a)(iv)) | 320 | hours |
| but did take | 328 | hours |
| Variance in hours | 8 | hours (A) |
| × standard cost per hour | × £8 | |
| | £64 | (A) |

(v) **Fixed overhead expenditure variance**

| | £ | |
|---|---|---|
| Budgeted fixed overhead expenditure (from (a)(vi)) | 14,400 | |
| Actual fixed overhead expenditure (from (a)(vii)) | 16,250 | |
| | 1,850 | (A) |

(vi) **Fixed overhead volume variance**

| | £ | |
|---|---|---|
| Actual production at standard rate (40 barrels × £320) | 12,800 | |
| Budgeted production at standard rate (45 barrels × £320) | 14,400 | |
| | 1,600 | (A) |

(vii) **Fixed overhead efficiency variance**

| | | |
|---|---|---|
| 40 barrels should take (× 16 hours) (from (a)(viii)) | 640 | hours |
| but did take | 656 | hours |
| Variance in hours | 16 | hours (A) |
| × standard rate per hour | × £20 | |
| | £320 | (A) |

(viii) **Fixed overhead capacity variance**

| | | |
|---|---|---|
| Budgeted machine hours (from (a)(v)) | 720 | |
| Actual machine hours | 656 | |
| Variance in hours | 64 | (A) |
| × standard absorption rate per hour | × £20 | |
| | £1,280 | (A) |

**(c) Reconciliation statement – five weeks ended 31 May 20X8**

|  |  | £ |  |
|---|---|---|---|
| Standard absorption cost of actual production (from (a)(ix)) |  | 39,360 |  |

|  | £ (F) | £ (A) |  |  |
|---|---|---|---|---|
| Variances |  |  |  |  |
| Material price | 615 |  |  |  |
| Material usage |  | 600 |  |  |
| Labour rate |  | 164 |  |  |
| Labour efficiency |  | 64 |  |  |
| Fixed overhead expenditure |  | 1,850 |  |  |
| Fixed overhead efficiency |  | 320 |  |  |
| Fixed overhead capacity |  | 1,280 |  |  |
|  | 615 | 4,278 | 3,663 | (A) |

|  | £ |
|---|---|
| Actual absorption cost of actual production (from (a)(x)) | 43,023 |

**(d) MEMO**

To: Judith Green, production manager

From: Accounting technician

Date: 7 August 20X5

Subject: **Croxton Ltd – analysis of variances for 5 weeks ended 31 May 20X8**

Following our recent meeting, I set out below some issues to consider in relation to our discussions.

(i) **Revised standard material price per litre** = £60 × 133/140 = £57

(ii) **Subdivision of material price variance**

|  | £ | £ |
|---|---|---|
| 410 litres were expected to have cost (at the original standard of £60 per litre) | 24,600 |  |
| but should then have been expected to have cost (at the revised standard of £57 per litre) | 23,370 |  |
| Variance due to the change in the price index |  | 1,230 (F) |
| 410 litres should have cost, if the revised standard of £57 had been used | 23,370 |  |
| but did cost | 23,985 |  |
| Variance due to other reasons |  | 615 (A) |
| Total material price variance |  | 615 (F) |

(iii) **Reasons for the occurrence of the material price variance**

A favourable material price variance of £615 was reported for the five weeks ended 31 May 20X8. The standard price used as the basis for this calculation was out of date, however, and was too high. If a more realistic standard had been used, the actual cost was in fact greater than the standard cost, not less than the standard cost. The purchasing department had therefore purchased material at a price greater than the realistic standard (although at a price lower than the out of date standard).

The purchasing department have therefore been inefficient, not efficient.

(iv) **Implications of one scrapped barrel**

(1) **Material usage variance**

The material usage variance shows that 10 litres more than standard were used. As the standard usage per barrel is 10 litres it is possible that the scrapped barrel is the reason for this adverse variance.

(2) **Labour efficiency variance**

The labour efficiency variance shows that eight hours more than standard were worked. As a standard eight hours should be worked per barrel it is possible that the scrapped barrel is the reason for this adverse variance.

(3) **Labour rate variance**

328 hours were actually worked during the five weeks. Overtime is paid on hours in excess of 320 hours, and hence an overtime premium of eight hours × £8 = £64 was paid in the period. Suppose the eight hours of overtime were worked because one barrel was scrapped (see (2) above). The total labour rate variance is £164 and so there is still £164 − £64 = £100 of the variance not explained by the scrapping of the barrel. This £100 would be due to other, unexplained reasons.

(v) **Why the fixed overheads might not be controllable by the processing department**

(1) The apportionment of both budgeted and fixed overheads to the department is done on the arbitrary basis of budgeted machine hours. Budgeted machine hours are determined by budgeted production volume, which is outside the control of the processing department.

(2) The actual overheads apportioned to the processing department are a share of total fixed overheads. The processing department is unable to control the fixed overheads incurred in other parts of Croxton Ltd, however.

**Note**. Only one reason was required for (v).

........................................................................................

## Task 6.13

**(a) (i)** (1) Actual number of meals served = 4 meals × 7 days × 648 guests

= 18,144 meals

(2) Standard number of meals
for actual number of guests = 3 meals × 7 days × 648 guests

= 13,608 meals

(3) Actual hourly rate of pay = £5,280 ÷ 1,200 hours

= £4.40 per hour

(4)  Standard hours allowed for
actual number of guests       = (648 guests × 3 meals × 7 days)
                                ÷ 12 meals per hour

                              = 1,134 hours

(5)  Standard fixed overhead per guest = budgeted overheads ÷
                                         budgeted number of guests

                              = £38,340 ÷ 540 = £71 per guest

(6)  Total standard cost for actual number of guests

|  | £ |
|---|---|
| Meal costs (13,608 meals × £3 per meal) | 40,824 |
| Catering staff costs (1,134 hours × £4 per hour) | 4,536 |
| Fixed overhead costs (648 × £71 per guest) | 46,008 |
| Total standard cost | 91,368 |

**(ii)**  (1)

|  | £ |
|---|---|
| 18,144 meals should cost (× £3) | 54,432 |
| but did cost | 49,896 |
| **Material price variance for meals served** | 4,536 (F) |

(2)

|  |  |
|---|---|
| 648 guests should have used ((a)(i)(2)) | 13,608 meals |
| but did use ((a)(i)(1)) | 18,144 meals |
| Usage variance in meals | 4,536 meals (A) |
| × standard cost per meal | × £3 |
| **Material usage variance for meals served** | £13,608 (A) |

(3)

|  | £ |
|---|---|
| 1,200 hrs worked should have cost (× £4/hr) | 4,800 |
| but did cost | 5,280 |
| **Labour rate variance for catering staff** | 480 (A) |

(4)

|  |  |
|---|---|
| Meals for 648 guests should have taken ((a)(i)(4)) | 1,134 hours |
| but did take | 1,200 hours |
| Labour efficiency variance in hours | 66 hours (A) |
| × standard rate per hour | × £4 |
| **Labour efficiency variance for catering staff** | £264 (A) |

(5)

|  | £ |
|---|---|
| Budgeted fixed overhead expenditure | 38,340 |
| Actual fixed overhead expenditure | 37,800 |
| **Fixed overhead expenditure variance** | 540 (F) |

(6)

| | |
|---|---:|
| Actual number of guests | 648 |
| Budgeted number of guests | 540 |
| Volume variance – number of guests | 108 |
| × standard fixed overhead per guest ((a)(i)(5)) | × £71 |
| **Fixed overhead volume variance** | £7,668 (F) |

(iii) **Bare Foot Hotel complex**

**Standard cost reconciliation for seven days ended 27 November 20X8**

Budgeted number of guests        540

Actual number of guests          648

| | £ | | £ | |
|---|---:|---|---:|---|
| **Standard cost for 648 guests** ((a)(i)(6)) | | | 91,368 | |
| **Cost variances** | | | | |
| Material price variance ((a)(ii)(1)) | 4,536 | (F) | | |
| Material usage variance ((a)(ii)(2)) | 13,608 | (A) | | |
| | | | 9,072 | (A) |
| Catering labour rate variance ((a)(ii)(3)) | 480 | (A) | | |
| Catering labour efficiency variance ((a)(ii)(4)) | 264 | (A) | | |
| | | | 744 | (A) |
| Fixed overhead expenditure variance ((a)(ii)(5)) | 540 | (F) | | |
| Fixed overhead volume variance ((a)(ii)(6)) | 7,668 | (F) | | |
| | | | 8,208 | (F) |
| **Actual cost for 648 guests** | | | 92,976 | |

**Note**. (A) denotes adverse variance, (F) denotes favourable variance.

**(b) MEMO**

To: Alice Groves, general manager
From: Assistant management accountant
Date: xx.xx.xx
Subject: **Performance report for seven days ended 27 November 20X8**

This memorandum deals with a number of issues arising from the standard cost reconciliation statement prepared for the seven days ended 27 November 20X8.

**(i) Subdivision of the catering labour efficiency variance**

The adverse catering labour efficiency variance of £264 can be divided into that part due to guests taking more meals than planned and that part due to other efficiency reasons.

| | |
|---|---:|
| Standard hours allowed for 648 guests taking 3 meals ((a)(i)(4)) | 1,134 hours |
| Standard hours allowed for 648 guests taking 4 meals = (648 guests × 4 meals × 7 days) ÷ 12 meals per hour | 1,512 hours |
| Excess hours due to guests taking more meals than planned | 378 hours (A) |
| × standard rate per hour | × £4 |
| **Efficiency variance due to guests taking more meals than planned** | £1,512 (A) |
| Standard hours allowed for 648 guests taking 4 meals (from above) | 1,512 hours |
| Actual hours worked | 1,200 hours |
| Efficiency variance due to other reasons (in hours) | 312 hours (F) |
| × standard rate per hour | × £4 |
| **Catering labour efficiency variance due to other reasons** | £1,248 (F) |

**(ii) The meaning of the fixed overhead capacity and efficiency variances**

The fixed overhead absorption rate for our hotel is based on the budgeted overhead expenditure for the period, divided by the budgeted number of guests.

$$\text{Fixed overhead absorption rate} = \frac{\text{budgeted fixed overhead}}{\text{budgeted number of guests}}$$

If the actual overhead, or the actual number of guests, or both, are different from budget then over or under absorption of overhead may occur, so that there may be a fixed overhead variance.

A **volume variance** arises when the activity level is different from that budgeted, in our case if the actual number of guests is different from the budgeted number. In some organisations it may be possible to sub-divide the volume variance into two parts: the capacity variance and the efficiency variance.

The **capacity variance** arises when the utilisation of the available capacity is higher or lower than budgeted. It is usually calculated as the difference between budgeted and actual hours worked, multiplied by the fixed overhead absorption rate. Under or over utilisation of capacity can potentially lead to under– or over-absorbed overhead.

The **efficiency variance** arises when employees are working at a more or less efficient rate than standard to produce a given output. Producing output at a faster or slower rate could also potentially lead to under– or over-absorbed overhead.

### (iii) Calculating the fixed overhead capacity and efficiency variances for the Bare Foot Hotel complex

The above descriptions of the fixed overhead capacity and efficiency variances highlight the need to be able to measure hours of work so that the volume variance can be subdivided.

It is not feasible to do this for the Bare Foot Hotel complex. We do have a measure of hours worked within the catering activity, but a large proportion of overheads are incurred on entertainment, for which we have no record of hours worked.

The absence of an activity measure based on hours worked therefore makes it difficult and meaningless to subdivide the fixed overhead volume variance into its capacity and efficiency elements.

## Task 6.14

**Total direct material variance**

The total direct material variance simply compares the **flexed budget** for materials with the actual cost incurred. The flexed budget is the total budgeted cost of materials for the actual production; 21,000 units in this example. It is incorrect to calculate the variance as £74,500 adverse by comparing the actual cost of £954,500 with the budgeted cost of £880,000.

The flexing of the budget calculates the **quantity of materials** which are expected to be used to produce the **actual production**. Therefore, the expected usage of materials to produce 21,000 units is £924,000 (if 80,000 kgs costing £880,000 is required to make 20,000 units then it follows, assuming that the material cost and quantity is perfectly variable, that to make 21,000 units requires 84,000 kilograms at a cost of £11 per kilogram (£880,000/80,000)).

This flexed budget can now be **compared with the actual** costs to produce the total material variance of £30,500. This variance is adverse because the **actual cost was greater than the flexed budgeted cost**.

This total variance can now be split into two elements:

- The variance due to the price being different to that which was expected. The material price variance.

- The variance due to the quantity of material used per unit of production being different to that which was expected. The material usage variance.

The expected (standard or budgeted or planned) price is £11 per kilogram (£880,000/80,000) and therefore the expected cost of 83,000 kilograms must be 83,000 kilograms at £11 per kilogram. This is £913,000.

The price variance can now be calculated by taking the actual cost (price paid) for the 83,000 kilograms and comparing this to the expected cost. This results in £913,000, compared to £954,500: a variance of £41,500. This variance is adverse because the **actual cost is greater than the expected cost**.

The material usage variance is calculated by taking the quantity of materials which would be expected to be used to produce the actual volume of production. In this case 21,000 units were produced and the expected quantity of materials for each unit is 4 kilograms (80,000 kilograms/20,000 units). Therefore, to produce 21,000 units requires 84,000 kilograms of material. Compare this to the actual quantity used of 83,000 kilograms produces a variance of 1,000 kilograms. This is favourable and needs to be **valued at the expected cost** of £11 per kilogram.

The usage variance is always **valued at the standard cost** (expected/planned or budgeted) because the price variance has already been isolated. If both variances have been calculated correctly they should reconcile back to the total materials variance. In this example, the price of £41,500 adverse less £11,000 favourable is reconciled to the total variance of £30,500.

## Task 6.15

### POL89 price variance

The POL89 price variance is likely to be favourable.

This is due to a reduction in price of 18% during the quarter, resulting in the actual price being lower than the standard price.

### POL89 usage variance

The POL89 usage variance is likely to be favourable.

The purchase of a higher quality product would usually be expected to result in less wastage, and therefore the actual quantity used would be lower than the standard usage.

The usage and price variances are often linked when a higher priced and therefore higher quality product may reduce wastage costs, however in this case the higher quality is probably due to the advances in production of POL89 and so is unlikely to be linked with the POL89 price variance.

Employees may be demotivated from the lack of pay rise but the new material usage control policy recently implemented should keep material usage favourable.

## Direct labour efficiency variance

The direct labour efficiency variance is likely to be adverse, with each unit taking more hours to manufacture than expected.

Efficiency will be affected by the demotivational effects of the suspension of the pay rise.

In addition the cancelled order means that production will be lower by 25% during the quarter and there is likely to be idle time for employees which will have an adverse effect on the labour efficiency.

## Fixed overhead expenditure variance

The fixed overhead expenditure variance is likely to be adverse, due to costs of recalibrating the machines and the repair of the defective machine. Therefore the actual fixed overheads will be higher than expected.

## Fixed overhead volume variance

The fixed overhead volume variance is likely to be adverse because the actual volume produced is likely to be 25% lower than the forecast volume due to the cancellation of the order for 3,000 units. Therefore overheads are likely to be under-absorbed.

## Chapter 7

### Task 7.1

| Organisation | Possible productivity measures |
|---|---|
| Taxi firm | • Number of fares per shift<br>• Number of miles per shift |
| Hospital | • Out-patients seen per day |
| Motorbike courier service | • Miles per week<br>• Number of packages per day |
| Firm of accountants | • Chargeable hours as a percentage of total hours |
| Retail store | • Sales per employee<br>• Sales per square foot of shop floor |
| Maker of hand-made pottery | • Number of pots thrown per day<br>• Number of pots painted per day |

### Task 7.2

The total value added is £394,200

The value added per employee is £26,280

**Workings**

|  | £ |
|---|---|
| Sales | 1,447,600 |
| Less:  cost of materials | (736,500) |
|  cost of services | (316,900) |
| Total value added | 394,200 |
| Value added per employee | £394,200/15 |
|  | £26,280 |

## Task 7.3

### (a)

|  | Calculation | Explanation |
|---|---|---|
| Efficiency ratio | 92.61% | As the efficiency ratio is less than 100% this indicates that the workforce have not worked as efficiently as was anticipated. The actual hours worked are more than the standard hours for that level of production. |
| Capacity ratio | 102.22% | The capacity ratio indicates whether as many hours have been worked as were budgeted for. In this instance the capacity ratio is greater than 100% meaning that the number of hours worked was more than those budgeted for. |
| Production volume ratio | 94.67% | The production volume ratio is an indicator of how the volume of actual production compares to the budgeted level of output. In this instance as the production volume ratio is below 100% this indicates that the actual level of output was below the budgeted level. |

### Workings

Efficiency ratio $= \dfrac{\text{Standard hours for actual production}}{\text{Actual hours worked}} \times 100$

$= \dfrac{14{,}200 \times 3}{46{,}000} \times 100$

$= 92.61\%$

Capacity ratio $= \dfrac{\text{Actual hours worked}}{\text{Budgeted hours}} \times 100$

$= \dfrac{46{,}000}{15{,}000 \times 3} \times 100$

$= 102.22\%$

Production volume ratio $= \dfrac{\text{Actual output}}{\text{Budgeted output}} \times 100$

$= \dfrac{14{,}200}{15{,}000} \times 100$

$= 94.67\%$

(b) Hours worked @ 95% efficiency $= \dfrac{14{,}200 \times 3}{0.95}$

$= 44{,}842$

Hours saved (46,000 − 44,842) $= 1{,}158$ hours

## Task 7.4

| | |
|---|---|
| Gross profit margin | 38.00% |
| Operating profit margin | 12.70% |
| Return on capital employed | 14.40% |
| Asset turnover | 1.13 |
| Non-current asset turnover | 1.38 |
| Current ratio | 3.19 |
| Quick ratio | 2.19 |
| Receivables' collection period | 55 days |
| Inventory holding period in days | 41 days |
| Payables' payment period | 42 days |
| Interest cover | 9.35 times |
| Gearing ratio | 34.53% |

**Workings**

**(a)** (i) Gross profit margin

$$= \frac{\text{Gross profit}}{\text{Revenue}} \times 100$$

$$= \frac{1{,}007{,}200}{2{,}650{,}400} \times 100$$

$$= 38.00\%$$

(ii) Operating profit margin

$$= \frac{\text{Operating profit}}{\text{Revenue}} \times 100$$

$$= \frac{336{,}600}{2{,}650{,}400} \times 100$$

$$= 12.70\%$$

(iii) Return on capital employed

$$= \frac{\text{Operating profit}}{\text{Non-current assets + Net current assets}} \times 100$$

$$= \frac{336{,}600}{2{,}337{,}500} \times 100$$

$$= 14.40\%$$

(iv) Asset turnover

$$= \frac{\text{Revenue}}{\text{Capital employed}}$$

$$= \frac{2{,}650{,}400}{2{,}337{,}500}$$

$$= 1.13$$

(v)   Non-current asset turnover   $= \dfrac{\text{Revenue}}{\text{Non-current assets}}$

$= \dfrac{2,650,400}{1,920,400}$

$=$ 1.38

(vi)  Current ratio   $= \dfrac{\text{Current assets}}{\text{Current liabilities}}$

$= \dfrac{607,400}{190,300}$

$=$ 3.19

(vii)  Quick ratio   $= \dfrac{\text{Current assets} - \text{Inventory}}{\text{Current liabilities}}$

$= \dfrac{607,400 - 191,200}{190,300}$

$=$ 2.19

(viii) Receivables' collection period   $= \dfrac{\text{Receivables}}{\text{Revenue}} \times 365$

$= \dfrac{399,400}{2,650,400} \times 365$

$=$ 55 days

(ix)  Inventory days   $= \dfrac{\text{Average inventory}}{\text{Cost of sales}} \times 365$

$= \dfrac{(180,000 + 191,200)/2}{1,643,200} \times 365$

$=$ 41 days

(x)   Payables' payment period   $= \dfrac{\text{Payables}}{\text{Purchases}} \times 365$

$= \dfrac{190,300}{1,654,400} \times 365$

$=$ 42 days

(xi)  Interest cover   $= \dfrac{\text{Profit before interest}}{\text{Interest charge}}$

$= \dfrac{336,600}{36,000}$

$=$ 9.35

(xii) Gearing ratio $= \dfrac{\text{Total debt}}{\text{Share capital} + \text{Reserves}}$

$= \dfrac{600{,}000}{1{,}737{,}500}$

$= 34.53\%$

**(b)** Increase in cash balance $= \dfrac{£1{,}654{,}400}{365} \times (60 - 42)$

$= £81{,}587$

## Task 7.5

**(a)**

|  | July | Aug | Sept | Oct | Nov | Dec |
|---|---|---|---|---|---|---|
| Gross profit margin | 34% | 34% | 34% | 32% | 31% | 31% |
| Operating profit margin | 12% | 12% | 12% | 11% | 10% | 9% |
| Expenses to sales % | 22% | 22% | 22% | 21% | 21% | 22% |
| Return on capital employed (W1) | 15.2% | 14.6% | 13.1% | 11.6% | 10.9% | 10.0% |
| Asset turnover (W2) | 1.3 | 1.2 | 1.09 | 1.1 | 1.1 | 1.1 |

**(b)** Sales revenue decreased from July to September and then increased significantly until the end of the year. However the increase in sales has been at the cost of the gross profit margin which has decreased from 34% to 31%. Although the expenses to sales percentage has remained reasonably constant over the period, the operating profit margin has fallen due to the decrease in gross profit margin.

Return on capital employed fell dramatically in the first four months of the period although this was due to a significant decrease in asset turnover in that period more than a decline in profitability. The fall in return on capital employed continues in the last three months of the year due to the fall in operating profit margin; however the drop in return is not as bad as it might have been, as the asset turnover is again improving.

**Workings**

(1) Here, return on capital employed is calculated as

$$\text{ROCE} = \dfrac{\text{Profit before interest}}{\substack{\text{Capital employed} \\ \text{(shareholders funds} + \text{loan)}}} = \dfrac{(550 - 374 - 116)}{468 + 50} = 11.6\% \text{ for October, etc}$$

Alternatively, it may be computed as a return on net assets:

$$\text{RONA} = \frac{\text{Profit after interest}}{\text{Shareholders' funds}} = \frac{(550 - 374 - 116 - 3)}{468} = 12.2\% \text{ for October, etc}$$

(2) To be consistent with the ROCE definition used, asset turnover has been calculated as

$$\text{Asset turnover} = \frac{\text{Revenue}}{\text{Total capital employed}} = \frac{550}{468+50} = 1.06 \text{ for October, etc}$$

$$(\text{shareholders' funds} + \text{loan})$$

## Task 7.6

**(a)**

|  | North | South | Central |
|---|---|---|---|
| Gross profit margin | 32.0% | 30.0% | 35.0% |
| Operating profit margin | 18.0% | 11.1% | 13.4% |
| Return on capital employed | 16.0% | 9.0% | 14.0% |
| Asset turnover | 0.9 | 0.8 | 1.0 |
| Inventory holding in months | 0.7 months | 1.1 months | 1.0 months |
| Receivables' collection period in months | 1.4 months | 2.3 months | 1.6 months |
| Payables' payment period in months | 2.1 months | 1.3 months | 1.9 months |
| Units per square metre | 34.0 units | 25.5 units | 29.3 units |
| Units per employee | 944.4 units | 850.0 units | 820.0 units |
| Units per hour | 2.0 units | 1.8 units | 1.8 units |

**(b)** In terms of profitability North is clearly the most profitable with the highest operating profit margin and return on capital employed. However Central has a higher gross profit margin which may be due to production of a different product to North or due to higher local selling prices or lower purchasing prices for Central. Although Central's operating profit margin is significantly lower than North's its return on capital employed is not so different due to a higher asset turnover in Central. South seems to have profitability problems with gross and operating profit margins, asset turnover and return on capital employed significantly lower than those of the other two divisions.

North again appears to have the best working capital control with the lowest inventory holding and receivables' collection period and the longest payables' payment period. Central's working capital control appears to be adequate but again there are questions to be asked at South with a relatively long receivables' collection period and a month shorter payables' payment period.

Finally, whichever way productivity is measured, the productivity at North is significantly greater than at either of the other two divisions. Central makes the same number of units per hour as South but less per employee, indicating that there could be room for improvement in employee productivity at Central.

**Workings**

|  | North £ | South £ | Central £ |
|---|---|---|---|
| *Statement of profit or loss (Income statement )* |  |  |  |
| Revenue | 870,000 | 560,000 | 640,000 |
| COS: Opening inventory | 34,000 | 41,000 | 34,000 |
| Purchases | 590,000 | 380,000 | 420,000 |
| Closing inventory | (32,000) | (29,000) | (38,000) |
|  | 592,000 | 392,000 | 416,000 |
| Gross profit | 278,000 | 168,000 | 224,000 |
| Expenses | (121,000) | (106,000) | (138,000) |
| Operating profit | 157,000 | 62,000 | 86,000 |
| *Statement of financial position* |  |  |  |
| Receivables | 100,100 | 107,300 | 87,600 |
| Payables | (103,400) | (42,600) | (66,700) |
| Other net assets | 983,300 | 625,300 | 594,100 |
| Capital | 980,000 | 690,000 | 615,000 |

|  | North | South | Central |
|---|---|---|---|
| Gross profit margin | 278/870 | 168/560 | 224/640 |
| Operating profit margin | 157/870 | 62/560 | 86/640 |
| Return on capital employed | 157/980 | 62/690 | 86/615 |
| Asset turnover | 870/980 | 560/690 | 640/615 |
| Inventory holding in months (using average inventory) | 33/592 × 12 | 35/392 × 12 | 36/416 × 12 |
| Receivables' collection period in months | 100.1/870 × 12 | 107.3/560 × 12 | 87.6/640 × 12 |
| Payables' payment period in months | 103.4/592 × 12 | 42.6/392 × 12 | 66.7/416 × 12 |
| Units per square metre | 17,000/500 | 10,200/400 | 12,300/420 |
| Units per employee | 17,000/18 | 10,200/12 | 12,300/15 |
| Units per hour | 17,000/8,500 | 10,200/5,800 | 12,300/7,000 |

## Task 7.7

**(a)** Gross profit

= 380,000 × 0.48

= £182,400

**(b)** Sales

= £425,000/0.34

= £1,250,000

**(c)** Gross profit

= £85,000 × 0.40

= £34,000

Operating profit

= £85,000 × 0.115

= £9,775

Expenses

= £34,000 − £9,775

= £24,225

**(d)** Capital employed

= £100,000/0.116

= £862,069

**(e)** Asset turnover

= 0.10/0.08

= 1.25

**(f)** Average inventory

= (£158,000 + £182,000)/2

= £170,000

Cost of sales

= £158,000 + £560,000 − £182,000

= £536,000

| | | |
|---|---|---|
| Inventory turnover | = | £536,000/£170,000 |
| | = | 3.2 times |
| **(g)** Sales | = | £96,000/48 × 365 |
| | = | £730,000 |

## Task 7.8

**(a)**

| | Y/e 31 Dec 20X8 | Y/e 31 Dec 20X7 |
|---|---|---|
| Gross profit margin | 45.3% | 42.4% |
| Operating profit margin (Operating profit/Revenue) | 18.3% | 17.0% |
| Return on capital employed (Operating profit/ Share capital + Retained earnings + Loan) | 14.7% | 13.9% |
| Asset turnover | 0.80 | 0.82 |
| Non-current asset turnover | 0.85 | 0.89 |
| Current ratio | 1.75 | 2.3 |
| Quick ratio | 1.2 | 1.6 |
| Receivables' collection period | 40 days | 44 days |
| Inventory holding | 31 days | 36 days |
| Payables' payment period | 61 days | 51 days |
| Interest cover | 11.0 | 9.6 |
| Gearing ratio (Total debt/Share capital + Retained earnings) | 25% | 27.8% |

**(b)** Return on capital employed has increased over the two-year period and this is solely due to increased profitability as both the asset turnover and non-current asset turnover have decreased over the period. There has been a significant increase in gross profit margin in 20X8 and, although operating profit margin has also increased, it has not done so at the rate of the gross profit margin, indicating that expenses are in fact increasing at a faster rate than sales. This may be due to a large advertising campaign which has increased costs but allowed the gross profit margin to increase or some similar reason.

As well as an increase in sales and profitability there also appears to be general improvement in the working capital management. Both the current and quick ratios have fallen but are still at acceptable levels. The receivables' collection period and inventory holding period have both been reduced by a few days and in combination with the increase in the payables' payment period by 10 days this will have a significant positive effect on the cash flows of the business.

The level of gearing does not appear to be a problem, as the gearing ratios are quite low and the interest cover is quite high.

## Task 7.9

(a) To:       Angela Wade

From:    A Technician

Date:    xx.xx.xx

Subject:  **West Ltd and East Ltd – Performance Report**

(i) **Return on net assets (RONA)**

The RONA is a key financial ratio which shows the amount of profit which has been made in relation to the amount of resources invested. It also gives some idea of how efficiently the company has been operating.

$$RONA = \frac{\text{Operating profit}}{\text{Net assets}}$$

$$RONA \text{ (West Ltd)} = \frac{3,068}{15,340} = 0.2 \times 100\% = 20\%$$

$$RONA \text{ (East Ltd)} = \frac{2,795}{6,500} = 0.43 \times 100\% = 43\%$$

(ii) **Net asset turnover**

The net asset turnover is one of the main ratios for the statement of financial position, and is a measure of how well the assets of a business are being used to generate sales.

$$\text{Asset turnover} = \frac{\text{Net revenue}}{\text{Net assets}}$$

$$\text{Asset turnover (West Ltd)} = \frac{17,910}{15,340} = 1.17 \text{ times}$$

$$\text{Asset turnover (East Ltd)} = \frac{17,424}{6,500} = 2.68 \text{ times}$$

(iii) **Operating profit margin**

The operating profit margin ratio is a measure of overall profitability and it provides a measure of performance for management. Unsatisfactory operating profit margins are investigated by management, and are generally followed by control action. Increasing selling prices and reducing costs will have a direct effect on this ratio.

$$\text{Operating profit margin} = \frac{\text{Operating profit}}{\text{Net revenue}}$$

$$\text{Operating profit margin (West Ltd)} = \frac{3,068}{17,910} = 0.171 \times 100\% = 17.1\%$$

$$\text{Operating profit margin (East Ltd)} = \frac{2,795}{17,424} = 0.16 \times 100\% = 16\%$$

(b) **Measure of customer service: faulty sales**

The percentage of faulty sales as a measure of the level of customer service is calculated as:

$$\frac{\text{Returns}}{\text{Gross sales}}$$

$$\text{West Ltd} = \frac{100}{20,000} = 0.005 \times 100\% = 0.5\%$$

$$\text{East Ltd} = \frac{220}{22,000} = 0.01 \times 100\% = 1\%$$

(c) **Further measure of customer service**

Another possible measure of the level of customer service which could be derived from the accounting data is the number of days between order and delivery of goods.

This can be calculated as follows.

$$\frac{\text{Time between}}{\text{order and delivery}} = \frac{\text{Orders received in year-net sales ('000 litres)}}{\text{Net sales ('000 litres)}} \times 365 \text{ days}$$

$$\text{West Ltd} = \frac{20,173 - 19,900}{19,900} \times 365 \text{ days} = 5 \text{ days}$$

$$\text{East Ltd} = \frac{22,854 - 21,780}{21,780} \times 365 \text{ days} = 18 \text{ days}$$

The amount of money which the subsidiaries invest in research and development, and training could also provide a measure of customer service.

(d) **Limitations of financial ratios**

Financial ratios as a measure of performance are only concerned with the data recorded in the accounts. For example, East Ltd appears to be a much more efficient company than West Ltd based on its RONA and net asset turnover ratios. However, when calculations are made to measure customer service, West Ltd has far fewer days between order and delivery of goods, and half as many faulty sales (as a percentage of gross sales).

The financial ratios also treat research and development, and training costs as expenses which are written off to the statement of profit or loss (income statement). These expenses are likely to have an impact on the future profitability of the company, and are more of an investment than expense.

Both West Ltd and East Ltd use plant of similar size and technology. There is however, a large difference in the net book values of the plant, and hence a large difference in the net assets of each company.

East Ltd purchased its plant before West Ltd, and has a lower cost, and a higher depreciation to date than West Ltd. These differences arise mainly due to the fact that the accounts are prepared using historic cost accounting. The fact that East Ltd's net assets are so much lower than those of West Ltd, means that the RONA of East Ltd will be much higher than that of West Ltd.

## Task 7.10

### (a)

| Performance indicator | Workings | |
|---|---|---|
| Return on net assets | (Operating profit ÷ Net assets) × 100% <br><br> (975,000/4,875,000) × 100% | 20% |
| Net asset turnover | Revenue/Net assets <br><br> 3,900,000/4,875,000 | 0.8 |
| Operating profit margin | (Operating profit/Revenue) × 100% <br><br> (975,000/3,900,000) × 100% | 25% |
| Average age of receivables in months | (Receivables/Revenue) × 12 <br><br> (325,000/3,900,000) × 12 | 1 month |
| Average age of finished inventory in months | (Average finished goods inventory/Cost of sales) × 12 <br><br> (½ × (140,000 + 50,000)/840,000) × 12 | 1.4 months |

**(b) Briefing notes on the usefulness of performance indicators**

Prepared for Angela Frear

Prepared by Financial Analyst

Dated: xx.xx.xx

(i) **Return on net assets**

The return on net assets can be misleading.

(1) Profits should be related to average capital employed but we compute the ratio using year-end assets. Using year-end figures can distort trends and comparisons. If a new investment is undertaken near to a year end and financed, for example, by an issue of shares, the capital employed will rise by the finance raised but profits will only have a month or two of the new investment's contribution.

(2) The RONA would be higher if costs such as marketing, research and development and training were not treated as revenue expenditure but were viewed as investment for the future and were capitalised.

(ii) **Operating profit margin**

The operating profit margin can be manipulated in a number of ways. The following activities would result in short-term improvements in the margin, but probably at the expense of the organisation's long-term viability:

(1) Reducing expenditure on discretionary cost items such as research and development.

(2) Depreciating assets over a longer period of time, so that the depreciation charge is less.

(3) Choosing an alternative inventory valuation method to increase the value of closing inventory.

(iii) **Average delay in fulfilling orders**

|  | £ |
|---|---|
| Orders during the year | 4,550,000 |
| Revenue during the year | 3,900,000 |
| Unfulfilled orders | 650,000 |

Average delay = (£650,000/£3,900,000) × 12 months = 2 months

(iv) **Measures of customer satisfaction**

As well as the delay in fulfilling orders, other measures of customer satisfaction include the following.

- Repeat business ((£3,120,000/£3,900,000) × 100% = 80%)

- Cost of customer support per £ of revenue (£400,000/£3,900,000 = 10p)

- Cost of customer support per customer (information not available)

(v) **Measuring performance from an internal perspective**

A number of indicators may help to measure performance from an internal perspective.

- Training costs as a percentage of production costs ((£140,000/£930,000) × 100% = 15.05%)

- Reworked faulty production as a percentage of total production ((£37,200/£930,000) × 100% = 4%)

- Returns as a percentage of sales ((£100,000/£4m) × 100% = 2.5%)

The first indicator should be relatively high, the second and third as low as possible.

(vi) **Measuring the innovation and learning perspective**

The innovation and learning perspective could be measured with one of the following indicators.

- Revenue from new products as a percentage of total revenue ((£1.56m/£3.9m) × 100% = 40%)

- Research and development expenditure as a percentage of cost of production ((£750,000/£930,000) × 100% = 81%)

- Research and development expenditure as a percentage of revenue ((£750,000/£3.9m) × 100% = 19.2%)

**Note**. A fuller answer has been given here than was required in the task for assessment purposes, where in most cases only ONE point was required.

## Task 7.11

**(a)** (i) Gross profit margin $= \dfrac{£221,760}{£633,600} \times 100\% = 35\%$

(ii) Operating profit margin $= \dfrac{£76,032}{£633,600} \times 100\% = 12\%$

(iii) Return on capital employed $= \dfrac{£76,032}{£95,040} \times 100\% = 80\%$

(iv) Asset turnover $= \dfrac{£633,600}{£95,040} = 6.7$ times

(v) No. of passengers in the year $= \dfrac{\text{Revenue (turnover)}}{\text{Fare per passenger}} = \dfrac{£633,600}{£1}$

$= 633,600$ passengers

(vi) Total cost per mile $= \dfrac{£633,600 - £76,032}{356,400} = £1.56$

(vii) No. of journeys in the year $\quad = \dfrac{356{,}400 \text{ miles}}{18 \text{ miles per journey}} \quad = 19{,}800 \text{ journeys}$

No. of journeys per day $\quad = \dfrac{19{,}800}{360} \quad = 55 \text{ journeys}$

(viii) Maintenance cost per mile $\quad = \dfrac{£28{,}512}{356{,}400} \quad = £0.08$

(ix) Passengers per day $\quad = \dfrac{633{,}600 \text{ (from v))}}{360} \quad = 1{,}760 \text{ passengers}$

(x) Passengers per journey $\quad = \dfrac{1{,}760 \text{ (from(ix))}}{55 \text{ (from(vii))}} \quad = 32 \text{ passengers}$

(xi) Number of drivers $\quad = \dfrac{\text{Wages paid}}{\text{Wages per driver}} \quad = \dfrac{£142{,}000}{£14{,}200}$

$= 10 \text{ drivers}$

## (b) MEMO

To:        Chief executive

From:      Management accountant

Date:      xx.xx.xx

Subject:   **Performance of Travel Bus Ltd for the year to 30 November 20X8**

This memo addresses a number of issues concerning the productivity and profitability of Travel Bus Ltd.

### (i) Productivity and profitability

Productivity is the quantity of service produced (output) in relation to the resources put in (input). It measures how efficiently resources are being used.

An increase in productivity does not always lead to increased profitability. For example the number of passengers carried per driver, a measure of productivity, could increase. The extra passengers may have been attracted by offering substantial fare reductions, however, and this could lead to reduced profitability.

Another example might be an increase in productivity in terms of the number of journeys per bus. This increase in 'output' arising from the increase in productivity may not be saleable: the buses may be running empty. The revenue gained might be less than the additional costs incurred, leading to reduced profitability.

(ii)  **Driver productivity**

A possible measure of driver productivity is the number of miles per driver.

|  | 20X7 | 20X8 |
|---|---|---|
| Miles per driver | $\dfrac{324,000}{8} = 40,500$ | $\dfrac{356,400}{10} = 35,640$ |

The number of miles per driver has decreased between 20X7 and 20X8 and so, in terms of this measure of productivity, the drivers' claim that their productivity has increased is incorrect.

Even if the productivity had increased, the drivers might still be unable to claim that this had resulted in improved profitability. As discussed above, the extra miles might have been travelled with too few fare-paying passengers, so profitability would not necessarily have improved.

(iii)  **Reason for improved profitability**

A major reason for the improved profitability was the Council's decision not to charge for parking. This reduced the overall cost of using the service for passengers, and demand therefore increased considerably. Since many of the costs incurred by Travel Bus Ltd are fixed, costs did not increase at the same rate as revenue,and profitability improved.

(iv)  **Performance indicators to measure the satisfaction of passenger needs**

(1)  The satisfaction of passenger needs could be monitored by the number of passengers per journey.

|  | 20X7 | 20X8 |
|---|---|---|
| Number of passengers per journey | 30 | 32 |

Depending on the size of the buses, passenger needs may have been less satisfied during 20X8 because of more crowding or the need to stand because no seats were available.

Another measure of the satisfaction of passenger needs is the number of journeys per day.

|  | 20X7 | 20X8 |
|---|---|---|
| Number of journeys per day | 50 | 55 |

This increase probably led to reduced waiting times and so passenger needs may have been better satisfied in 20X8.

(2)  A measure of the satisfaction of customer needs that cannot be derived from the existing data is cleanliness of the buses.

Monitoring the cleaning cost per day or per bus might give some indication of the effort put into keeping the buses clean.

Another measure of the satisfaction of customer needs is punctuality of the buses and their adherence to published timetables.

Monitoring the percentage of buses arriving and departing within five minutes of their published time would give an indication of performance in this area.

**Note**. Only one measure required by the task

(v) **Monitoring the safety aspect of Travel Bus's operations**

(1) The safety aspect of Travel Bus's operations could be monitored by the maintenance cost per mile.

| | 20X7 | 20X8 |
|---|---|---|
| Maintenance cost per mile | £0.10 | £0.08 |

This has reduced, which may indicate a reduction in attention to safety, especially as maintenance costs are likely to increase as buses become older. No new buses have been added to the fleet (cost value of buses has remained at £240,000); the buses are older and likely to require more maintenance.

On the other hand, some of this reduction in the cost per mile may have been caused by the spreading of the fixed element of maintenance costs over a higher number of miles in the year 20X8.

Another indicator of attention to the safety aspect might be the average age of the buses. The depreciation charge for the year 20X8 was £12,000 (£180,000 – £168,000). On a cost value of £240,000, assuming straight line depreciation and no residual value, this suggests a useful life of 20 years. Accumulated depreciation of £180,000 means that the buses were on average 15 years old by the end of 20X6, and thus nearing the end of their useful lives.

(2) A measure of the safety aspect that cannot be derived from the existing data is the number of accidents per year.

Another measure could be the percentage of maintenance cost that is incurred to prevent faults compared with the percentage incurred to correct faults. This would indicate whether faults were being prevented before they occurred, or whether maintenance was being carried out 'after the event', which could compromise safety.

**Note**. Only one measure required by the task.

## Task 7.12

### (a) Budgeted statements of profit or loss (income statements)

|  | Pickmaster | Pickmaster 2 |
|---|---|---|
|  | £ | £ |
| Revenue | 1,125,000 | 1,125,000 |
| Cost of sales |  |  |
| Tea pickers | 150,000 | 150,000 |
| Tea processor operators (W) | 48,000 | 4,800 |
| Depreciation (W) | 16,000 | 72,000 |
| Seed and fertiliser costs | 75,000 | 75,000 |
| Total cost of sales | 289,000 | 301,800 |
| Gross profit | 836,000 | 823,200 |
| Administration costs | 150,000 | 135,000 |
| Distribution costs | 350,000 | 350,000 |
| Operating profit | 336,000 | 338,200 |

### Net assets at year end

|  | Pickmaster | Pickmaster 2 |
|---|---|---|
|  | £ | £ |
| Budgeted net assets | 935,500 | 935,500 |
| Operating profit | 336,000 | 338,200 |
|  | 1,271,500 | 1,273,700 |

### Workings

|  | Pickmaster | Pickmaster 2 |
|---|---|---|
|  | £ | £ |
| Tea processor operators (10 × £6 × 100 × 8) | 48,000 |  |
| (1 × £6 × 100 × 8) |  | 4,800 |
| Depreciation of tea machines (8 × £2,000) | 16,000 |  |
| (8 × £9,000) |  | 72,000 |

**Tutorial note.** The value of the new machines has not been included in the net asset figure as their purchase would have to be funded in some way ie bank loan, leasing, leading to an increase in liabilities which would cancel out the increase in asset values. This will not be an exact cancellation but we have no information about the method of funding.

**(b)**

|  | Pickmaster | Pickmaster 2 |
|---|---|---|
| Gross profit margin | 74.31% | 73.17% |
| Operating profit margin | 29.87% | 30.06% |
| Return on net assets | 26.43% | 26.55% |

## Workings

|  | Pickmaster | Pickmaster 2 |
|---|---|---|
|  | % | % |
| **(i) Gross profit margin** |  |  |
| $\dfrac{836,000}{1,125,000} \times 100$ | 74.31 |  |
| $\dfrac{823,200}{1,125,000} \times 100$ |  | 73.17 |
| **(ii) Operating profit margin** |  |  |
| $\dfrac{336,000}{1,125,000} \times 100$ | 29.87 |  |
| $\dfrac{338,200}{1,125,000} \times 100$ |  | 30.06 |
| **(iii) Return on net assets** |  |  |
| $\dfrac{336,000}{1,271,500} \times 100$ | 26.43 |  |
| $\dfrac{338,200}{1,273,700} \times 100$ |  | 26.55 |

**(c)**

REPORT

**To:** Managing Director

**From:** Accounting technician

**Date:** December 20X7

**Subject:** Purchase of new machinery

I have been asked to write this report with regard to the decision as to whether to replace our current tea machines with eight new Pickmaster machines or Pickmaster 2 machines.

## Performance indicators

(i) In terms of our profitability and return on net assets, there is little to be chosen between the two options. The Pickmaster machines give a slightly higher gross profit margin due to the much smaller depreciation charge, although costing more in terms of tea processor operators. However due to a reduction in administration costs if the Pickmaster 2 machines are purchased, then the gross profit and operating profit margins hardly differ under the two options. Equally the return on net assets under each of the two options is very similar.

## Other considerations

(ii) Firstly we need to consider the funding of the purchase of these machines. If the Pickmaster machines are purchased then they will cost £160,000 (8 × £20,000) but if the Pickmaster 2 machines are purchased then these will cost £720,000 (8 × £90,000). These purchases will have to be funded in some way such as a bank loan or by purchasing them under lease finance. In either event if the Pickmaster 2 machines are purchased then this will significantly increase the gearing of the organisation and incur high service costs in the form of interest payments on a loan or finance charges on a lease.

The second consideration is the relative benefits and costs of the two machines. The advantage of the Pickmaster 2 is that only 1 operator per day is required rather than 10. However these operators are employed as and when needed on temporary contracts, therefore if the harvest was low less operatives could be employed. However the depreciation charges on the machines at £72,000 (8 × £9,000) for the Pickmaster 2 machines compared to £16,000 (8 × £2,000) for the Pickmaster machines are fixed costs that will be incurred whatever the level of revenue and harvest. Therefore if there is a low harvest investment in the Pickmaster 2 machines will depress profit.

(**Tutorial note.** A third consideration might be the expected residual value of each type of machine at the end of the 10-year period but only two further considerations were required for the task).

## Conclusion

(iii) As the choice of machines has little effect on profit at the budgeted level but the Pickmaster 2 machines increase the risk of the operation, due to increased gearing and depreciation charges, then on balance purchase of the Pickmaster machines for £160,000 would be recommended.

# Task 7.13

## (a) Performance indicators

| | September | October | November |
|---|---|---|---|

**Profit margin**

$$\frac{£148,687}{£690,000} \times 100 \qquad \frac{£154,125}{£697,200} \times 100 \qquad \frac{£125,480}{£672,000} \times 100$$

$$= 21.55\% \qquad\qquad = 22.11\% \qquad\qquad = 18.67\%$$

**Direct material cost as a percentage of revenue**

$$\frac{£185,000}{£690,000} \times 100 \qquad \frac{£185,100}{£697,200} \times 100 \qquad \frac{£185,220}{£672,000} \times 100$$

$$= 26.81\% \qquad\qquad = 26.55\% \qquad\qquad = 27.56\%$$

**Direct labour cost as a percentage of revenue**

$$\frac{£274,313}{£690,000} \times 100 \qquad \frac{£275,975}{£697,200} \times 100 \qquad \frac{£279,300}{£672,000} \times 100$$

$$= 39.76\% \qquad\qquad = 39.58\% \qquad\qquad = 41.56\%$$

**Return on capital employed (ROCE)**

$$\frac{£148,687}{£1,211,000} \times 100 \qquad \frac{£154,125}{£1,218,700} \times 100 \qquad \frac{£125,480}{£1,204,700} \times 100$$

$$= 12.28\% \qquad\qquad = 12.65\% \qquad\qquad = 10.42\%$$

Alternatively:

$$\frac{£148,687}{£2,011,000} \times 100 \qquad \frac{£154,125}{£2,018,700} \times 100 \qquad \frac{£125,480}{£2,004,700} \times 100$$

$$= 7.39\% \qquad\qquad = 7.63\% \qquad\qquad = 6.26\%$$

**Meals produced as a percentage of orders**

$$\frac{115,500}{115,000} \qquad\qquad \frac{116,200}{117,000} \qquad\qquad \frac{117,600}{112,000}$$

$$= 100.43\% \qquad\qquad = 99.32\% \qquad\qquad = 105.00\%$$

**Meals produced as a percentage of capacity**

$$\frac{115,500}{125,000} \qquad\qquad \frac{116,200}{125,000} \qquad\qquad \frac{117,600}{125,000}$$

$$= 92.4\% \qquad\qquad = 92.96\% \qquad\qquad = 94.08\%$$

**(b)**

**REPORT**

To: Managing Director

From: Accounting Technician

Subject: Performance of the Catering Division

Date: 7 December 20X6

This report examines key areas of the performance of the catering division in November 20X6.

(1) Overall, the division performed significantly worse in November compared with the previous two months. Profit margin fell by 13% from 21.55% in October to 18.67%, and ROCE fell by 15% from 12.28% to 10.42% in the same period.

(2) The problem in the division arises from the difference between meals ordered and meals produced in November. 117,600 meals were produced, which was 5% greater than the number ordered of 112,000. As the meals are perishable, excess production one day cannot be used the next day, and so leads to wastage.

(3) The excess production in November meant that materials and labour costs were increased without the costs being recovered in increased sales.

(4) The division worked at 94.08% of capacity in the month. We would not expect full capacity at all times as work should only be done to fulfil orders placed.

**(c)**

|  |  | Renting | Purchasing |
|---|---|---|---|
| (i) |  | £ | £ |
|  | Revenue (120,000 × £6) | 720,000 | 720,000 |
|  | *Cost of sales* |  |  |
|  | Materials (120,000 × £2) | 240,000 | 240,000 |
|  | Labour (120,000 × £1.50) | 180,000 | 180,000 |
|  | Fixed overheads | 82,000 | 82,000 |
|  | Rent | 50,000 |  |
|  | Depreciation (£3m – £900,000)/(12 × 10 months) |  | 17,500 |
|  | Total cost of sales | 552,000 | 519,500 |
|  | **Profit** | 168,000 | 200,500 |
|  | **Net assets** |  |  |
|  | (£1,204,700 + £168,000) | 1,372,700 |  |
|  | (£1,204,700 + £1m + £200,500) |  | 2,405,200 |

|  |  | Renting | Purchasing |
|---|---|---|---|
| (ii) |  | Renting | Purchasing |
|  | **Profit margin =** | $\frac{£168,000}{£720,000} \times 100$ | $\frac{£200,500}{£720,000} \times 100$ |
|  |  | = 23.33% | = 27.85% |
|  | **ROCE =** | $\frac{£168,000}{£1,372,700} \times 100$ | $\frac{£200,500}{£2,405,200} \times 100$ |
|  |  | = 12.24% | = 8.34% |

(iii) Renting the machine gives a higher ROCE than buying the machine because the higher profit earned with a bought machine is outweighed by the large increase in net assets. Therefore the machine should be rented rather than bought. However, the ROCE is not necessarily improved when compared with the figures for October to November 20X6, and further consideration should be given to whether the machine is obtained at all.

## Task 7.14

**(a) Sales price and sales volume:**

The sales price is higher for S1 which will improve the gross profit margin for S1. However, the sales volume is higher for S2, which will improve the gross profit margin for this product as there are fixed production costs that remain constant. This is because these costs will be spread over more units therefore increasing the gross profit per unit.

**(b) Material cost:**

The material cost per unit is constant which therefore has no effect on the gross profit margin.

**(c) Fixed production cost:**

The fixed production cost is constant which means that the increased volume will reduce the fixed cost per unit. This is because the fixed costs are being spread over more units. A lower fixed cost per unit will increase the gross profit margin for S2.

## Task 7.15

**(a)**

|  | Scenario 1 | Scenario 2 |
|---|---|---|
| Return on net assets | 11.96% | 9.52% |
| Inventory holding period in days | 50.00 | 45.29 |
| Sales price per unit | £14.00 | £12.00 |
| Full production cost per unit | £9.00 | £9.00 |

**Workings**

Return on net assets
Scenario 1 = £275,000/£2,298,400 × 100% = 11.96%
Scenario 2 = £200,000/£2,100,340 × 100% = 9.52%

Inventory holding period
Scenario 1 = £147,950/(£1,680,000 – £600,000) × 365 = 50.00 days
Scenario 2 = £167,500/(£1,800,000 – £450,000) × 365 = 45.29 days

Sales price per unit
Scenario 1 = £1,680,000/120,000 = £14.00
Scenario 2 = £1,800,000/150,000 = £12.00

Full production cost per unit
Scenario 1 = (£1,680,000 – £600,000)/120,000 = £9.00
Scenario 2 = (£1,800,000 – £450,000)/150,000 = £9.00

**(b)**

|  | Scenario 3 |
|---|---|
| Net assets (£) | 175,000 |
| Return on net assets (%) | 13 |
| Profit margin (%) | 14 |
| Gearing (%) | 32.75 |
| Profit (to the nearest £) | 22,750 |
| Sales revenue (to the nearest £) | 162,500 |

**Workings**

Profit (to the nearest £) = £175,000 × (13/100) = £22,750

Sales revenue (to the nearest £) = £22,750 ÷ (14/100) = £162,500

**(c)**

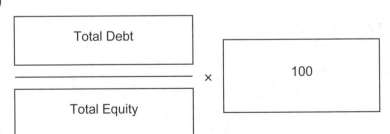

Total Debit / Total Equity × 100

**Or**

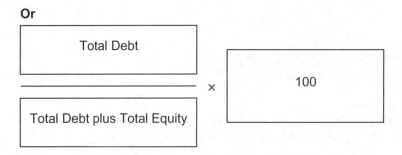

$$\frac{\text{Total Debt}}{\text{Total Debt plus Total Equity}} \times \boxed{100}$$

. . . . . . . . . . . . . . . . . . . . . . . . . . . . . . . . . . . . . . . . . . . . . . . . . . . . . . . . . . . . . . . . . . . . . . . . . .

## Task 7.16

**(a)**

|  | Company A | Company B |
|---|---|---|
| Selling price per unit | 42 | 35 |
| Labour cost per unit | 18 | 12 |
| Fixed production cost per unit | 3.50 | 3.00 |
| Selling and distribution costs as a % of revenue | 2.38 | 3.43 |
| Gross profit margin % | 32.14 | 40 |
| Profit margin % | 21.19 | 24 |
| Return on net assets % | 9 | 19.60 |

**Workings**

Selling price per unit Company A $\frac{37,800,000}{900,000} = £42$

Selling price per unit Company B $\frac{49,000,000}{1,400,000} = £35$

Labour cost per unit Company A $\frac{16,200,000}{900,000} = £18$

Labour cost per unit Company B $\frac{16,800,000}{1,400,000} = £12$

Fixed production cost per unit Company A $\frac{3,150,000}{900,000} = £3.50$

Fixed production cost per unit Company B $\frac{4,200,000}{1,400,000} = £3$

Selling and distribution costs as a % of revenue Company A $\left(\dfrac{900,000}{37,800,000}\right) \times 100 = 2.38\%$

Selling and distribution costs as a % of revenue Company B $\left(\dfrac{1,680,000}{49,000,000}\right) \times 100 = 3.43\%$

Gross profit margin % Company A $\left(\dfrac{12,150,000}{37,800,000}\right) \times 100 = 32.14\%$

Gross profit margin % Company B $\left(\dfrac{19,600,000}{49,000,000}\right) \times 100 = 40\%$

Profit margin % Company A $\left(\dfrac{8,010,000}{37,800,000}\right) \times 100 = 21.19\%$

Profit margin % Company B $\left(\dfrac{11,760,000}{49,000,000}\right) \times 100 = 24\%$

Return on net assets % Company A $\left(\dfrac{8,010,000}{89,000,000}\right) \times 100 = 9\%$

Return on net assets % Company B $\left(\dfrac{11,760,000}{60,000,000}\right) \times 100 = 19.6\%$

(b)

| Ratio | Year 1 % | Year 2 % |
|---|---|---|
| Labour efficiency ratio | 96.25 | 105.37 |

**Workings**

Year 1 $\left(\dfrac{(37,200 \times 0.8)}{30,920}\right) \times 100 = 96.25\%$

Year 2 $\left(\dfrac{(51,000 \times 0.8)}{38,720}\right) \times 100 = 105.37\%$

# Chapter 8

## Task 8.1

The net present value of the investment is £(5,682)

**Workings**

**Net present value**

| Year | Cash flow £ | Discount factor @ 7% | Present value £ |
|---|---|---|---|
| 0 | (84,000) | 1.000 | (84,000) |
| 1 | 26,000 | 0.935 | 24,310 |
| 2 | 30,000 | 0.873 | 26,190 |
| 3 | 21,000 | 0.816 | 17,136 |
| 4 | 14,000 | 0.763 | 10,682 |
| Net present value | | | (5,682) |

## Task 8.2

The net present value of the potential investment is £41,591.

**Workings**

**Net present value**

| Year | Cash flow £ | Discount factor @ 12% | Present value £ |
|---|---|---|---|
| 0 | (355,000) | 1.000 | (355,000) |
| 1 (47 + 60) | 107,000 | 0.893 | 95,551 |
| 2 (55 + 60) | 115,000 | 0.797 | 91,655 |
| 3 (68 + 60) | 128,000 | 0.712 | 91,136 |
| 4 (53 + 60) | 113,000 | 0.635 | 71,755 |
| 5 (22 + 60) | 82,000 | 0.567 | 46,494 |
| Net present value | | | 41,591 |

Note that depreciation is not a cash flow and having been charged in arriving at the profit figure must be added back to find the cash inflow in each year.

## Task 8.3

Under traditional costing methods the costs of a product are only recorded and analysed once production of the product has begun. However, it is recognised that a large proportion of the costs of a product are incurred before production has started in the early stages of the product life cycle. Life cycle costing recognises all of these pre-production costs of the product such as:

- Design costs
- Prototyping

- Programming
- Process design
- Equipment acquisition

The aim of life cycle costing is to ensure that all the costs of the product are accumulated over the whole of its life cycle in order to ensure that all costs are covered by revenue from the product.

## Task 8.4

**(a)** The product life cycle is generally thought to split naturally into five separate stages:

- Development
- Launch
- Growth
- Maturity
- Decline

During the development and launch stage of the product's life there are large outgoings in terms of development expenditure, non-current assets necessary for production, the building up of inventory levels and advertising and promotion expenses. It is likely that even after the launch sales will be quite low and the product will be making a loss at this stage.

If the launch of the product is successful then during the growth stage there will be fairly rapid increases in sales and a move to profitability as the costs of the earlier stages are covered. However, these sales increases are not likely to continue indefinitely.

In the maturity stage of the product demand for the product will probably start to slow down and become more constant. In many cases this is the stage where the product is modified or improved in order to sustain demand and this may then see a small surge in sales.

At some point in a product's life, unless it is a consumable item such as chocolate bars, the product will reach the end of its sales life, this is known as the decline stage. The market will have bought enough of the product and sales will decline. This is the point where the business should consider no longer producing the product.

**(b)** If the future demand for a product is to be forecast using time series analysis it is obviously important that the stage in the product life cycle that has been reached is taken into account. For example, if the trend is based upon the growth stage whereas in fact the product is moving into the maturity stage then the trend would show an overly optimistic forecast for sales.

## Task 8.5

Target cost = Market price – Desired profit margin

= £50 – (£50 × 20%)

= £50 – £10

= £40

........................................................................................

## Task 8.6

Target cost = Price – Desired profit margin

= £25 – (£25 × 70%)

= £7.50 per unit

Sales price per unit = £250,000/10,000 = £25

........................................................................................

## Task 8.7

**(a)**

|  | Sales price £40 | Sales price £50 |
|---|---|---|
| The target total production cost per unit | £28 | £35 |
| The target fixed production cost per unit | £16 | £22 |
| The target fixed production cost | £8,000,000 | £9,460,000 |

**Workings**

Target total production cost per unit
Sales price £40 = £40 × 70/100 = £28
Sales price £50 = £50 × 70/100 = £35

Target fixed production cost per unit
Sales price £40 = £28 – £12 = £16
Sales price £50 = £35 – £13 = £22

Target fixed production cost
Sales price £40 = £16 per unit × 500,000 = £8,000,000
Sales price £50 = £22 per unit × 430,000 = £9,460,000

**(b)** Alpha should set the price at £50 ▼ in order to achieve the target profit margin.

........................................................................................

## Task 8.8

**(a)** The profit achieved is £ [ 120,000 ] .

**(b)** The profit achieved is £ [ 80,000 ] .

**(c)** The profit achieved is £ [ 100,000 ] .

**(d)** The sales price per unit will need to be £ [ 62.50 ] to achieve a profit margin of 20%.

**(e)** The sales price to achieve a mark up of 30% is £ [ 104 ] .

### Workings

**(a)** 6,000 × £90 = £540,000. Less: 6,000 × £70 = £420,000. Profit £120,000

**(b)** 8,000 × £70 = £560,000. Less: 8,000 × £60 = £480,000. Profit £80,000

**Note**. The £60 cost per unit includes £30 fixed costs (£240,000/8,000).

**(c)** 6,000 × £70 = £420,000. Less: 6,000 × £70 = £420,000. Profit £0

Breakeven on the 6,000 units manufactured and sold at £70

Profit of £25 per unit on the units from overseas, 4,000 × £25 = £100,000

**(d)** $\dfrac{£50}{(1-0.2)}$ = £62.50. Proof: £62.50 less £50 = £12.50

Check: Profit margin: $\left(\dfrac{12.50}{62.50}\right)$ × 100 = 20%

**(e)** £80/100 × 130 = £104

..........................................................................................................

## Task 8.9

**(a)**

| Year | 0 | 1 | 2 | 3 | 4 | 5 |
|---|---|---|---|---|---|---|
| Cash flow (£) | (400,000) | (50,000) | (52,500) | (55,125) | (55,125) | (20,125) |
| Discounted factor | 1 | 0.952 | 0.907 | 0.864 | 0.823 | 0.784 |
| Present value (£) | (400,000) | (47,600) | (47,618)* | (47,628) | (45,368)* | (15,778) |
| Net present cost (£) | (603,992) | | | | | |

**Workings**

*Note that the question states that you should 'round to the nearest whole pound'.

The figures are clearly signposted in the question.

Note that Year 5 cash flow figure includes the cash inflow for the residual value, so is calculated as £55,125 – £35,000 = £20,125.

**(b)**

| Year | 0 | 1 | 2 | 3 | 4 | 5 |
|---|---|---|---|---|---|---|
| Cash flow (£) | (140,000) | (140,000) | (140,000) | (140,000) | (140,000) | 0 |
| Discounted factor | 1 | 0.952 | 0.907 | 0.864 | 0.823 | 0.784 |
| Present value (£) | (140,000) | (133,280) | (126,980) | (120,960) | (115,220) | 0 |
| Net present cost (£) | (636,440) | | | | | |

**Workings**

Ensure you enter the annual lease payments in the correct years. The lease fee is paid in advance (so the year 1 fee is paid in year 0). The lease is for five years, so the final year fee will be paid in advance in year 4.

**(c)** Based on the calculations it is best to [ purchase ] as this saves

£ [ 32,448 ].

**Workings**

£636,440 – £603,992 = £32,448

# Chapter 9

## Task 9.1

**(a)** The price of job HMG/012 based upon direct costs plus 50% mark-up is £457,500

The price of job CFG/013 based upon direct costs plus 50% mark-up is £279,000

|  | HMG/012 £ | CFG/013 £ |
|---|---|---|
| Equipment cost | 175,000 | 120,000 |
| Direct labour cost | 130,000 | 66,000 |
| Total direct cost | 305,000 | 186,000 |
| Mark up | 50% | 50% |
| Price | £457,500 | £279,000 |

**(b) Calculation of cost per unit of cost driver**

| Activity | Budgeted cost pool £ | Cost driver | Cost driver units pa | Cost per unit of cost driver £ |
|---|---|---|---|---|
| Design department | 675,000 | Design hours | 25,000 | 27.00 |
| Site engineers | 370,000 | Miles travelled | 185,000 | 2.00 |
| Purchasing department | 105,000 | Items purchased | 15,000 | 7.00 |
| Payroll department | 75,000 | Direct hours | 300,000 | 0.25 |
| Site management | 750,000 | Direct hours | 300,000 | 2.50 |
| Post-installation inspection | 80,000 | Items purchased | 20,000 | 4.00 |

| Cost pool | Working | Total cost HMG/012 | Total cost CFG/013 |
|-----------|---------|--------------------|--------------------|
| | | £ | £ |
| Design department | £27 × 1,280/620 | 34,560 | 16,740 |
| Site engineers | £2 × (320 × 30)/(90 × 10) | 19,200 | 1,800 |
| Purchasing department | £7 × 650/410 | 4,550 | 2,870 |
| Payroll department | £0.25 × 10,000/6,000 | 2,500 | 1,500 |
| Site management | £2.50 × 10,000/6,000 | 25,000 | 15,000 |
| Post-installation inspection | £4 × 650/410 | 2,600 | 1,640 |
| **Total cost** | | 88,410 | 39,550 |

## Task 9.2

| | Server allocated overheads £ | PC allocated overheads £ |
|---|---|---|
| Set-up costs | 10,000 | - |
| Rent and power (production area) | 24,000 | 96,000 |
| Rent (stores area) | 25,000 | 25,000 |
| Salaries of stores issue staff | 8,000 | 32,000 |
| Total overheads | 67,000 | 153,000 |

**Workings**

**Reallocation of Little Ltd's budgeted total fixed annual overheads between server and PC production**

BPP
LEARNING MEDIA

## Step 1. Calculation of cost per cost driver

| | Budgeted total annual overheads | Cost driver | Number of cost drivers | Cost per cost driver |
|---|---|---|---|---|
| Set-up costs | 10,000 | Number of set-ups | 5 | 2,000.00 |
| Rent and power (production area) | 120,000 | Number of wks' production | 50 | 2,400.00 |
| Rent (stores area) | 50,000 | Floor area of stores (m²) | 800 | 62.50 |
| Salaries of store issue staff | 40,000 | No of issues of inventory | 10,000 | 4.00 |
| | 220,000 | | | |

## Step 2. Reallocation of overheads based on costs per cost driver

| Server | (i) Number of cost drivers | (ii) Cost per cost driver £ | (i) × (ii) Allocated overheads £ |
|---|---|---|---|
| Set-up costs | 5 | 2,000.00 | 10,000 |
| Rent and power (production area) | 10 | 2,400.00 | 24,000 |
| Rent (stores area) | 400 | 62.50 | 25,000 |
| Salaries of store issue staff | 2,000 | 4.00 | 8,000 |
| | | | 67,000 |

| PC | (i) Number of cost drivers | (ii) Cost per cost driver £ | (i) × (ii) Allocated overheads £ |
|---|---|---|---|
| Set-up costs | 0 | 2,000.00 | – |
| Rent and power (production area) | 40 | 2,400.00 | 96,000 |
| Rent (stores area) | 400 | 62.50 | 25,000 |
| Salaries of store issue staff | 8,000 | 4.00 | 32,000 |
| | | | 153,000 |

## Task 9.3

|  | Plastic allocated overheads £ | Metal allocated overheads £ |
|---|---|---|
| Power for machinery | 50,000 | 60,000 |
| Rent of factory | 100,000 | 20,000 |
| Canteen costs | 32,000 | 8,000 |
| Total overheads | 182,000 | 88,000 |

**Workings**

**Calculation of cost per cost driver**

|  | Budgeted overheads | Cost driver | Number of cost drivers | Cost per cost driver |
|---|---|---|---|---|
| Power for machinery | 110,000 | Number of machine hours | 5,500 | 20 |
| Rent of factory | 120,000 | Floor space | 1,200 | 100 |
| Canteen costs | 40,000 | Number of employees | 250 | 160 |

**Reallocation of overheads based on costs per cost driver**

| Plastic | (i) | (ii) | (i) × (ii) |
|---|---|---|---|
|  | Number of cost drivers | Cost per cost driver £ | Allocated overheads £ |
| Power for machinery | 2,500 | 20 | 50,000 |
| Rent of factory | 1,000 | 100 | 100,000 |
| Canteen costs | 200 | 160 | 32,000 |
|  |  |  | 182,000 |

| Metal | (i) | (ii) | (i) × (ii) |
|---|---|---|---|
|  | Number of cost drivers | Cost per cost driver £ | Allocated overheads £ |
| Power for machinery | 3,000 | 20 | 60,000 |
| Rent of factory | 200 | 100 | 20,000 |
| Canteen costs | 50 | 160 | 8,000 |
|  |  |  | 88,000 |

# Chapter 10

## Task 10.1

The break even point in units is 100,000 units

The margin of safety in units is 15,000 units

The margin of safety as a percentage of budgeted sales is 13%

**Workings**

Breakeven point $= \dfrac{£1,100,000}{£28 - £17}$

$= 100,000$ units

Margin of safety (units) = Budgeted sales − Breakeven sales

$= (115,000 - 100,000)$ units

$= 15,000$ units

Margin of safety (% budgeted sales) $= \dfrac{115,000 - 100,000}{115,000} \times 100\%$

$= 13\%$

## Task 10.2

Breakeven point in units $\qquad\qquad = 5,000$ units

Breakeven point in sales revenue $\quad = £80,000$

**Workings**

Contribution per unit $= £(16 - 8) = £8$

Contribution required to breakeven = fixed costs = £40,000

Breakeven point $= \dfrac{\text{Fixed costs}}{\text{Contribution per unit}}$

$= \dfrac{£40,000}{£8}$

$= 5,000$ units

Sales revenue at breakeven point $= 5,000$ units $\times £16$ per unit

$= £80,000$

## Task 10.3

Units = 500

Sales revenue = £40,000

**Workings**

Margin of safety = Budgeted sales volume – Breakeven sales volume

Breakeven sales volume = $\dfrac{\text{Fixed costs}}{\text{Contribution per unit}}$

$= \dfrac{£110,000}{£55}$

= 2,000 units

Therefore, margin of safety (units) = 2,500 units – 2,000 units

= 500 units

Therefore, margin of safety (sales revenue) = Margin of safety (units) × Selling price per unit

= 500 units × £80

= £40,000

## Task 10.4

The number of units of the product that the business must sell in order to make a target profit of £300,000 is 46,667 units.

**Workings**

Target profit units = $\dfrac{£540,000 + £300,000}{£83 - 65}$

= 46,667 units

## Task 10.5

The sales revenue required in order to make a target profit of £250,000 is £2,560,000.

**Workings**

Profit volume ratio = $\dfrac{£40 - 28}{£40} \times 100\%$ = 30%

Target profit sales revenue = $\dfrac{£518,000 + £250,000}{0.3}$ = £2,560,000

## Task 10.6

| Product | Units |
|---------|-------|
| B | 800 |
| A | 1,000 |
| C | 50 |

**Workings**

**Contribution per kg**

|  | A | B | C |
|---|---|---|---|
| Contribution | £12 | £16 | £16 |
| Kg per unit | 2 | 1 | 4 |
| Contribution per kg | £6 | £16 | £4 |
| Ranking | 2 | 1 | 3 |

**Production plan**

|  | Units | Kg used | Cumulative kg used |
|---|-------|---------|---------------------|
| B | 800 | 800 | 800 |
| A | 1,000 | 2,000 | 2,800 |
| C (balance) | 50 | 200 | 3,000 |
|  |  | 3,000 |  |

## Task 10.7

| Product | Units |
|---------|-------|
| T | 8,000 |
| R | 20,000 |
| S | 12,000 |

The contribution that will be earned under this production plan is £540,000.

## Workings

### Identify the limiting factor

Materials – at maximum demand

$(4 \times 20,000) + (5 \times 25,000) + (3 \times 8,000) = 229,000$ kg

Labour hours – at maximum demand

$(2 \times 20,000) + (3 \times 25,000) + (3 \times 8,000) = 139,000$ hours

Machine hours – at maximum demand

$(4 \times 20,000) + (3 \times 25,000) + (2 \times 8,000) = 171,000$ hours

Therefore the only limiting factor is labour hours.

### Contribution per labour hour

|  | R | S | T |
|---|---|---|---|
| Contribution | £11 | £14 | £19 |
| Labour hours | 2 | 3 | 3 |
| Contribution per labour hour | £5.50 | £4.67 | £6.33 |
| Ranking | 2 | 3 | 1 |

### Production plan

|  | Units | Labour hours used | Cumulative labour hours used |
|---|---|---|---|
| T | 8,000 | 24,000 | 24,000 |
| R | 20,000 | 40,000 | 64,000 |
| S (balance) | 12,000 | 36,000 | 100,000 |
|  |  | 100,000 |  |

### Contribution earned

|  | £ |
|---|---|
| R (20,000 × £11) | 220,000 |
| S (12,000 × £14) | 168,000 |
| T (8,000 × £19) | 152,000 |
|  | 540,000 |

# Task 10.8

(a) **Complete the following table**

|  | Product X | Product Y |
|---|---|---|
| The contribution per unit is | 45 | 57 |
| The contribution per kilogram of materials | 7.5 | 7.13 |

**Workings**

Contribution = selling price – variable costs

Contribution for X = £100 – £55 = £45

Contribution for Y = £135 – £78 = £57

Contribution for X per kg of material = £45 $\div \dfrac{£30}{£5}$ = £7.50

Contribution for Y per kg of material = £57 $\div \dfrac{£40}{£5}$ = £7.125 = £7.13 to the nearest penny.

(b) **The optimal production order for products X, and Y is**

| Product X then Product Y ▼ |

(c) **Complete the table below for the optimal production mix**

|  | Product X | Product Y |
|---|---|---|
| Production in units | 3,500 | 3,000 |

**Working**

(3,500 × 6kg) + (3,000 × 8kg) = 45,000kg

(d) **Complete the table below for the total contribution for each product.**

|  | Product X | Product Y |
|---|---|---|
| Total contribution | 157,500 | 171,000 |

## Task 10.9

**(a)**

|  | Product Tig | Product Tag |
|---|---|---|
| The contribution per unit is | 1,200 | 1,350 |
| The contribution per kilogram of materials is | 200 | 180 |

**Workings**

Contribution per unit

Product Tig = £4,000 – £2,800 = £1,200
Product Tag = £4,950 – £3,600 = £1,350

Contribution per kilogram of material
Product Tig = £1,200/6kg = £200
Product Tag = £1,350/7.5kg = £180

**(b)** The optimal production order for products Tig and Tag is Tig then Tag. ▼

(based on the contribution per kilogram of material calculated in part (a)).

**(c)**

|  | Product Tig | Product Tag |
|---|---|---|
| Production in units | 200 | 240 |

Supply is limited to 3,000 kilograms of material

Product Tig then Tag (based on part (b)).

200 units of Tig × 6kg per unit = 1,200kg (so 1,800kg remaining to produce Tag)

1,800kg/7.5kg per unit = 240 units of Tag

**(d)**

|  | Product Tig £ | Product Tag £ |
|---|---|---|
| Total contribution | 240,000 | 324,000 |

Product Tig = 200 units × £1,200 = £240,000

Product Tag = 240 units × £1,350 = £324,000

**(e)**

| Should Alpha purchase the additional material? | Give a reason |
|---|---|
| Yes ▼ | The additional cost per kilogram is less than the contribution per kilogram. ▼ |

**Answer bank**

# AAT AQ2016 SAMPLE ASSESSMENT
## Management Accounting:
## Decision and Control

**Time allowed: 2.5 hours**

# Management Accounting: Decision and Control
## AAT sample assessment

## Task 1 (16 marks)

A manufacturer of a single product has supplied the budget information below for the next quarter end.

| | |
|---|---|
| Materials per unit | 2.55 kg at £3.20 per kg |
| Rent per quarter | £7,450 |
| Leased machines | £7,522 for every 5,000 units produced |
| Maintenance | £2,150 per quarter plus £2.07 per unit |

(a) **Calculate the budgeted quarterly costs of production for the following activity levels to the nearest pound, and classify each cost.**

| Cost | Quarterly production | | Cost Classification |
|---|---|---|---|
| | 3,800 units | 15,900 units | |
| | £ | £ | |
| Direct Materials | | | ▼ |
| Rent | | | ▼ |
| Leased machines | | | ▼ |
| Maintenance | | | ▼ |

**Drop-down list:**

Fixed
Semi-variable
Stepped
Variable

You have been supplied with the following information about a factory's overheads.

| Units produced | Total overheads £ |
|---|---|
| 19,000 | 295,000 |
| 23,900 | 324,400 |

The fixed portion of the overheads increases by £12,000 when more than 30,000 units are produced.

Variable costs reduce by £1 per unit for units produced in excess of 25,000 units.

(b) Calculate the total fixed and variable overheads for the following production levels.

Enter your answers to the nearest pound.

| Units | Fixed £ | Variable £ |
|---|---|---|
| 21,000 | | |
| 36,000 | | |

## Task 2 (12 marks)

The production information below relates to Apricot Ltd, a business that packages apricots.

| | Budget | Actual |
|---|---|---|
| Production – cartons | 5,000 | 6,000 |
| Apricots – kilograms (kg) | 50,000 | 70,000 |
| Apricots – £ | 25,000 | 40,000 |
| Direct labour – hours | 1,000 | 800 |
| Direct labour – £ | 10,000 | 8,000 |

(a) For each variance below, show the variance amount and whether the variance is adverse, favourable or whether there is no variance.

| Variance | Variance amount £ | Adverse/favourable/ no variance |
|---|---|---|
| Apricots usage | | ▼ |
| Direct labour efficiency | | ▼ |

**Drop-down list:**

Adverse
Favourable
No variance

(b) Complete the reconciliation statement below.

Indicate any negative figures by using a minus sign.

| | £ |
|---|---|
| **Standard direct cost of actual production** | |
| Apricot price variance | 5,000 |
| Apricots usage variance | |
| Direct labour rate variance | 0 |
| Direct labour efficiency variance | |
| **Actual direct cost of production** | |

Another business, Blueberry Ltd, has supplied you with the following information.

|  | £ | Hours |
|---|---|---|
| Favourable material price variance | 168 | |
| Standard cost per kilogram of material | 12 | |
| Actual cost of material | 900 | |
| Adverse labour rate variance | 536 | |
| Actual labour hours | | 668 |
| Actual cost of labour | 12,560 | |

(c) **Complete the following two sentences.**

The actual quantity of material used is ☐ kg.

The standard labour rate is £ ☐ per hour.

## Task 3 (12 marks)

The table below shows selected management accounting information for a bus company. Fixed overheads are absorbed based on budgeted operating kilometres. Fuel and labour are variable costs.

| | **Budget** | | **Actual** | |
|---|---|---|---|---|
| Journeys | | 7,000 | | 5,000 |
| Operating kilometres | | 140,000 | | 100,000 |
| | | £ | | £ |
| Fuel | 12,460 litres | 15,000 | 11,000 | 14,000 |
| Labour | 35,000 hours | 350,000 | 25,000 hours | 250,000 |
| Fixed overheads | | 140,000 | | 125,000 |

(a) **Complete the table below.**

| | | |
|---|---|---|
| Standard litres of fuel for 5,000 journeys | [ ] litres | |
| Standard labour hours for 5,000 journeys | [ ] hours | |
| Fixed overheads volume variance | £ [ ] | [ ▼ ] |
| Standard operating kilometres for 5,000 journeys | [ ] kilometres | |
| Standard fixed overheads costs absorbed by the 5,000 journeys | £ [ ] | |
| Total fixed overheads variance | £ [ ] | [ ▼ ] |

**Drop-down list:**

Adverse
Favourable
No variance

(b) **Answer the following questions about variances.**

Which of the following situations would probably cause an adverse fixed overhead **expenditure** variance?

[ ▼ ]

**Drop-down list:**

Appointment of new factory manager
Decrease in annual rent
Lower production volume than standard
Sale of production machinery

Which of the following situations would probably cause an adverse fixed overhead **capacity** variance?

[ ▼ ]

**Drop-down list:**

Appointment of new factory manager
Bulk discounts on material
Machine breakdowns
Purchase of new machinery

## Task 4 (12 marks)

The following budgeted figures refer to a factory producing a single product.

Overheads are absorbed on a budgeted production basis.

Inventory is valued on a FIFO basis.

| | Month 1 | Month 2 | Month 3 |
|---|---|---|---|
| Operating inventory (units) | 0 | | |
| Selling price (£) | 110 | 100 | 90 |
| Production (units) | 10,000 | 10,000 | 10,000 |
| Sales (units) | 8,000 | 9,000 | 11,000 |
| Direct materials (£ per unit) | 15 | 15 | 15 |
| Direct labour (£ per unit) | 10 | 10 | 10 |
| Other variable production costs (£) | 230,000 | 230,000 | 250,000 |
| Fixed production costs (£) | 450,000 | 450,000 | 450,000 |

Complete the table below. If any answer is zero, enter '0' into the relevant cell.

- **For the sales to fixed overheads rows, use positive numbers only (do not use minus signs).**

- **For the final row, record any loss figure with a minus sign.**

| | Absorption costing | | Marginal costing | |
|---|---|---|---|---|
| | Month 2 (£) | Month 3 (£) | Month 2 (£) | Month 3 (£) |
| Sales – month 2 | | | | |
| Sales – month 3 | | | | |
| Opening inventory | | | | |
| Production costs | | | | |
| Closing inventory | | | | |
| Cost of sales | | | | |
| Fixed overheads | | | | |
| Profit/(Loss) | | | | |

# Task 5 (12 marks)

(a) Insert the appropriate three month moving averages into the table below.

| Month | Sales (units) | Three month moving average (units) |
|---|---|---|
| December | 5,760 | |
| January | 5,820 | |
| February | 5,760 | |
| March | 6,600 | |
| April | 6,120 | |
| May | 6,150 | |
| June | 6,330 | |

(b) Complete the following sentences.

Seasonal variation equals actual data at a point, less [　　　　▼] data at the same point.

Drop-down list:

budget
cost
indexed
trend

The observation that traffic volumes are higher during daylight hours is an example of

[　　　　▼] .

Drop-down list:

long term cycles
random variations
seasonal variations
underlying trends

The information below relates to production costs and the RPI Index.

(c) Restate the following costs at January prices to the nearest pound.

| Month | Actual costs (£) | RPI | Costs at January prices (£) |
|---|---|---|---|
| January | 129,000 | 170 | |
| March | 132,000 | 172 | |
| June | 135,000 | 174 | |

**(d)  Complete the following sentences.**

The prediction of a figure outside of a data range already observed is known as

[ ▼ ] .

**Drop-down list:**

extrapolation
interpolation
linear regression
random variation

The effect of long term economic movements is known as [ ▼ ] variations.

**Drop-down list:**

average
cyclical
random
seasonal

A business's production costs vary linearly according to the regression equation $y = a + bx$, where $x$ = production volume. Total production costs of 200 units and 2,000 units are £5,000 and £14,000 respectively.

**(e)  Calculate the values of a and b.**

Value of a: [          ]

Value of b: [          ]

## Task 6 (24 marks)

Ezo Ltd has provided the following management accounting information pertaining to its operations during the prior month.

| | £ |
|---|---|
| Standard cost of actual production | 600,000 |
| **Variances** | |
| Materials price | 25,000 |
| Materials usage | (7,000) |
| Labour rate | 10,000 |
| Labour efficiency | (10,000) |
| Fixed overhead expenditure | (7,000) |
| Fixed overhead capacity | (5,000) |
| Fixed overhead efficiency | (6,000) |
| Actual cost of production | 600,000 |

**Recent events**

Storage facilities:

Alternative storage facilities were rented at the beginning of last month leading to lower monthly payments.

Machinery:

At the beginning of last month, an investment was made in more modern and efficient machinery which has a much higher depreciation charge.

Staff upgrade:

Due to the acquisition of the new machinery at the beginning of last month, a number of technology engineers were hired to operate the machinery, enabling the business to lay off a number of unskilled workers.

(a) **Write a memo to a colleague, explaining how each of the three recent events described above would have affected the variances in the reconciliation statement. Include suggestions regarding future budget amendments.**

To:     Colleague                         Subject:   Variance explanations
From:  Accounting Technician          Date:      XX/XX/20XX

**Storage facilities**

**Machinery**

**Staff upgrade**

The factory manager receives a bonus based on net labour variances. The bonus is only paid if the net variance is zero or favourable.

**(b)  Briefly explain any ethical conflicts and goal congruence issues that may arise.**

## Task 7 (18 marks)

**(a)  Complete the statement below.**

An activity where there is opportunity for reducing the cost without reducing a product's value to the customer is a [          ▼] activity.

**Drop-down list:**
benchmark
life cycle
non-value-added
value-added

A small business has supplied the following information:

|  | £ |
|---|---|
| Turnover | 1,500,000 |
| Cost of materials used | 700,000 |
| Cost of bought in services | 300,000 |
| Number of employees | 10 |

**(b) Use the information provided to complete the statements below.**

The total value added is £ [          ]

Value added per employee is a measure of [          ▼] .

**Drop-down list:**

capacity
gearing
net profit
productivity

A business with receivables of £120,000 and receivables collection days of 30, operates on a gross profit margin of 25% and a net profit margin of 15%. Fixed production overheads constitute 40% of the cost of sales.

**(c) Complete the profit and loss account below using the following performance indicators.**

**Enter ALL figures as positive numbers – do not enter negative figures.**

|  | £ |
|---|---|
| Sales | |
| Variable production costs | |
| Fixed production costs | |
| Cost of sales | |
| Gross profit | |
| Non-production costs | |
| Net profit | |

Kumquat Ltd has supplied the following extracts from its management accounts which are based on a 365 day year.

|  | £ |
|---|---|
| Revenue | 1,350,400 |
| Opening inventory | 122,658 |
| Purchases | 849,200 |
| Closing inventory | 110,000 |
| Receivables | 369,973 |
| Payables | 118,063 |

**(d) Calculate the following ratios using the above figures.**

**All answers must be to the nearest whole day and based on averages where applicable.**

|  | Inventory holding period | Payables payment period |
|---|---|---|
| Days | | |

(e)  **Complete the following sentence.**

The "innovation and learning perspective" is associated with the concept of

[                    ▼] .

**Drop-down list:**

efficiency
gearing
the balanced scorecard
value added

·······································································································

## Task 8 (15 marks)

A company manufactures two products, the Jackal and the Hyena.

The information below relates to the next reporting period.

| Per unit | Jackal (£) | Hyena (£) |
|---|---|---|
| Direct materials at £5 per kg | 10 | 15 |
| Direct labour at £6 per hour | 6 | 12 |
| Variable overheads | 2 | 4 |
| Fixed production overheads | 2.27 | 3.63 |
| Selling price | 25 | 40 |
| | **Units** | **Units** |
| Sales demands | 5,000 | 10,000 |

As a result of recent transport strikes, materials are limited to 55,000 kg and labour hours are limited to 20,000.

(a)  **Complete the table below for the next period calculating the optimal unit production.**

| | Jackal | Hyena |
|---|---|---|
| Total materials required (kg) | | |
| Total labour hours required | | |
| Contribution per unit (£) | | |
| Contribution per limiting factor (£) (to TWO decimal places) | | |
| Optimal production (units) | | |

**(b)** **What is the maximum that would be paid for each of the following?**

5,000 kg of additional material:   £ _____

5,000 hours of additional labour:  £ _____

Buffalo Ltd is considering acquiring new equipment to improve productivity.

The table below shows how having the new equipment would compare with the current situation.

| | Current situation | Proposed situation with new equipment |
|---|---|---|
| Direct materials per unit | 3 kg at £5 | Usage down by 15% |
| Direct labour per unit | 6 hours at £10 | Time down by 20% |
| Sales | 5,000 units at £150 | No change |
| Fixed costs | £277,500 | Up by £79,500 |

**(c)** **Calculate the profit figures for the current and proposed situations and indicate whether or not the equipment should be acquired.**

| | Current situation (£) | Proposed situation with new equipment (£) |
|---|---|---|
| Profit | | |

It [ _____ ▼ ] be better to acquire the new equipment.

**Drop-down list:**

would
would not

## Task 9 (15 marks)

Herb Ltd manufactures two products, Rose and Thyme.

The two overhead activities, production set-ups and materials handling, have budgets of £600,000 and £400,000 respectively.

Rose and Thyme use three hours and two hours of labour per unit respectively.

Further information has been provided below.

|  | Rose | Thyme |
|---|---|---|
| Direct materials – £ per unit | 2.10 | 3.33 |
| Direct labour – £ per unit | 30 | 20 |
| Number of material requisitions | 400 | 1,200 |
| Number of production set-ups | 150 | 450 |
| Budgeted production – units | 50,000 | 25,000 |

(a) **Complete the table below using Activity Based Costing (ABC) principles.**

|  | £ | Rose (£) | Thyme (£) |
|---|---|---|---|
| Cost driver – per material requisition |  |  |  |
| Cost driver – per production set-up |  |  |  |
| Total materials handling |  |  |  |
| Total production set-ups |  |  |  |

(b) **Calculate the fixed overheads assuming they are absorbed on a budgeted labour hours basis.**

|  | Rose (£) | Thyme (£) |
|---|---|---|
| Fixed overheads |  |  |

(c) **Using the information from (a) and (b) calculate the total cost per unit using ABC and the traditional method to two decimal places.**

|  | Rose (£) | Thyme (£) |
|---|---|---|
| Total unit – ABC |  |  |
| Total unit cost – labour hours |  |  |

(d) **Complete the following sentence.**

In ABC systems overheads are allocated to each major activity rather than to each

[        ▼ ].

**Drop-down list:**
department
investment centre
product
unit

## Task 10 (24 marks)

A business operates two departments, Charlie and Delta.

It has supplied the following information for last month:

|  | Charlie | Delta |
| --- | --- | --- |
| Sales volume (units) | 35,000 | 30,000 |
| Selling price (£ per unit) | 6 | 6 |
| Variable production costs (£ per unit) | 3.50 | 1.00 |
| Fixed overheads (£) | 43,750 | 120,000 |

The finance manager would like you to:

- Calculate the contribution per unit, break-even point and margin of safety for each department

- Draft a report in which you provide an analysis of these figures as per the given section headings

**Calculations:**

|  | Charlie | Delta |
| --- | --- | --- |
| Contribution per unit (£) |  |  |
| Break-even point (units) |  |  |
| Margin of safety (%) |  |  |

**Report:**

| To: | Finance Manager | Subject: | Charlie and Delta |
| --- | --- | --- | --- |
| From: | Accounting Technician | Date: | Today |

**Provide an evaluation of the differences in contribution between the two departments.**

**Implications of the differences in break-even point between the two departments.**

**Which department has the better margin of safety and why?**

**Comment on the results from a risk perspective and suggest any potential ways of reducing it.**

# AAT AQ2016 SAMPLE ASSESSMENT
## Management Accounting:
## Decision and Control

# ANSWERS

# Management Accounting: Decision and Control
## AAT sample assessment

## Task 1 (16 marks)

(a) Calculate the budgeted quarterly costs of production for the following activity levels to the nearest pound, and classify each cost.

| | Quarterly production | | Cost Classification |
|---|---|---|---|
| Cost | 3,800 units | 15,900 units | |
| | £ | £ | |
| Direct Materials | 31,008 | 129,744 | Variable ▼ |
| Rent | 7,450 | 7,450 | Fixed ▼ |
| Leased machines | 7,522 | 30,088 | Stepped ▼ |
| Maintenance | 10,016 | 35,063 | Semi-variable ▼ |

You have been supplied with the following information about a factory's overheads.

| Units produced | Total overheads £ |
|---|---|
| 19,000 | 295,000 |
| 23,900 | 324,400 |

The fixed portion of the overheads increases by £12,000 when more than 30,000 units are produced.

Variable costs reduce by £1 per unit for units produced in excess of 25,000 units.

(b) Calculate the total fixed and variable overheads for the following production levels.

Enter your answers to the nearest pound.

| Units | Fixed £ | Variable £ |
|---|---|---|
| 21,000 | 181,000 | 126,000 |
| 36,000 | 193,000 | 205,000 |

## Task 2 (12 marks)

The production information below relates to Apricot Ltd, a business that packages apricots.

|  | Budget | Actual |
| --- | --- | --- |
| Production – cartons | 5,000 | 6,000 |
| Apricots – kilograms (kg) | 50,000 | 70,000 |
| Apricots – £ | 25,000 | 40,000 |
| Direct labour – hours | 1,000 | 800 |
| Direct labour – £ | 10,000 | 8,000 |

(a) **For each variance below, show the variance amount and whether the variance is adverse, favourable or whether there is no variance.**

| Variance | Variance amount £ | Adverse/favourable/ no variance |
| --- | --- | --- |
| Apricots usage | 5,000 | Adverse ▼ |
| Direct labour efficiency | 4,000 | Favourable ▼ |

(b) **Complete the reconciliation statement below.**

**Indicate any negative figures by using a minus sign.**

|  | £ |
| --- | --- |
| **Standard direct cost of actual production** | 42,000 |
| Apricot price variance | 5,000 |
| Apricots usage variance | 5,000 |
| Direct labour rate variance | 0 |
| Direct labour efficiency variance | -4,000 |
| **Actual direct cost of production** | 48,000 |

Another business, Blueberry Ltd, has supplied you with the following information.

|  | £ | Hours |
| --- | --- | --- |
| Favourable material price variance | 168 |  |
| Standard cost per kilogram of material | 12 |  |
| Actual cost of material | 900 |  |
| Adverse labour rate variance | 536 |  |
| Actual labour hours |  | 668 |
| Actual cost of labour | 12,560 |  |

(c) **Complete the following two sentences.**

The actual quantity of material used is  89  kg.

The standard labour rate is £ 18  per hour.

# Task 3 (12 marks)

**(a) Complete the table below.**

| | | |
|---|---|---|
| Standard litres of fuel for 5,000 journeys | 8,900 | litres |
| Standard labour hours for 5,000 journeys | 25,000 | hours |
| Fixed overheads volume variance | £ 40,000 | Adverse ▼ |
| Standard operating kilometres for 5,000 journeys | 100,000 | kilometres |
| Standard fixed overheads costs absorbed by the 5,000 journeys | £ 100,000 | |
| Total fixed overheads variance | £ 25,000 | Adverse ▼ |

**(b) Answer the following questions about variances.**

Which of the following situations would probably cause an adverse fixed overhead **expenditure** variance?

Appointment of new factory manager. ▼

Which of the following situations would probably cause an adverse fixed overhead **capacity** variance?

Machine breakdowns. ▼

## Task 4 (12 marks)

Complete the table below. If any answer is zero, enter '0' into the relevant cell.

- For the sales to fixed overheads rows, use positive numbers only (do not use minus signs).

- For the final row, record any loss figure with a minus sign.

| | Absorption costing | | Marginal costing | |
|---|---|---|---|---|
| | Month 2 (£) | Month 3 (£) | Month 2 (£) | Month 3 (£) |
| Sales – month 2 | 900,000 | | 900,000 | |
| Sales – month 3 | | 990,000 | | 990,000 |
| Opening inventory | 186,000 | 279,000 | 96,000 | 144,000 |
| Production costs | 930,000 | 950,000 | 480,000 | 500,000 |
| Closing inventory | 279,000 | 190,000 | 144,000 | 100,000 |
| Cost of sales | 837,000 | 1,039,000 | 432,000 | 544,000 |
| Fixed overheads | 0 | 0 | 450,000 | 450,000 |
| Profit/(Loss) | 63,000 | -49,000 | 18,000 | -4,000 |

## Task 5 (12 marks)

(a) Insert the appropriate three month moving averages into the table below.

| Month | Sales (units) | Three month moving average (units) |
|---|---|---|
| December | 5,760 | |
| January | 5,820 | 5,780 |
| February | 5,760 | |
| March | 6,600 | 6,160 |
| April | 6,120 | |
| May | 6,150 | 6,200 |
| June | 6,330 | |

**(b) Complete the following sentences.**

Seasonal variation equals actual data at a point, less | trend ▼ | data at the same point.

The observation that traffic volumes are higher during daylight hours is an example of | seasonal variations. ▼ |

The information below relates to production costs and the RPI Index.

**(c) Restate the following costs at January prices to the nearest pound.**

| Month | Actual costs (£) | RPI | Costs at January prices (£) |
|-------|------------------|-----|------------------------------|
| January | 129,000 | 170 | 129,000 |
| March | 132,000 | 172 | 130,465 |
| June | 135,000 | 174 | 131,897 |

**(d) Complete the following sentences.**

The prediction of a figure outside of a data range already observed is known as | extrapolation. ▼ |

The effect of long term economic movement is known as | cyclical ▼ | variations.

A business's production costs vary linearly according to the regression equation $y = a + bx$, where x = production volume. Total production costs of 200 units and 2,000 units are £5,000 and £14,000 respectively.

**(e) Calculate the values of a and b.**

Value of a: | 4,000 |

Value of b: | 5 |

## Task 6 (24 marks)

> The notes below cover a range of possible points that you may include in your written response.
>
> These examples are not intended to be exhaustive and other valid comments may be relevant.

**(a)**

### Storage facilities

> The reduction in rent would have reduced fixed overhead expenditure and is reflected in the favourable fixed overhead expenditure variance.
>
> The fixed overhead standard cost should be amended in view of this saving.

### Machinery

> The new machinery was more efficient and should lead to favourable labour efficiency and favourable fixed overhead efficiency variances.
>
> The increased depreciation however, will increase fixed overhead expenditure.
> Once these are known the standards can be amended.

### Staff upgrade

> The higher skilled staff – probably responsible for the favourable labour efficiency variance.
>
> They are also likely to have led to the favourable materials usage variance
>
> If fixed overheads are absorbed on a labour hours basis
>
> Then this would also be the reason for the favourable fixed overhead efficiency variance.
>
> However, the new staff would have caused the adverse labour rate variance as they are likely to be on a much higher wage rate per hour.
>
> Any overtime worked by the new staff could have led to the favourable capacity variance.
>
> If new staff are permanent – standard labour rate & hours should be updated.

**(b)**

> Mention of Integrity, Objectivity and Professionalism
> Self-interest versus goal-congruence
> Laying off of unskilled staff versus retraining
> Hiring expensive staff rather than retaining cheaper staff

## Task 7 (18 marks)

**(a)  Complete the statement below.**

An activity where there is opportunity for reducing the cost without reducing a product's value to the customer is a | non-value-added ▼ | activity.

A small business has supplied the following information:

|                            | £          |
|----------------------------|------------|
| Turnover                   | 1,500,000  |
| Cost of materials used     | 700,000    |
| Cost of bought in services | 300,000    |
| Number of employees        | 10         |

**(b)  Use the information provided to complete the statements below.**

The total value added is £ | 500,000 | .

Value added per employee is a measure of | productivity. ▼ |

**(c)  Complete the profit and loss account below using the following performance indicators.**

**Enter ALL figures as positive numbers – do not enter negative figures.**

|                          | £         |
|--------------------------|-----------|
| Sales                    | 1,460,000 |
| Variable production costs | 657,000  |
| Fixed production costs    | 438,000   |
| Cost of sales            | 1,095,000 |
| Gross profit             | 365,000   |
| Non-production costs     | 146,000   |
| Net profit               | 219,000   |

Kumquat Ltd has supplied the following extracts from its management accounts which are based on a 365 day year.

|                   | £         |
|-------------------|-----------|
| Revenue           | 1,350,400 |
| Opening inventory | 122,658   |
| Purchases         | 849,200   |
| Closing inventory | 110,000   |
| Receivables       | 369,973   |
| Payables          | 118,063   |

(d)  Calculate the following ratios using the above figures.

All answers must be to the nearest whole day and based on averages where applicable.

|  | Inventory holding period | Payables payment period |
|---|---|---|
| Days | 49 | 51 |

(e)  Complete the following sentence.

The "innovation and learning perspective" is associated with the concept of

the balanced scorecard.  ▼

. . . . . . . . . . . . . . . . . . . . . . . . . . . . . . . . . . . . . . . . . . . . . . . . . . . . . . . . . . . . . . . . . . . . . . . . . . . . . . . . . . . . . . . . . .

## Task 8 (15 marks)

(a)  Complete the table below for the next period calculating the optimal unit production.

|  | Jackal | Hyena |
|---|---|---|
| Total materials required (kg) | 10,000 | 30,000 |
| Total labour hours required | 5,000 | 20,000 |
| Contribution per unit (£) | 7 | 9 |
| Contribution per limiting factor (£) (to TWO decimal places) | 7.00 | 4.50 |
| Optimal production (units) | 5,000 | 7,500 |

(b)  What is the maximum that would be paid for each of the following?

5,000 kg of additional material:  £ ☐ 0

5,000 hours of additional labour:  £ ☐ 22,500

Buffalo Ltd is considering acquiring new equipment to improve productivity.

The table below shows how having the new equipment would compare with the current situation.

|  | Current situation | Proposed situation with new equipment |
|---|---|---|
| Direct materials per unit | 3 kg at £5 | Usage down by 15% |
| Direct labour per unit | 6 hours at £10 | Time down by 20% |
| Sales | 5,000 units at £150 | No change |
| Fixed costs | £277,500 | Up by £79,500 |

(c) Calculate the profit figures for the current and proposed situations and indicate whether or not the equipment should be acquired.

|  | Current situation (£) | Proposed situation with new equipment (£) |
|---|---|---|
| Profit | 97,500 | 89,250 |

It [ would not ▼ ] be better to acquire the new equipment.

## Task 9 (15 marks)

Herb Ltd manufactures two products, Rose and Thyme.

The two overhead activities, production set-ups and materials handling, have budgets of £600,000 and £400,000 respectively.

Rose and Thyme use three hours and two hours of labour per unit respectively.

Further information has been provided below.

|  | Rose | Thyme |
|---|---|---|
| Direct materials – £ per unit | 2.10 | 3.33 |
| Direct labour – £ per unit | 30 | 20 |
| Number of material requisitions | 400 | 1,200 |
| Number of production set-ups | 150 | 450 |
| Budgeted production – units | 50,000 | 25,000 |

(a) Complete the table below using Activity Based Costing (ABC) principles.

|  | £ | Rose (£) | Thyme (£) |
|---|---|---|---|
| Cost driver – per material requisition | 250 |  |  |
| Cost driver – per production set-up | 1,000 |  |  |
| Total materials handling |  | 100,000 | 300,000 |
| Total production set-ups |  | 150,000 | 450,000 |

(b) Calculate the fixed overheads assuming they are absorbed on a budgeted labour hours basis.

|  | Rose (£) | Thyme (£) |
|---|---|---|
| Fixed overheads | 750,000 | 250,000 |

(c) **Using the information from (a) and (b) calculate the total cost per unit using ABC and the traditional method to two decimal places.**

|  | Rose (£) | Thyme (£) |
|---|---|---|
| Total unit – ABC | 37.10 | 53.33 |
| Total unit cost – labour hours | 47.10 | 33.33 |

(d) **Complete the following sentence.**

In ABC systems overheads are allocated to each major activity rather than to each

| department. ▼ |
|---|

## Task 10 (24 marks)

|  | Charlie | Delta |
|---|---|---|
| Contribution per unit (£) | 2.50 | 5.00 |
| Break-even point (units) | 175,000 | 24,000 |
| Margin of safety (%) | 50 | 20 |

> The notes below cover a range of possible points that you may include in your written response.
>
> These examples are not intended to be exhaustive and other valid comments may be relevant.

**Provide an evaluation of the differences in contribution between the two departments.**

> The main reason is because of the much higher variable costs in Charlie/lower variable costs in Delta.
>
> On an initial reading this might look much better for Delta because it has the higher contribution.
>
> Mention of difference in operating gearing
>
> The selling price has no effect on the differing contributions as it is the same for both products

**Implications of the differences in break-even point between the two departments.**

Despite lower contribution per unit Charlie has a lower break-even point because of less fixed costs.

This means Charlie has enough contribution to easily cover the fixed costs.

This means Charlie doesn't have to sell as many units to cover the fixed costs/Delta would have to sell many more units (6,500 more) than Charlie.

**Which department has the better margin of safety and why?**

Charlie has a much higher margin of safety for two main reasons.

Firstly, it has a much higher sales volume

Secondly, it has a lower break-even point and thus can suffer a bigger drop in volume before breaking-even.

Delta's volume only needs to fall by 6,000 less units before it breaks-even and faces the prospect of losses.

**Comment on the results from a risk perspective and suggest any potential ways of reducing it.**

From a risk perspective, Charlie is the safer option

Its sales volume would have to fall by half before it hit problems.

Ways of reducing the risk include, cutting back on fixed costs, reducing variable costs or increasing sales price/volume.

Delta is the riskier option and would need further investigation but

Delta would be much more profitable if sales increased significantly.

# BPP PRACTICE ASSESSMENT 1
# MANAGEMENT ACCOUNTING:
# DECISION AND CONTROL

**Time allowed: 2.5 hours**

# Management Accounting Decision & Control: BPP practice assessment 1

## Task 1

RD Ltd manufactures rubberised asphalt and operates a standard costing system.

The standard cost card for the coming month is being prepared and you have been given the following information.

- 50 tonnes of CR materials will be transferred from the CR Division of the company at a cost of £474 per tonne.

- 200 tonnes of asphalt material will be purchased at a cost of £150 per tonne.

- Labour required to produce 250 tonnes of output is 800 hours.

- Labour cost is £10 per hour.

- Fixed running costs of the machines are £150,000 per month.

- Budgeted production is 250 tonnes per month.

- Fixed production overheads are absorbed on the basis of tonnes.

**Complete the standard cost card for the production of 250 tonnes of rubberised asphalt.**

|  |  | Quantity | Unit price | Total cost |
|---|---|---|---|---|
|  |  |  | £ | £ |
| CR materials | tonnes |  |  |  |
| Asphalt | tonnes |  |  |  |
| Direct labour | hours |  |  |  |
| Fixed production overheads | tonnes |  |  | _____ |
| Standard cost |  |  |  | ═══════ |

## Task 2

The budgeted activity and actual results for a business for the month of May 20X8 are as follows:

|  |  | Budget |  | Actual |
|---|---|---|---|---|
| Production (tonnes) |  | 200 |  | 210 |
| Direct labour | 600 hours | £4,800 | 600 hours | £5,100 |

**Complete the following sentences.**

The standard labour rate per hour is £ [        ] per hour.

The standard labour hours for actual production is [        ] hours.

The direct labour rate variance is £ [        ] (Adverse/Favourable).

The direct labour efficiency variance is £ [        ] (Adverse/Favourable).

## Task 3

A business has a single product into which fixed overheads are absorbed on the basis of labour hours. The standard cost card shows that fixed overheads are to be absorbed on the basis of 8 labour hours per unit at a rate of £10.00 per hour. The budgeted level of production is 100,000 units.

The actual results for the period were that fixed overheads were £7,800,000 and that the actual hours worked were 820,000 and the actual units produced were 98,000.

**Calculate the following variances.**

| | Variance £ | Adverse/Favourable |
|---|---|---|
| Fixed overhead expenditure variance | | |
| Fixed overhead volume variance | | |
| Fixed overhead efficiency variance | | |
| Fixed overhead capacity variance | | |

## Task 4

ABC Ltd manufactures one product, the ZZ. The company operates a standard costing system and analysis of variances is made every month. The standard cost card for the ZZ is as follows:

|  | £ |
|---|---|
| Direct materials 0.5 kg at £4.00 per kg | 2.00 |
| Direct wages 2 hours at £8.00 per hour | 16.00 |
| Variable overheads 2 hours at £0.30 per hour | 0.60 |
|  | 18.60 |

BPP
LEARNING MEDIA

The budgeted production was for 5,100 units in the month of June. The actual costs during the month of June for the production of 4,850 units were as follows:

|  | £ |
|---|---|
| Direct materials 2,300 kg | 9,800 |
| Direct labour 8,500 hours paid | £67,800 |
| Actual operating hours amounted to 8,000 hours |  |
| Variable overheads | 2,600 |

The following variances have been calculated.

| | |
|---|---|
| Materials price | £600 Adv |
| Materials usage | £500 Fav |
| Labour rate | £200 Fav |
| Labour efficiency | £13,600 Fav |
| Idle time variance | £4,000 Adv |
| Variable overhead expenditure | £200 Adv |
| Variable overhead efficiency | £510 Fav |

**Calculate the standard cost of 4,850 units of production and insert the variances in the correct place in the following operating statement. Total the variances and reconcile the standard cost of actual production to the actual cost of actual production.**

|  | Favourable £ | Adverse £ | Total £ |
|---|---|---|---|
| **Standard cost of actual production** |  |  |  |
| **Variances** |  |  |  |
| Materials price |  |  |  |
| Materials usage |  |  |  |
| Labour rate |  |  |  |
| Labour efficiency |  |  |  |
| Labour idle time |  |  |  |
| Variable overhead expenditure |  |  |  |
| Variable overhead efficiency | _____ | _____ | _____ |
| **Total variances** |  |  |  |
| **Actual cost of actual production** |  |  |  |

## Task 5

A company imports tea from India and the historical cost per kilogram is shown below.

|  | June X7 £ | July X7 £ | Aug X7 £ | Sept X7 £ | Oct X7 £ | Nov X7 £ |
|---|---|---|---|---|---|---|
| Cost per kg of tea | 4.95 | 4.97 | 4.99 | 5.05 | 5.08 | 5.10 |

(a) The price per kilogram at January 20X7 was £4.80.

**Convert the costs per kilogram for June and November to index numbers using January 20X7 as the base year.**

| June cost |  |
|---|---|
| November cost |  |

(b) It is expected that the index number for tea for January 20X8 will be 108.25.

**What is the expected cost per kilogram for January 20X8?**

£5.52 ☐

£5.36 ☐

£5.20 ☐

£5.40 ☐

(c) **The percentage increase in the price of tea from January 20X7 to January 20X8 is:**

8.33% ☐

7.69% ☐

5.80% ☐

5.58% ☐

## Task 6

You are employed as part of the management accounting team in a large industrial company. The production director, who has only recently been appointed, is unfamiliar with fixed overhead variances. Because of this, the group management accountant has asked you to prepare a report to the production director.

Your report should do the following.

(a) Outline the similarities and differences between fixed overhead variances and other cost variances such as the material and labour variances.

(b) Explain what is meant by the fixed overhead expenditure, volume, capacity and efficiency variances, and show, by way of examples, how these can be of help to the production director in the planning and controlling of the division.

**REPORT**

To: Production Director

From: Assistant Management Accountant

Date: xx/xx/xx

Subject: **Fixed overhead variances**

**Similarities between fixed overhead variances and other variances**

The meaning of fixed overhead variances

Fixed overhead variances and planning and control

## Task 7

Given below is a summary of the performance of a business for the last two years:

|  | 20X6 | 20X7 |
| --- | --- | --- |
|  | £'000 | £'000 |
| Sales | 1,420 | 1,560 |
| Cost of sales | 850 | 950 |
| Expenses | 370 | 407 |
| Interest | – | 7 |
| Share capital and reserves | 1,500 | 1,600 |
| Long term loan | – | 100 |
| Non-current assets | 1,100 | 1,300 |
| Receivables | 155 | 198 |
| Inventory | 105 | 140 |
| Payables | 140 | 162 |
| Bank balance | 280 | 224 |

**For each of the two years complete the table to calculate the performance measures. Give your answers to TWO decimal places.**

|  | 20X6 | 20X7 |
| --- | --- | --- |
| Gross profit margin |  |  |
| Operating profit margin |  |  |
| Return on capital employed |  |  |
| Asset turnover |  |  |
| Non-current asset turnover |  |  |
| Current ratio |  |  |
| Quick ratio |  |  |
| Receivables' collection period |  |  |
| Inventory holding in days |  |  |
| Payables' payment period |  |  |

## Task 8

A business sells a single product and has budgeted sales of 130,000 units for the next period. The selling price per unit is £56 and the variable costs of production are £36. The fixed costs of the business are £2,000,000.

**Complete the following sentences. Give your answers to the nearest whole number.**

The breakeven point in units is [          ] units.

The margin of safety in units is [          ] units.

The margin of safety as a percentage of budgeted sales is [          ] %.

........................................................................................

## Task 9

HM Ltd is considering purchasing a new machine to reduce the labour time taken to produce one of its products. The machine would cost £300,000. The labour time would be reduced from five hours to two hours without compromising quality and the failure rates will remain at zero.

The discount factors you will need are shown below.

| Year | Discount factor 5% |
|---|---|
| 0 | 1.000 |
| 1 | 0.952 |
| 2 | 0.907 |
| 3 | 0.864 |
| 4 | 0.823 |
| 5 | 0.784 |

(a) **Calculate the discounted lifecycle cost of the machine based upon the following:**

  (i)   Purchase price of £300,000

  (ii)  Annual running costs of £30,000 for the next 5 years

  (iii) A residual value of £50,000 at the end of the 5 years

| Year | 0 | 1 | 2 | 3 | 4 | 5 |
|---|---|---|---|---|---|---|
| | £'000 | £'000 | £'000 | £'000 | £'000 | £'000 |
| Purchase price | | | | | | |
| Running cost | | | | | | |
| Residual value | ___ | ___ | ___ | ___ | ___ | ___ |
| Net cost | | | | | | |
| Discount factor | | | | | | |
| Present cost | | | | | | |

The discounted lifecycle cost of the machine is £ [ ]

(b) **Calculate the discounted labour savings based upon annual production of 5,000 units, a three hour saving per unit and a labour rate of £7 per hour.**

| Year | 0 | 1 | 2 | 3 | 4 | 5 |
|---|---|---|---|---|---|---|
| | £'000 | £'000 | £'000 | £'000 | £'000 | £'000 |
| Labour cost Saving | | | | | | |
| Discount factor | | | | | | |
| Present value | | | | | | |

The discounted labour savings are £ [ ]

## Task 10

HE Ltd has been reviewing the quality of the solar panels that it produces and has engineered two new products, the SP2000 and the SP3000.

The SP2000 is a low quality product with an economic life of 5 years. The SP3000 is a high quality product with an economic life of 20 years.

The Sales Director has provided information about the expected demand and price for the SP2000 and SP3000 for the coming year.

- SP2000 will be priced at £200 per panel and demand is expected to be around 9,000 units per year.

- SP3000 will be priced at £300 per panel and demand is expected to be around 5,000 units per year.

## Forecast statement of profit or loss (income statement)

|  | SP2000<br>9,000 units | SP3000<br>5,000 units |
|---|---|---|
| Volume |  |  |
|  | £ | £ |
| Revenue | 1,800,000 | 1,500,000 |
| **Cost of production** |  |  |
| Direct materials (glass) | 540,000 | 300,000 |
| Direct labour | 126,000 | 175,000 |
| Fixed production overheads | 120,000 | 120,000 |
| Total cost of sales | 786,000 | 595,000 |
| **Gross profit** | **1,014,000** | **905,000** |
| Selling and distribution costs | 400,000 | 400,000 |
| Administration costs | 200,000 | 200,000 |
| **Operating profit** | **414,000** | **305,000** |

## Extracts from the forecast statement of financial position

|  | £ | £ |
|---|---|---|
| Inventory of material (glass) | 60,000 | 60,000 |
| Inventory of finished goods | NIL | NIL |
| Net assets | 2,014,000 | 1,905,000 |

(a) **Complete the table to calculate the following performance indicators for BOTH products. Give your answers to TWO decimal places.**

|  | SP2000 | SP3000 |
|---|---|---|
| Gross profit margin |  |  |
| Operating profit margin |  |  |
| Direct materials cost per unit |  |  |
| Direct labour cost per unit |  |  |
| Fixed production overheads cost per unit |  |  |
| Return on net assets |  |  |
| Raw materials holding period in days |  |  |

(b) **Draft a report for the Finance Director covering the following:**

(i) An explanation of why the gross profit margin is different for each product. Your answer should refer to the following and explain their effect on the gross profit margin:

- Sales price per unit
- Materials, labour and fixed cost per unit

(ii) An assessment of the return on net assets for each product.

**From:** A Student

**To:** Finance Director

**Sent:** 1 December 20X8

**Subject:** Performance indicators

(i) **Gross profit margin**

(ii) **Return on net assets**

# BPP PRACTICE ASSESSMENT 1
# MANAGEMENT ACCOUNTING:
# DECISION AND CONTROL

## ANSWERS

# Management Accounting Decision & Control: BPP practice assessment 1

## Task 1

Standard cost card for production of 250 tonnes of rubberised asphalt:

|  |  | Quantity | Unit price | Total cost |
|---|---|---|---|---|
|  |  |  | £ | £ |
| CR material | tonnes | 50 | 474 | 23,700 |
| Asphalt | tonnes | 200 | 150 | 30,000 |
| Direct labour | hours | 800 | 10 | 8,000 |
| Fixed production overheads | tonnes | 250 | 600 | 150,000 |
| Standard cost |  |  |  | 211,700 |

## Task 2

The standard labour rate per hour is **£8** per hour.

The standard labour hours for actual production is **630** hours.

The direct labour rate variance is **£300 Adverse**.

The direct labour efficiency variance is **£240 Favourable**.

### Workings

| Standard labour rate per hour | = | Budgeted labour cost/Budgeted labour hours |
|---|---|---|
|  | = | £4,800 / 600 |
|  | = | £8 per hour |
| Standard labour hours for actual production | = | Standard labour hour per tonne × Actual production |
|  | = | 600 hours/200 tonnes × 210 tonnes |
|  | = | 630 hours |

## Direct labour rate variance

|  | £ |
|---|---|
| 600 should have cost (× £8) | 4,800 |
| But did cost | 5,100 |
| Labour rate variance | 300 Adv |

## Direct labour efficiency variance

|  |  |
|---|---|
| 210 tonnes should have taken (×3) | 630 hours |
| But did take | 600 hours |
| Efficiency variance in hours | 30 Fav |
| × standard rate per hour | × £8 |
| Labour efficiency variance | 240 Fav |

••••••••••••••••••••••••••••••••••••••••••••••••••••••••••••••••••••••••••••••••••••••

## Task 3

|  | Variance £ | Adverse/Favourable |
|---|---|---|
| Fixed overhead expenditure variance | 200,000 | Favourable |
| Fixed overhead volume variance | 160,000 | Adverse |
| Fixed overhead efficiency variance | 360,000 | Adverse |
| Fixed overhead capacity variance | 200,000 | Favourable |

### Workings

### Fixed overhead expenditure variance

|  | £ |
|---|---|
| Budgeted fixed overhead 100,000 units × 8 hours × £10.00 | 8,000,000 |
| Actual fixed overhead | 7,800,000 |
| Expenditure variance | 200,000 (F) |

## Fixed overhead volume variance

|  | £ |
|---|---|
| Standard hours for actual production @ standard OAR 98,000 units × 8 hours × £10.00 | 7,840,000 |
| Standard hours for budgeted production @ standard OAR 100,000 units × 8 hours × £10.00 | 8,000,000 |
| Volume variance | 160,000 (A) |

## Fixed overhead efficiency variance

|  | Hours |
|---|---|
| Actual units should take (98,000 × 8 hrs) | 784,000 |
| But did take | 820,000 |
| Fixed overhead efficiency variance in hours | 36,000 Adv |
| × standard fixed overhead absorption rate per hour | × £10 |
| Fixed overhead efficiency variance in £ | 360,000 Adv |

## Fixed overhead capacity variance

|  | Hours |
|---|---|
| Budgeted hours of work (100,000 × 8hrs) | 800,000 |
| Actual hours of work | 820,000 |
| Fixed overhead capacity variance | 20,000 Fav |
| × standard fixed overhead absorption rate per hour | × £10 |
| Fixed overhead capacity variance in £ | £200,000 Fav |

## Task 4

|  | Favourable £ | Adverse £ | Total £ |
|---|---|---|---|
| Standard cost of actual production (4,850 units × £18.60) |  |  | 90,210 |
| **Variances** |  |  |  |
| Materials price |  | 600 |  |
| Materials usage | 500 |  |  |
| Labour rate | 200 |  |  |
| Labour efficiency | 13,600 |  |  |

BPP
LEARNING MEDIA

|  | Favourable £ | Adverse £ | Total £ |
|---|---|---|---|
| Labour idle time |  | 4,000 |  |
| Variable overhead expenditure |  | 200 |  |
| Variable overhead efficiency | 510 |  |  |
| Total variances | 14,810 | 4,800 | 10,010 (F) |
| Actual cost of actual production (9,800 + 67,800 +2,600) |  |  | 80,200 |

## Task 5

(a)

| June cost | 103.13 |
|---|---|
| November cost | 106.25 |

June = $\dfrac{£4.95}{£4.80} \times 100 = 103.13$

November = $\dfrac{£5.10}{£4.80} \times 100 = 106.25$

(b)  January X8 cost = $\dfrac{£4.80 \times 108.25}{100} = £5.20$

(c)  Percentage increase  = $\dfrac{£5.20 - £4.80}{£4.80} \times 100$

= 8.33%

## Task 6

REPORT

To:          Production Director

From:      Assistant Management Accountant

Date:       xx/xx/xx

Subject:   **Fixed overhead variances**

This memorandum provides information on fixed overhead variances. In particular it covers the similarities between fixed overhead variances and other cost variances, the meaning of the various fixed overhead variances and the ways in which such variances can be of assistance in the planning and the controlling of the division.

### Similarities between fixed overhead variances and other variances

The fixed overhead expenditure variance is the difference between the budgeted fixed overhead expenditure and actual fixed overhead expenditure. It is therefore similar to the material price and labour rate variances in that it shows the effect on costs and hence profit of paying more or less than anticipated for resources used.

Material usage and labour efficiency variances show the effect on costs and hence profit of having used more or less resource than should have been used for the actual volume of production. Fixed overheads should remain constant within the relevant range of production, however; they should not change simply because budgeted and actual production volumes differ. Fixed overhead variances similar to material usage and labour efficiency variances (reflecting the difference between the actual fixed overhead expenditure and the fixed overhead expenditure which should have been incurred at the actual volume of production) cannot therefore occur.

### The meaning of fixed overhead variances

Whereas labour and material total variances show the effect on costs and hence profit of the difference between what the actual production volume should have cost and what it did cost (in terms of labour or material), if an organisation uses standard absorption costing (as we do), the fixed overhead total variance is the difference between actual fixed overhead expenditure and the fixed overhead absorbed (the under- or over-absorbed overhead).

The total under- or over-absorption is made up of the fixed overhead expenditure variance and the fixed overhead volume variance. The volume variance shows that part of the under- or over-absorbed overhead which is due to any difference between budgeted production volume and actual production volume.

The volume variance can be further broken down into an efficiency variance and a capacity variance. The capacity variance shows how much of the under- or over-absorbed overhead is due to working the labour force or plant more or less than planned, whereas the efficiency variance shows the effect of the efficiency of the labour force or plant.

The volume variance and its two subdivisions, the efficiency variance and the capacity variance, measure the extent of under or over absorption due to production volume being different to that planned. Material usage and labour efficiency variances, on the other hand, measure the effect of usage being different from that expected for the actual volume achieved.

### Fixed overhead variances and planning and control

The fixed overhead volume variance and its subdivisions are perhaps misleading as variances for management control, because unlike expenditure variances or variable cost efficiency variances, they are not a true reflection of the extra or lower cash spending by an organisation as a result of the variance occurring. However, the fixed overhead efficiency and capacity variances are of some relevance for planning and control. They provide some measure of the difference between budgeted production volume and actual production volume, and management should obviously be interested in whether budgeted output was achieved, and if not, why not. A favourable efficiency variance might indicate an efficient workforce whereas an unfavourable capacity variance might indicate plant breakdowns or strikes. The existence of a fixed overhead volume variance can therefore be important; it is only the monetary value given to it that can be misleading.

The fixed overhead expenditure variance highlights the effect on costs and hence profit of changes to the level of overheads. For overhead expenditure variances to have any practical value as a planning or control measure, the variance for each overhead cost centre needs to be calculated, and reported to the manager responsible. Within each overhead cost centre, the manager should be able to analyse the total variance into indirect material cost variances, indirect labour cost variances and excess or favourable spending on other items, such as depreciation, postage, telephone charges and so on. Managers can then, for example, consider other suppliers, reconsider pricing structures of products and the like.

## Task 7

|  | *20X6* | *20X7* |
|---|---|---|
| Gross profit margin | 40.14% | 39.10% |
| Operating profit margin | 14.08% | 13.01% |
| Return on capital employed | 13.33% | 11.94% |
| (**Note**. Total CE used ie share capital and reserves + long term loan.) | | |
| Asset turnover | 0.95 | 0.92 |
| Non-current asset turnover | 1.29 | 1.20 |
| Current ratio | 3.86 | 3.47 |
| Quick ratio | 3.11 | 2.60 |
| Receivables' collection period | 39.84 days | 46.33 days |
| Inventory holding in days | 45.09 days | 53.79 days |
| Payables' payment period | 60.12 days | 62.24 days |

## Workings

|  | *20X6* | *20X7* |
|---|---|---|
| Gross profit margin | 570/1,420 | 610/1,560 |
| Operating profit margin | 200/1,420 | 203/1,560 |
| Return on capital employed | 200/1,500 | 203/1,700 |
| (**Note**. Total CE used ie share capital & reserves + long term loan.) | | |

| Asset turnover | 1,420/1,500 | 1,560/1,700 |
|---|---|---|
| Non-current asset turnover | 1,420/1,100 | 1,560/1,300 |
| Current ratio | 540/140 | 562/162 |
| Quick ratio | 435/140 | 422/162 |
| Receivables' collection period | 155/1,420 × 365 | 198/1,560 × 365 |
| Inventory holding in days | 105/850 × 365 | 140/950 × 365 |
| Payables' payment period | 140/850 × 365 | 162/950 × 365 |

## Task 8

The breakeven point in units is 100,000 units

The margin of safety in units is 30,000 units

The margin of safety as a percentage of budgeted sales is 23%

**Workings**

$$\text{Breakeven point} = \frac{£2,000,000}{£56 - £36}$$

$$= 100,000 \text{ units}$$

Margin of safety (units) = Budgeted sales – breakeven sales

$$= (130,000 - 100,000) \text{ units}$$

$$= 30,000 \text{ units}$$

$$\text{Margin of safety (\% budgeted sales)} = \frac{130,000 - 100,000}{130,000} \times 100\%$$

$$= 23\%$$

## Task 9

(a)

| Year | 0 | 1 | 2 | 3 | 4 | 5 |
|---|---|---|---|---|---|---|
| | £'000 | £'000 | £'000 | £'000 | £'000 | £'000 |
| Purchase price | 300 | | | | | |
| Running cost | | 30 | 30 | 30 | 30 | 30 |
| Residual value | — | — | — | — | — | (50) |
| Net cost | 300 | 30 | 30 | 30 | 30 | (20) |

| Discount factor | 1.000 | 0.952 | 0.907 | 0.864 | 0.823 | 0.784 |
|---|---|---|---|---|---|---|
| Present cost | 300 | 28.560 | 27.210 | 25.920 | 24.690 | (15.680) |

The discounted lifecycle cost of the machine is £390,700.

(b)

| Year | 0 | 1 | 2 | 3 | 4 | 5 |
|---|---|---|---|---|---|---|
| | £'000 | £'000 | £'000 | £'000 | £'000 | £'000 |
| Labour cost Saving (W1) | 0 | 105 | 105 | 105 | 105 | 105 |
| Discount factor | 1.000 | 0.952 | 0.907 | 0.864 | 0.823 | 0.784 |
| Present value | | 99.960 | 95.235 | 90.720 | 86.415 | 82.320 |

The discounted labour savings are £454,650

**Workings**

3 hours saving per unit × 5000 units × £7 = £105,000

## Task 10

(a)

| | SP2000 | SP3000 |
|---|---|---|
| Gross profit margin | 56.33% | 60.33% |
| Operating profit margin | 23.00% | 20.33% |
| Direct materials cost per unit | £60.00 | £60.00 |
| Direct labour cost per unit | £14.00 | £35.00 |
| Fixed production overheads cost per unit | £13.33 | £24.00 |
| Return on net assets | 20.56% | 16.01% |
| Raw materials holding period in days | 40.56 days | 73.00 days |

## Workings

| | SP2000 | SP3000 |
|---|---|---|
| Note all monetary amounts in '000 for (i) and (ii) | | |
| (i) = Gross Profit/Turnover × 100 | Gross profit margin<br><br>(1,014/1,800) × 100<br><br>= 56.33% | (905/1,500) × 100<br><br>= 60.33% |
| (ii) = Operating Profit/Turnover × 100 | Operating profit margin<br><br>(414/1,800) × 100<br><br>= 23.00% | (305/1,500) × 100<br><br>= 20.33% |
| (iii) = Direct materials cost/Sales units | Direct materials cost per unit<br><br>£540,000/9,000 = £60.00 | £300,000/5,000 = £60.00 |
| (iv) = Direct labour cost/Sales units | Direct labour cost per unit<br><br>£126,000/9,000 = £14.00 | £175,000/5,000 = £35.00 |
| (v) = Fixed prod'n o/hds cost/Sales units | Fixed production overheads cost per unit<br><br>£120,000/9,000 = £13.33 | £120,000/5,000 = £24.00 |
| (vi) = Operating profit/Net assets × 100 | Return on net assets<br><br>£414,000/£2,014,000<br><br>× 100 = 20.56% | £305,000/£ 1,905,000<br><br>× 100 = 16.01% |
| (vii) = (Inventory of material/Direct materials) × 365 | Inventory holding<br><br>£60,000/£540,000 × 365<br><br>= 40.56 days | £60,000/£300,000 × 365<br><br>= 73.00 days |

(b)

> **From:**      A Student
>
> **To:**      Finance Director
>
> **Sent:**      1 December 20X8
>
> **Subject:**      Performance indicators
>
> (i) **Gross profit margin**
>
> The gross margin for the SP3000 is higher than the SP2000 by 4%.
>
> This difference can be explained by differences in the selling price per unit and the cost of production of each unit.
>
> The selling price of the SP3000 is £300 per unit whereas the selling price of the SP2000 is £200 per unit. If the cost of production for both products was the same then the SP3000 would have a higher gross margin.
>
> The cost of production of the two products should be compared:
>
> - The direct material cost of glass is constant at £60 per unit and so does not affect the margin.
>
> - The direct labour cost per unit is much higher for the SP3000. This will reduce the gross margin for the SP3000.
>
> - The fixed costs per unit are also higher for the SP3000 because less volume is produced (£24 per unit as opposed to £13.33 per unit for SP2000). Again this will reduce the margin for the SP3000.
>
> The higher unit selling price of the SP3000 more than outweighs the additional costs per unit and hence the SP3000 has a higher gross margin.
>
> (ii) **Return on net assets**
>
> The SP2000 has a higher return on net assets than the SP3000 because its operating profits are larger relative to its net assets. Thus it generates an additional £109,000 but only uses an additional £109,000 of net assets.

# BPP PRACTICE ASSESSMENT 2
# MANAGEMENT ACCOUNTING:
# DECISION AND CONTROL

**Time allowed: 2.5 hours**

# Management Accounting Decision & Control: BPP practice assessment 2

## Task 1

The bagging division of a tea company operates a standard costing system. The standard cost card for the coming months is being prepared and you have been provided with the following information.

- Loose tea is expected to cost £5 per kilogram.
- 1,000 tea bags require 3 kilograms of loose tea.
- Tea bags cost 0.6 pence per bag.
- One machine can package 5,000 bags per hour and requires one operator who costs £10 per hour.
- Budgeted labour hours are 4,000 per month.
- Fixed production overheads are £200,000 per month.
- Budgeted production is 20,000 batches of 1,000 tea bags per month.
- Fixed production overheads are absorbed on the basis of direct labour hours.

**Prepare the standard cost card for the production of 1,000 tea bags.**

| Standard cost card for 1,000 tea bags | £ |
|---|---|
| Direct materials | |
| Direct materials | |
| Direct labour | |
| Fixed overhead | |
| Total standard cost | |

## Task 2

The standard direct materials cost for a business's product is:

14.4 kg @ £5.00 per kg = £72.00

During the month of May production was 9,200 units of the product and the actual materials cost was £671,600 for 135,500 kg. The price of the materials has been unexpectedly increased to £5.70 per kg for the whole month.

**The total materials price variance is £ [          ]**

**The non-controllable element of the materials price variance that has been caused by the price increase is £ [          ]**

**The controllable element of the materials price variance caused by other factors is**

£ [          ]

## Task 3

A business produces a single product in its factory which has two production departments, cutting and finishing. In the following quarter it is anticipated that 200,000 units of the product will be produced. The expected costs are:

| | |
|---|---|
| Direct materials | £10 per unit |
| Direct labour | 3 hours cutting @ £8.00 per hour |
| | 1 hour finishing @ £9.00 per hour |
| Variable overheads cutting | £444,000 |
| finishing | £382,000 |
| Fixed overheads    cutting | £240,000 |
| finishing | £110,000 |

Overheads are absorbed on the basis of direct labour hours.

(a) **The absorption cost per unit is**

£45.65

£46.60

£47.13

£48.88

(b) **The marginal cost per unit is**

£45.65

£46.60

£47.13

£48.88

## Task 4

A company budgeted to produce 80,000 of its product with a standard cost of £4.60 per unit but in fact produced 84,000 units.

The actual costs of production were:

| | |
|---|---|
| Materials | 278,850 |
| Packaging | 8,800 |
| Labour | 17,100 |
| Fixed overheads | 85,000 |

The variances for the period have already been calculated:

| Materials price | Zero | |
|---|---|---|
| Materials usage | £1,650 | Adverse |
| Packaging price | £400 | Adverse |
| Packaging usage | Zero | |
| Labour rate | £900 | Favourable |
| Labour efficiency | £1,200 | Adverse |
| Fixed overhead expenditure | £5,000 | Adverse |
| Fixed overhead efficiency | £6,000 | Adverse |
| Fixed overhead capacity | £10,000 | Favourable |

**Calculate the budgeted cost for 84,000 units and then complete the table with the variances to reconcile to the actual cost of production.**

| Budgeted cost for actual production | | | |
|---|---|---|---|
| **Variances** | **Favourable** | **Adverse** | |
| Materials price | | | |
| Materials usage | | | |
| Packaging price | | | |
| Packaging usage | | | |
| Labour rate | | | |
| Labour efficiency | | | |
| Fixed overhead expenditure | | | |
| Fixed overhead efficiency | | | |
| Fixed overhead capacity | | | |
| Total variance | | | |
| **Actual cost of actual production** | | | |

## Task 5

(a) Given below are the production cost figures for the last nine months.

**Calculate a three month moving average for these figures.**

|  | Production costs | Three month moving total | Three month moving average |
|---|---|---|---|
|  | £ | £ | £ |
| March | 226,500 |  |  |
| April | 245,300 |  |  |
| May | 240,800 |  |  |
| June | 231,400 |  |  |
| July | 237,600 |  |  |
| August | 246,000 |  |  |
| September | 241,200 |  |  |
| October | 242,300 |  |  |
| November | 247,500 |  |  |
| December | 249,300 |  |  |

(b) **The three month moving average represents which of the following?**



**Picklist:**

Cyclical variations
Random variations
Seasonal variations
Trend

## Task 6

You are employed as an accounting technician at BeThere Airlines, a company that operates flights across Europe. The company has several divisions including a catering division operating from Manchester. The catering division produces meals daily for the flights. Currently all meals produced are used only on BeThere flights.

The company operates an integrated standard cost system in which:

- Purchases of materials are recorded at standard cost
- Direct material costs and direct labour costs are variable
- Production overheads are fixed and absorbed using direct labour hours

The budgeted activity and actual results for November 20X6 are as follows:

|  |  | Budget |  | Actual |
|---|---|---|---|---|
| Production (meals) |  | 112,000 |  | 117,600 |
| Direct materials | 56,000 kg | £224,000 | 61,740 kg | £185,220 |
| Direct labour | 28,000 hours | £252,000 | 27,930 hours | £279,300 |
| Fixed overheads |  | £84,000 |  | £82,000 |
| Total cost |  | £560,000 |  | £546,520 |

(a) **Calculate the following information for November (to two decimal places):**

   (i)    Standard price of materials per kilogram
   (ii)   Standard usage of materials per meal
   (iii)  Standard labour rate per hour
   (iv)   Standard labour hours per meal
   (v)    Budgeted overhead absorption rate per hour
   (vi)   Overheads absorbed into actual production
   (vii)  The total standard cost of actual production

(b) **Calculate the following variances for November:**

   (i)    Direct material price variance
   (ii)   Direct material usage variance
   (iii)  Direct labour rate variance
   (iv)   Direct labour efficiency variance
   (v)    Fixed overhead expenditure variance
   (vi)   Fixed overhead volume variance
   (vii)  Fixed overhead capacity variance
   (viii) Fixed overhead efficiency variance

(c) **Prepare a report to the managing director giving ONE possible reason for each of the following variances you calculated in (b).**

   (i)    Direct material price variance
   (ii)   Direct material usage variance
   (iii)  Direct labour rate variance
   (iv)   Direct labour efficiency variance

# REPORT

**To:**      Managing Director

**From:**    Accounting Technician

**Subject:**  Reasons for the variances

**Date:**    14 December 20X6

## Direct material price variance

## Direct material usage variance

## Direct labour rate variance

## Direct labour efficiency variance

........................................................................................................

## Task 7

The production figures for January for a factory are as follows.

| | |
|---|---|
| Budgeted production in units | 12,000 |
| Actual production in units | 11,250 |
| Labour hours worked | 30,000 |
| Standard hours for each unit | 2 |

**Calculate the efficiency, capacity and activity ratios for January (give answers to two decimal places).**

The efficiency ratio is [          ] %

The capacity ratio is [          ] %

The activity ratio is [          ] %

## Task 8

(a)  The following information relates to one period for a single product produced by a company.

Expected sales revenue = £400,000
Selling price per unit = £40 per unit
Variable cost = £18 per unit
Fixed costs = £99,000

**The breakeven point both in terms of units and sales revenue is:**

| Breakeven point in units | Breakeven point in sales revenue | |
|---|---|---|
| 4,500 units | £99,000 | ☐ |
| 4,500 units | £180,000 | ☐ |
| 2,475 units | £99,000 | ☐ |
| 2,475 units | £180,000 | ☐ |

(b)  Company X sells product Y for £28 per unit. Variable costs of production are £23 per unit. The company has fixed overheads of £440,000 and has budgeted to sell 95,000 units of the product in the next year.

**The margin of safety as a percentage (to two decimal places) is** [          ] %

## Task 9

A company is developing a new product to monitor energy consumption. There are currently several other companies manufacturing similar products which sell for a price of £25 each. The company wishes to make a margin of 30%.

**The target cost of each new product is £** [                    ]

---

## Task 10

Voltair Ltd has developed a domestic wind turbine. A colleague has prepared forecast information based upon two scenarios. The forecast statements of profit or loss (income statements) and statements of financial position for both scenarios are shown below.

- Scenario 1 is to set the price at £1,250 per unit with sales of 10,000 units each year.
- Scenario 2 is to set the price at £1,000 per unit with sales of 14,000 units each year.

**Forecast statement of profit or loss (income statement)**

|                               | Scenario 1 | Scenario 2 |
|-------------------------------|-----------:|-----------:|
|                               | £000       | £000       |
| Revenue                       | 12,500     | 14,000     |
| Cost of production:           |            |            |
| Direct (raw) materials        | 3,000      | 4,200      |
| Direct labour                 | 2,000      | 2,800      |
| Fixed production overheads    | 3,000      | 3,000      |
| Total cost of sales           | 8,000      | 10,000     |
| Gross profit                  | 4,500      | 4,000      |
| Selling and distribution costs| 1,000      | 1,000      |
| Administration costs          | 750        | 750        |
| Operating profit              | 2,750      | 2,250      |
| Interest payable              | 600        | 600        |
| Net profit                    | 2,150      | 1,650      |

**Extracts from the forecast statement of financial position**

|  | £000 | £000 |
|---|---|---|
| Non-current assets | 20,000 | 20,000 |
| Current assets | 5,000 | 5,500 |
| Current liabilities | 4,600 | 5,800 |
| Long-term loans | 12,000 | 11,300 |
|  | 8,400 | 8,400 |
| Represented by: |  |  |
| Share capital | 5,650 | 6,150 |
| Reserves | 2,750 | 2,250 |
|  | 8,400 | 8,400 |

(a) **Calculate the following performance indicators for each scenario. Give your answer to TWO decimal places:**

 (i) Gross profit margin
 (ii) Net profit margin
 (iii) Direct materials cost per unit
 (iv) Direct labour cost per unit
 (v) Fixed production cost per unit
 (vi) Gearing ratio
 (vii) Interest cover

(b) **Draft a report for the Finance Director covering the following:**

 (i) An explanation of why the gross profit margin is different in each scenario. Your answer should refer to the following:

   • Sales price per unit
   • Materials, labour and fixed cost per unit

 (ii) An assessment of the level of gearing and interest cover and whether it is a problem for the business.

## REPORT

**To:** Finance Director   **Subject:** Gross profit margin, gearing and interest cover

**From:** AAT Trainee   **Date:** 16 June 20X8

**(i) Gross profit margin**

**(ii) Gearing and interest cover**

# BPP PRACTICE ASSESSMENT 2
# MANAGEMENT ACCOUNTING:
# DECISION AND CONTROL

## ANSWERS

# Management Accounting Decision & Control: BPP practice assessment 2

## Task 1

| Standard cost card for 1,000 tea bags | |
|---|---|
| | £ |
| Direct materials – tea (3kg × £5) | 15.00 |
| Direct materials – bags (1,000 × £0.006) | 6.00 |
| Direct labour $\left(\dfrac{1,000}{5,000 \text{ hours}} \times £10\right)$ | 2.00 |
| Fixed overhead $\left(\dfrac{0.2 \text{ hours} \times £200,000}{4,000 \text{ hours}}\right)$ | 10.00 |
| Total standard cost | 33.00 |

····································································································

## Task 2

The total materials price variance is £5,900 Favourable.

The non-controllable element of the materials price variance that has been caused by the price increase is £94,850.

The controllable element of the materials price variance caused by other factors is £100,750.

**Workings**

**Total materials price variance**

| | £ |
|---|---|
| Standard cost for actual quantity 135,500 × £5 | 677,500 |
| Actual cost | 671,600 |
| | 5,900 (F) |

**Planning variance caused by price increase**

|  | £ |
|---|---|
| Standard cost for actual quantity 135,500 × £5.00 | 677,500 |
| Adjusted cost for actual quantity 135,500 × £5.70 | 772,350 |
|  | 94,850 (A) |

**Control variance caused by other factors**

|  | £ |
|---|---|
| Adjusted cost for actual quantity 135,500 × £5.70 | 772,350 |
| Actual cost | 671,600 |
|  | 100,750 (F) |

## Task 3

(a) £48.88
(b) £47.13

**Workings**

(a) **Absorption costing**

|  | £ |
|---|---|
| Direct materials | 10.00 |
| Direct labour – cutting (3 × £8.00) | 24.00 |
|                Finishing | 9.00 |
| Variable overheads: |  |
|   Cutting (£444,000/600,000) × 3 hrs | 2.22 |
|   Finishing (£382,000/200,000) × 1hr | 1.91 |
| Fixed overheads: |  |
|   Cutting (£240,000/600,000) × 3 hrs | 1.20 |
|   Finishing (£110,000/200,000) × 1 hr | 0.55 |
|  | 48.88 |

(b) **Marginal costing**

|  | £ |
|---|---|
| Direct materials | 10.00 |
| Direct labour – Cutting (3 × £8.00) | 24.00 |
|                Finishing | 9.00 |

Variable overheads:

| | |
|---|---:|
| Cutting (£440,000/600,000) × 3 hrs | 2.22 |
| Finishing (£382,000/200,000) × 1 hr | 1.91 |
| | 47.13 |

## Task 4

| | £ | £ | £ |
|---|---|---|---|
| **Budgeted cost for actual production (84,000 × £4.60)** | | | **386,400** |
| **Variances** | **Favourable** | **Adverse** | |
| Materials price | – | – | |
| Materials usage | | 1,650 | |
| Packaging price | | 400 | |
| Packaging usage | – | – | |
| Labour rate | 900 | | |
| Labour efficiency | | 1,200 | |
| Fixed overhead expenditure | | 5,000 | |
| Fixed overhead efficiency | | 6,000 | |
| Fixed overhead capacity | 10,000 | | |
| Total variance | 10,900 | 14,250 | 3,350 |
| **Actual cost of actual production** (£278,850 + £8,800 + £17,100 + £85,000) | | | 389,750 |

# Task 5

(a)

|  | Production costs | Three month moving total | Three month moving average |
|---|---|---|---|
|  | £ | £ | £ |
| March | 226,500 |  |  |
| April | 245,300 | 712,600 | 237,533 |
| May | 240,800 | 717,500 | 239,167 |
| June | 231,400 | 709,800 | 236,600 |
| July | 237,600 | 715,000 | 238,333 |
| August | 246,000 | 724,800 | 241,600 |
| September | 241,200 | 729,500 | 243,167 |
| October | 242,300 | 731,000 | 243,667 |
| November | 247,500 | 739,100 | 246,367 |
| December | 249,300 |  |  |

(b)    The correct answer is: Trend

# Task 6

(a)  (i)    Standard price of materials per kg    $= \dfrac{\text{Budgeted total materials cost}}{\text{Budgeted total materials usage in kg}}$

$= \dfrac{£224,000}{56,000}$

$= £4 \text{ per kg}$

(ii)    Standard usage of materials per meal    $= \dfrac{\text{Budgeted total materials usage in kg}}{\text{Production (meals)}}$

$= \dfrac{56,000}{112,000}$

$= 0.5 \text{ kg}$

(iii)  Standard labour rate per hour

$$= \frac{\text{Budgeted total labour cost}}{\text{Budgeted total labour hours}}$$

$$= \frac{£252,000}{28,000}$$

$$= £9 \text{ per hour}$$

(iv)  Standard labour hours per meal

$$= \frac{\text{Budgeted total labour hours}}{\text{Production (meals)}}$$

$$= \frac{28,000}{112,000}$$

$$= 0.25 \text{ hours (or 15 minutes)}$$

(v)  Budgeted overhead absorption rate per hour

$$= \frac{\text{Budgeted total overhead cost}}{\text{Budgeted total labour hours}}$$

$$= \frac{£84,000}{28,000}$$

$$= £3 \text{ per hour}$$

(vi)  Overheads absorbed into actual production

$$= 27,930 \text{ hours} \times £3$$

$$= £83,790$$

(vii)  Total standard cost of actual production

$$= £560,000 \times \frac{117,600}{112,000}$$

$$= £588,000$$

Alternatively:

|  | Standard cost per meal |
|---|---|
|  | £ |
| Direct material (0.5 kg × £4) | 2.00 |
| Direct labour (0.25 hours × £9) | 2.25 |
| Fixed overheads (0.25 hours × £3) | 0.75 |
|  | 5.00 |

Total standard cost of actual production

$$= 117,600 \text{ meals} \times £5 \text{ per meal}$$

$$= £588,000$$

(b)   Variance calculations:

|  |  | £ |
|---|---|---:|
| (i) | **Direct material price variance** | |
| | 61,740kg should have cost (× £4) | 246,960 |
| | But did cost | 185,220 |
| | | 61,740 (F) |
| (ii) | **Direct material usage variance** | |
| | 117,600 meals should have used (× 0.5 kg) | 58,800 |
| | But did use | 61,740 |
| | Variance in kg | 2,940 |
| | at standard cost (× £4) | × £4 |
| | | 11,760 (A) |
| (iii) | **Direct labour rate variance** | |
| | 27,930 hours should have cost (× £9) | 251,370 |
| | But did cost | 279,300 |
| | | 27,930 (A) |
| (iv) | **Direct labour efficiency variance** | |
| | 117,600 meals should have taken (× 0.25 hrs) | 29,400 |
| | But did take | 27,930 |
| | Variance in hrs | 1,470 |
| | at standard cost (× £9) | × £9 |
| | | 13,230 (F) |
| (v) | **Fixed overhead expenditure variance** | |
| | Budgeted fixed overhead | 84,000 |
| | Actual fixed overhead | 82,000 |
| | | 2,000 (F) |

(vi)     **Fixed overhead volume variance**

|  |  |
|---|---|
| Actual production volume at standard rate<br>(117,600 × 0.25 × £3) | 88,200 |
| Budgeted production volume at standard rate<br>(112,000 × 0.25 × £3) | 84,000 |
|  | 4,200 (F) |

**Tutorial note**. This is a favourable variance because a greater production volume has been achieved than was budgeted for. The two variances below are a further analysis of the volume variance and the sum of the two will therefore equal the volume variance. The capacity variance looks at how the actual production hours differ from the originally budgeted hours. The efficiency variance compares actual with the flexed budget, and is the same type of calculation as the labour efficiency variance.

£

(vii)    **Fixed overhead capacity variance**

|  |  |
|---|---|
| Budgeted hours of work | 28,000 |
| Actual hours of work | 27,930 |
|  | 70 |
| at standard rate | × £3 |
|  | 210 (A) |

(viii)   **Fixed overhead efficiency variance**

|  |  |
|---|---|
| Actual units should take (117,600 × 0.25) | 29,400 |
| But did take | 27,930 |
|  | 1,470 |
| at standard rate (× £3) | × £3 |
|  | 4,410 (F) |

(c)
REPORT

**To:**       Managing Director

**From:**     Accounting Technician

**Subject:**  Reasons for the variances

**Date:**     14 December 20X6

Having investigated the materials and labour variances calculated for November 20X6, I can suggest the following possible causes.

(i)   Direct materials price variance £61,740 (F)

   This variance resulted from the purchase of materials at £3 per kg rather than the standard cost of £4 per kg. This material was cheaper and possibly of a lower quality.

(ii)  Direct material usage variance £11,760 (A)

   The actual usage was worse than expected, and this could have been a consequence of buying inferior material.

(iii) Direct labour rate variance £27,930 (A)

   Direct workers were actually paid at £10 per hour, whilst we had only budgeted for a rate of £9 per hour. It is possible that the workers used were more skilled than we planned for.

(iv)  Direct labour efficiency variance £13,230 (F)

   Actual production required fewer hours than were expected which is consistent with using more highly-skilled staff.

**Tutorial note**. There is more than one possible reason for each of the above variances, and marks would have been awarded for any reasonable suggestions.

........................................................................................

## Task 7

$$\text{Efficiency ratio} = \frac{\text{Standard hours for actual production}}{\text{Actual hours worked}} \times 100$$

$$= \frac{11{,}250 \text{ units} \times 2 \text{ hours per unit}}{30{,}000} \times 100$$

$$= \frac{22{,}500}{30{,}000} \times 100$$

$$= 75.00\%$$

$$\text{Capacity ratio} = \frac{\text{Actual hours worked}}{\text{Budgeted hours}} \times 100$$

$$= \frac{30,000}{12,000\,\text{units} \times 2\,\text{hours}} \times 100$$

$$= \frac{30,000}{24,000} \times 100$$

$$= 125.00\%$$

$$\text{Activity ratio} = \frac{\text{Standard hours for actual production}}{\text{Budgeted hours}} \times 100$$

$$= \frac{11,250\,\text{units} \times 2\,\text{hours}}{12,000\,\text{units} \times 2\,\text{hours}} \times 100$$

$$= \frac{22,500}{24,000} \times 100$$

$$= 93.75\%$$

## Task 8

(a) Breakeven point in units: 4,500 units and breakeven point in sales revenue: £180,000

**Workings**

Contribution per unit = £(40 − 18) = £22

Contribution required to breakeven = fixed costs = £99,000

$$\text{Breakeven point} = \frac{\text{Fixed costs}}{\text{Contribution per unit}}$$

$$= \frac{£99,000}{£22}$$

$$= 4,500\ \text{units}$$

Sales revenue at breakeven point = 4,500 units × £40 per unit

$$= £180,000$$

(b)    Margin of safety = 7.37%

**Workings**

Breakeven point = $\dfrac{£440,000}{£28 - £23}$

= 88,000 units

Margin of safety = $\dfrac{95,000 - 88,000}{95,000}$ × 100 = 7.37%

## Task 9

Target cost  =    Market price – Desired profit margin

=    £25 – (£25 × 30%)

=    £25 – £7.50

=    £17.50

# Task 10

(a)

|  | Scenario 1 | Scenario 2 |
|---|---|---|
| **(i) Gross profit margin** | | |
| = Gross Profit/ Revenue (turnover) × 100 | (4,500/12,500) × 100 = 36.00% | (4,000/14,000) × 100 = 28.57% |
| **(ii) Net profit margin** | | |
| = Net Profit/ Revenue × 100 | (2,150/12,500) × 100 = 17.20% | (1,650/14,000) × 100 = 11.79% |
| **(iii) Direct materials cost per unit** | | |
| = Direct materials cost/Sales units | £3,000,000/10,000 = £300.00 | £4,200,000/14,000 = £300.00 |
| **(iv) Direct labour cost per unit** | | |
| = Direct labour cost/Sales units | £2,000,000/10,000 = £200.00 | £2,800,000/14,000 = £200.00 |
| **(v) Fixed production cost per unit** | | |
| = Fixed production cost/ Sales units | £3,000,000/10,000 = £300.00 | £3,000,000/14,000 = £214.29 |
| **(vi) Gearing** | | |
| = Total debt/(Total debt + Share capital + Reserves) | 12,000/(12,000 + 8,400)= (0.59 or 58.82%) | 11,300/(11,300 + 8,400)= 0.57 or 57.36% |

Alternative answer for gearing:

| Gearing | | |
|---|---|---|
| = Total debt/ (Share capital + Reserves) | 12,000/8,400 = | 11,300/8,400 = |
| | (1.43 or 142.86%) | (1.35 or 134.52%) |
| **(vii) Interest cover** | | |
| = Operating profit /Interest payable | 2,750/600 = 4.58 | 2,250/600 = 3.75 |

(b)                                    REPORT

**To:**    Finance Director  **Subject:** Gross profit margin, gearing and interest cover

**From:**  AAT Trainee        **Date:** 16 June 20X8

(i)   **Gross profit margin**

The gross profit margin for scenario 1 is 36% and scenario 2 is 28.57%. Direct materials and labour are the same under both scenarios so that the higher gross profit margin for scenario 1 must be as a result of differences in sales price per unit or fixed production overheads. In fact the fixed costs per unit are higher under scenario 1 because less volume is produced (£300 per unit as opposed to £214.29 per unit for scenario 2). Therefore the reason for the higher gross margin is the higher price per unit (£1,250 and £1,000 respectively).

(ii)  **Gearing and interest cover**

The level of gearing for both scenarios is at a similar level and there appears to be reasonable security in the form of non-current assets. Everything else being equal, the higher the gearing ratio the higher the risk. This is because long term loans have interest payments that have to be made from operating profit. However, the gearing indicator cannot be considered in isolation. Voltair's ability to service the debt is also important.

The level of interest cover shows how many times Voltair can pay its interest payable out of operating profit. For scenario 1 the profit is 4.58 times greater than interest payable. This falls slightly to 3.75 times for scenario 2 due to the fall in profits, as the interest payable is constant under both scenarios.

Both scenarios have a relatively high interest cover and this does not appear to be a problem for the business.

# BPP PRACTICE ASSESSMENT 3
# MANAGEMENT ACCOUNTING:
# DECISION AND CONTROL

**Time allowed: 2.5 hours**

# Management Accounting Decision & Control: BPP practice assessment 3

## Task 1

A business produces one product which requires the following inputs:

| | |
|---|---|
| Direct materials | 3 kg @ £6.20 per kg |
| Direct labour | 7 hours @ £8.00 per hour |
| Rent/rates | £24,000 per quarter |
| Leased delivery vans | £1,000 for every 900 units of production |
| Warehouse costs | £10,000 per quarter plus £2.00 per unit |

**Complete the table to show the total cost of production and the cost per unit at each of the quarterly production levels.**

| Production level – units | Total cost of production – £ | Cost per unit – £ |
|---|---|---|
| 2,000 | | |
| 3,000 | | |
| 4,000 | | |

## Task 2

(a) A company purchases 14,000 kg of material at a cost of £58,000. The standard cost per kg is £4.

**The total materials price variance is**

| | |
|---|---|
| £14,000 | |
| £2,000 | |
| £58,000 | |
| £4.14 | |

The variance is [ ▼ ]

**Picklist:**

Adverse
Favourable

(b) A company purchases 10,000 kgs of material at a cost of £22,000. The budgeted production was 6,000 units which requires 9,000 kgs of material at a total standard cost of £18,000. The actual production was 6,500 units.

**The material usage variance is**

500 kg

250 kg

£500

£250

The variance is [ ▼ ]

**Picklist:**

Adverse
Favourable

(c) Extracts from Drizzle Co's records from last period are as follows:

| | Budget | Actual |
|---|---|---|
| Production | 1,925 units | 2,070 units |
| Variable production overhead cost | £13,475 | £13,455 |
| Labour hours worked | 3,850 | 2,990 |

**The variable production overhead expenditure variance for the last period is**

£ [ ]

The variance is [ ▼ ]

**Picklist:**

Adverse
Favourable

## Task 3

The budgeted activity and actual results for a business for the month of May 20X8 are as follows:

| | | Budget | | Actual |
|---|---|---|---|---|
| Production (tonnes) | | 200 | | 210 |
| Direct labour | 600 hours | £4,800 | 600 hours | £5,100 |
| Fixed overheads | | £90,000 | | £95,000 |

**Complete the table to calculate the following:**

| | £ |
|---|---|
| Budgeted overhead absorption rate per tonne | |
| Overheads absorbed into actual production | |
| Fixed overhead expenditure variance | |
| Fixed overhead volume variance | |

## Task 4

(a) The standard labour cost for one unit of product Z is £24 (3 hours @ £8 per hour). The budgeted level of production is 14,000 units.

Actual results for the period are:

Production    13,200 units

Labour        18,600 hours costing £111,600

**Prepare a reconciliation of the budgeted labour cost with the actual labour cost using the labour cost variances.**

| | | | |
|---|---|---|---|
| Standard cost of labour for actual production | | | |
| Variances | Favourable | Adverse | |
| Direct labour rate variance | | | |
| Direct labour efficiency variance | | | |
| Total variance | | | |
| Actual cost of labour for actual production | | | |

(b) **Which variances would not be included in an operating statement prepared under a system of marginal costing?**

Fixed overhead efficiency variance and fixed overhead capacity variance ☐

Fixed overhead expenditure variance and fixed overhead volume variance ☐

Fixed overhead expenditure variance and fixed overhead efficiency variance ☐

Fixed overhead expenditure variance and fixed overhead capacity variance ☐

(c)   The standard material content of one unit of product A is 25kgs of material X which should cost £10 per kilogram. In March 20X4, 6,250 units of product A were produced and there was an adverse material usage variance of £7,500.

**The quantity of material X used in March 20X4 is** [            ] **kg**

## Task 5

A material which is derived from soft fruit is either imported or purchased from UK farmers by a company. The price of the material fluctuates month by month depending on the time of year. The cost information for the four months ending August 20X6 is given below.

|  | May X6 | June X6 | July X6 | August X6 |
|---|---|---|---|---|
| Cost per 1,000 kg | £1,000 | £900 | £700 | £800 |

The underlying cost does not change during the period May to August. The change in cost over the four months is due only to the seasonal variations which are given below.

|  | May X6 | June X6 | July X6 | August X6 |
|---|---|---|---|---|
| Seasonal variations | £200 | £100 | −£100 | £0 |

(a)   **Complete the table to calculate the underlying cost per 1,000 kilograms for the period May to August 20X6.**

|  | May 20X6 £ | June 20X6 £ | July 20X6 £ | Aug 20X6 £ |
|---|---|---|---|---|
| Cost per 1,000 kg |  |  |  |  |
| Seasonal variation |  |  |  |  |
| Trend |  |  |  |  |

(b)   Indications are that the underlying cost per 1,000 kilograms for the period May 20X7 to August 20X7 will be £850.

**The percentage increase in the underlying cost from 20X6 to 20X7 is** [            ] **%**

(c)   **Complete the table to calculate the forecast cost per 1,000 kilograms for the period May 20X7 to August 20X7 using the underlying cost and the seasonal variations given above.**

|  | May 20X7 | June 20X7 | July 20X7 | Aug 20X7 |
|---|---|---|---|---|
|  | £ | £ | £ | £ |
| Trend |  |  |  |  |
| Seasonal variation |  |  |  |  |
| Cost per 1,000 kg |  |  |  |  |

## Task 6

Given below is the operating statement for a manufacturing business for the last month:

### Reconciliation of standard cost of actual production to actual cost – March 20X9

|  | Variances | | |
|---|---|---|---|
|  | Favourable | Adverse |  |
|  | £ | £ | £ |
| Standard cost of actual production |  |  | 672,500 |
| **Variances:** |  |  |  |
| Materials price |  | 24,300 |  |
| Materials usage | 6,780 |  |  |
| Labour rate |  | 10,600 |  |
| Labour efficiency | 10,300 |  |  |
| Fixed overhead expenditure | 7,490 |  |  |
| Fixed overhead capacity | 4,800 |  |  |
| Fixed overhead efficiency | 6,100 |  |  |
|  | 35,470 | 34,900 | (570) |
| Actual cost of production |  |  | 671,930 |

A number of factors about the month's production have been discovered:

- At the end of the previous month a new warehouse had been purchased which has meant a saving in warehouse rental.

- Six new machines were installed at the start of the month which are more power efficient than the old machines, but also more expensive, causing a larger depreciation charge.

- There was an unexpected increase in the materials price during the month and when other suppliers were contacted it was found that they were all charging approximately the same price for the materials.

- A higher than normal skilled grade of labour was used during the month due to staff shortages. The production process is a skilled process and the benefit has been that these employees, although more expensive, have produced the goods faster and with less wastage. This particular group of employees are also keen to work overtime and, as the business wishes to build up inventory levels, advantage of this has been taken.

**Prepare a report for the production director.**

Your report should do the following:

(a)    Suggest what effect the combination of the factors given above might have had on the reported variances.

(b)    Make suggestions as to any action that should be taken in light of these factors.

**REPORT**

**To:**        Production Director

**From:**    Management Accountant

**Date:**     xx/xx/xx

**Subject:**  March 20X9 variances

**New warehouse**

**New machines**

**Price increase**

**Skilled labour**

# Task 7

Given below are the production figures for a factory for the last four months.

| | November | December | January | February |
|---|---|---|---|---|
| Output in units | 64,300 | 68,900 | 62,100 | 60,200 |
| Budgeted output | 65,000 | 65,000 | 60,000 | 62,000 |
| Hours worked | 98,200 | 107,300 | 90,200 | 92,000 |

The standard time for each unit of production is 1.5 hours.

**Complete the table to calculate the following performance indicators for each of the four months. Give your answer to ONE decimal place.**

| | November | December | January | February |
|---|---|---|---|---|
| Actual hours per unit | | | | |
| Efficiency ratio | | | | |
| Capacity ratio | | | | |
| Activity ratio | | | | |

.........................................................................................

# Task 8

Voltair Ltd has developed a domestic wind turbine. A colleague has prepared forecast information based upon two scenarios. The forecast statement of profit or loss (income statement) for both scenarios is shown below.

- Scenario 1 is to set the price at £1,250 per unit with sales of 10,000 units each year.
- Scenario 2 is to set the price at £1,000 per unit with sales of 14,000 units each year.

| Forecast statement or profit or loss (income statement) | | |
|---|---|---|
| | Scenario 1 | Scenario 2 |
| | £'000 | £'000 |
| Revenue (turnover) | 12,500 | 14,000 |
| Cost of production | | |
| Direct (raw) materials | 3,000 | 4,200 |
| Direct labour | 2,000 | 2,800 |
| Fixed production overheads | 3,000 | 3,000 |
| Cost of sales | 8,000 | 10,000 |

| Forecast statement or profit or loss (income statement) | | |
|---|---|---|
| | Scenario 1 | Scenario 2 |
| Gross profit | 4,500 | 4,000 |
| Selling and distribution costs | 1,000 | 1,000 |
| Administration costs | 750 | 750 |
| Operating profit | 2,750 | 2,250 |
| Interest payable | 600 | 600 |
| Net profit | 2,150 | 1,650 |

The Managing Director has been in talks with a Romanian manufacturer who could produce the wind turbines. You have been asked to analyse the information in order to evaluate whether Voltair should contract out the manufacture of the turbines.

If the turbines are manufactured in Romania the costs and savings would be as follows:

- The cost of each turbine would be £650 including transport costs to the UK.

- The material and labour costs would be saved.

- The fixed production costs consist of £1.95 million of specific costs which would be avoided, and £1.05 million of allocated overheads which would not be avoided.

(a) **Complete the table to calculate the following information for the demand level of 10,000 turbines per annum.**

| | £ |
|---|---|
| Full production cost per turbine manufactured by Voltair | |
| Voltair's unavoidable fixed production cost per turbine if contracted out | |
| Voltair's avoidable production cost per turbine if contracted out | |

(b) **Complete the table to calculate the following information for the demand level of 14,000 turbines per annum.**

| | £ |
|---|---|
| Full production cost per turbine manufactured by Voltair | |
| Voltair's unavoidable fixed production cost per turbine if contracted out | |
| Voltair's avoidable production cost per turbine if contracted out | |

## Task 9

A company is reviewing various alternatives to determine whether it is possible to reduce monthly costs. The operations director is considering whether to invest in a new machine which:

- Could either be purchased for £3 million or rented for £50,000 per month
- Is expected to have a life of 10 years and a scrap value of £900,000

It is assumed under both options that:

- The maintenance cost of the machine is £50,000 per annum
- Decommissioning costs will be £100,000
- The machine will be used for 10 years

**Calculate the lifecycle cost of the TWO options outlined**

Ignore the time value of money and any opportunity costs when calculating the lifecycle cost.

........................................................................................

## Task 10

A division of Fooddrink Ltd is developing a new supplement and a colleague has prepared forecast information based upon two scenarios. The forecast statements of profit or loss (income statements), statements of financial position and performance ratios for both scenarios are shown below.

- Scenario 1 is to set the price at £10 per unit with sales of 120,000 units each year.
- Scenario 2 is to set the price at £5 per unit with sales of 360,000 units each year.

| | Scenario 1 | Scenario 2 |
|---|---|---|
| | **£000** | **£000** |
| **Budgeted statement of profit or loss (income statement)** | | |
| Revenue | 1,200 | 1,800 |
| Cost of production | | |
| Direct (raw) materials | 300 | 900 |
| Direct labour | 120 | 360 |
| Fixed production overheads | 360 | 360 |
| Total cost of sales | 780 | 1,620 |
| **Gross profit** | **420** | **180** |
| Selling and distribution costs | 74 | 122 |
| Administration costs | 100 | 100 |
| **Operating profit** | **246** | **(42)** |
| | | |

| | Scenario 1 | Scenario 2 |
|---|---|---|
| **Budgeted statement of financial position** | | |
| **Non-current assets** | | |
| Machinery | 1,600 | 1,600 |
| **Current assets** | | |
| Inventory of raw materials | 50 | 50 |
| Receivables | 150 | 150 |
| **Current liabilities** | | |
| Payables | 75 | 75 |
| | | |
| **Net current assets** | 125 | 125 |
| | | |
| Long-term loans | 754 | 1,042 |
| | | |
| **Net assets** | 971 | 683 |
| | | |
| Represented by: | | |
| Share capital | 725 | 725 |
| Operating profit for the year | 246 | (42) |
| **Share capital and reserves** | 971 | 683 |
| | Scenario 1 | Scenario 2 |
| **Performance ratios** | | |
| Gross profit margin | 35.00% | 10.00% |
| Operating profit margin | 20.50% | −2.33% (0%) |
| Direct materials as a percentage of revenue | 25.00% | 50.00% |
| Direct materials cost per unit | £2.50 | £2.50 |
| Return on net assets | 25.33% | −6.15% (0%) |

(a) **Draft a report for the finance director giving an explanation of why the following ratios have changed:**

   (i)   Gross profit margin
   (ii)  Operating profit margin
   (iii) Direct materials as a percentage of revenue

**To:**         Finance Director

**Subject:**   Differences in key performance indicators

**From:**     Accounting Technician

**Date:**      18 June 20X7

**Gross profit margin**

**Operating profit margin**

**Direct materials**

You have found that your colleague has made a few mistakes with the figures for Scenario 2. The impact on gross profit, operating profit and net assets for Scenario 2 is shown below.

- Recalculated gross profit = £540,000
- Recalculated operating profit = £318,000
- Recalculated net assets = £1,043,000

(b) **Recalculate the following ratios. Give your answers to TWO decimal places:**

    (i)    Gross profit margin
    (ii)   Operating profit margin
    (iii)  Return on net assets

(c) **Redraft your report for the finance director commenting on the ratios you recalculated in (b) above and recommend whether the price of the product should be set at £10 or £5.**

    **To:**         Financial Director

    **Subject:**    Differences in key performance indicators

    **From:**     Accounting Technician

    **Date:**      18 June 20X7

    **Gross profit margin**

**Operating profit margin**

**Return on net assets**

**Recommendations**

........................................................................................................

# BPP PRACTICE ASSESSMENT 3
# MANAGEMENT ACCOUNTING:
# DECISION AND CONTROL

## ANSWERS

# Management Accounting Decision & Control:
# BPP practice assessment 3

## Task 1

| Production level – units | Total cost of production – £ | Cost per unit – £ |
|---|---|---|
| 2,000 | 190,200 | 95.10 |
| 3,000 | 267,800 | 89.27 |
| 4,000 | 345,400 | 86.35 |

### Workings

| | 2,000 units £ | 3,000 units £ | 4,000 units £ |
|---|---|---|---|
| Direct materials 3kg × £6.20 × units | 37,200 | 55,800 | 74,400 |
| Direct labour 7 hours × £8.00 × units | 112,000 | 168,000 | 224,000 |
| Rent/rates | 24,000 | 24,000 | 24,000 |
| Leased delivery vans | 3,000 | 4,000 | 5,000 |
| Warehouse costs £10,000 + £2.00 × units | 14,000 | 16,000 | 18,000 |
| | 190,200 | 267,800 | 345,400 |
| Cost per unit | £95.10 | £89.27 | £86.35 |

## Task 2

(a) £2,000 Adverse

| | £ |
|---|---|
| 14,000 kg should have cost (× £4) | 56,000 |
| But did cost | 58,000 |
| Total materials price variance | 2,000 A |

(b) £500 Adverse

| | |
|---|---|
| 6,500 units should have used × 1.5 kgs | 9,750 kg |
| But did use | 10,000 kg |
| | 250 kg |
| @ standard rate per kg £2 | × £2 |
| Materials usage variance | £500 A |

(c)  £2,990 Adverse

Standard variable production overhead cost per hour = £13,475/3850 = £3.50

|  | £ |
|---|---|
| 2,990 hours of variable production overhead should cost (× £3.50) | 10,465 |
| But did cost | 13,455 |
| Variable production overhead expenditure variance | 2,990  A |

## Task 3

| Budgeted overhead absorption rate per tonne | £450 |
|---|---|
| Overheads absorbed into actual production | £94,500 |
| Fixed overhead expenditure variance | £5,000 Adverse |
| Fixed overhead volume variance | £4,500 Favourable |

### Workings

| Budgeted overhead absorption rate per tonne | = Fixed overheads/Budgeted output |
|---|---|
|  | = £90,000/200 tonnes |
|  | = £450 |
| Overheads absorbed into actual production | = Actual production × Absorption rate |
|  | = 210 units × £450 |
|  | = £94,500 |

Fixed overhead expenditure variance

|  | £ |
|---|---|
| Budgeted fixed overhead | 90,000 |
| Actual fixed overhead | 95,000 |
| Fixed overhead expenditure variance | 5,000 Adv |

Fixed overhead volume variance

|  | £ |
|---|---|
| Actual production at absorption rate per unit (210 × £450) | 94,500 |
| Budgeted production at absorption rate per unit | 90,000 |
| Fixed overhead volume variance | 4,500 Fav |

## Task 4

(a)

| Standard cost of labour for actual production | | | £316,800 |
|---|---|---|---|
| Variances | Favourable | Adverse | |
| Direct labour rate variance | £37,200 | | |
| Direct labour efficiency variance | £168,000 | | |
| Total variance | | | £(205,200) |
| Actual cost of labour for actual production | | | £111,600 |

**Workings**

Standard cost for actual units produced = 13,200 units × 3hrs × £8 = £316,800

| Labour rate variance | £ |
|---|---|
| 18,600 hrs should have cost (× £8) | 148,800 |
| But did cost | 111,600 |
| Rate variance | 37,200 (F) |

| Labour efficiency variance | |
|---|---|
| 13,200 units should have taken (× 3 hours) | 39,600 hrs |
| But did take | 18,600 hrs |
| | 21,000 (F) |
| At standard cost | × £8 |
| Usage variance | 168,000 (F) |

(b) The correct answer is: Fixed overhead efficiency variance and fixed overhead capacity variance.

Neither fixed overhead efficiency variance nor fixed overhead capacity variance (which together make up the fixed overhead volume variance) exist in a marginal costing system.

(c) The quantity used is 157,000kg.

**Workings**

| | |
|---|---|
| Standard material cost of actual production | £1,562,500 |
| 6,250 × 25kgs × £10 | |
| Usage variance (adverse) | £7,500 |
| So actual material used actually cost (at standard price per kg) | £1,570,000 |
| ÷ standard price per kg | ÷ £10 |
| Actual material used | 157,000 kg |

## Task 5

(a)

| | May 20X6 | June 20X6 | July 20X6 | Aug 20X6 |
|---|---|---|---|---|
| | £ | £ | £ | £ |
| Cost per 1,000 kgs | 1,000 | 900 | 700 | 800 |
| Seasonal variation | 200 | 100 | (100) | 0 |
| Trend | 800 | 800 | 800 | 800 |

**Tutorial note.** The underlying cost is the Trend.

(b) The percentage increase in the underlying cost from 20X6 to 20X7 is 6.25%

$$\left(\frac{(850-800)}{800}\right) \times 100 = 6.25\%$$

**Tutorial note.** The above calculation is the most normal way of calculating a change from one period to the next, as a percentage of the original figure.

(c)

| | May 20X7 | June 20X7 | July 20X7 | Aug 20X7 |
|---|---|---|---|---|
| | £ | £ | £ | £ |
| Trend | 850 | 850 | 850 | 850 |
| Seasonal variation | 200 | 100 | (100) | 0 |
| Cost per 1,000 kgs | 1,050 | 950 | 750 | 850 |

# Task 6

**REPORT**

**To:** Production Director

**From:** Management Accountant

**Date:** xx/xx/xx

**Subject:** March 20X9 variances

## New warehouse

This will have the effect of simply reducing the fixed overhead expense (assuming the rent saved exceeds any new depreciation charge) and therefore is part of the favourable fixed overhead expenditure variance. The standard fixed overhead cost should be adjusted to reflect the rental saving.

## New machines

The new machines use less power than the old ones therefore reducing the power costs element of the fixed overhead. The additional depreciation charge however will increase the fixed overhead expense. Once the reduction in power costs and increase in depreciation charge are known then the standard fixed overhead should be adjusted.

## Price increase

The price increase will be a cause of the adverse materials price variance. The price increase appears to be a permanent one as all suppliers have increased their prices, so the standard materials cost should be altered.

## Skilled labour

The use of the higher skilled labour will have been part of the cause of the favourable labour efficiency variance and the favourable materials usage variance. If the fixed overheads are absorbed on a labour hour basis then the efficiency of the skilled labour will also be a cause of the favourable fixed overhead efficiency variance. The additional expense of the skilled labour and the overtime that has been worked will have been causes of the adverse labour rate variance. The overtime may also have led to the favourable capacity variance as actual hours exceeded the budgeted hours. Unless the use of this grade of labour is likely to be a permanent policy, then there should be no change to the standard labour rate or hours.

BPP LEARNING MEDIA

## Task 7

|  | November | December | January | February |
|---|---|---|---|---|
| Actual hours per unit | 1.5 hours | 1.6 hours | 1. 5 hours | 1.5 hours |
| Efficiency ratio | 98.2% | 96.3% | 103.3% | 98.2% |
| Capacity ratio | 100.7% | 110.1% | 100.2% | 98.9% |
| Activity ratio | 98.9% | 106.0% | 103.5% | 97.1% |

| Workings | | November | December | January | February |
|---|---|---|---|---|---|
| (i) | | $\dfrac{98,200}{64,300}$ | $\dfrac{107,300}{68,900}$ | $\dfrac{90,200}{62,100}$ | $\dfrac{92,000}{60,200}$ |
| | Actual hours per unit | 1.53 hours per unit | 1.56 hours per unit | 1.45 hours per unit | 1.53 hours per unit |
| (ii) | | $\dfrac{64,300 \times 1.5}{98,200}$ | $\dfrac{68,900 \times 1.5}{107,300}$ | $\dfrac{62,100 \times 1.5}{90,200}$ | $\dfrac{60,200 \times 1.5}{92,000}$ |
| | Efficiency ratio | 98.2% | 96.3% | 103.3% | 98.2% |
| (iii) | | $\dfrac{98,200}{65,000 \times 1.5}$ | $\dfrac{107,300}{65,000 \times 1.5}$ | $\dfrac{90,200}{60,000 \times 1.5}$ | $\dfrac{92,000}{62,000 \times 1.5}$ |
| | Capacity ratio | 100.7% | 110.1% | 100.2% | 98.9% |
| (iv) | | $\dfrac{64,300}{65,000}$ | $\dfrac{68,900}{65,000}$ | $\dfrac{62,100}{60,000}$ | $\dfrac{60,200}{62,000}$ |
| | Activity ratio | 98.9% | 106.0% | 103.5% | 97.1% |

# Task 8

(a)

| Full production cost per turbine manufactured by Voltair | £800.00 |
|---|---|
| Voltair's unavoidable fixed production cost per turbine if contracted out | £105.00 |
| Voltair's avoidable production cost per turbine if contracted out | £695.00 |

(b)

| Full production cost per turbine manufactured by Voltair | £714.29 |
|---|---|
| Voltiar's unavoidable fixed production cost per turbine if contracted out | £75.00 |
| Voltaire's avoidable production cost per turbine if contracted out | £639.29 |

## Workings

(a) (i)  Full production cost per turbine based upon production of 10,000 turbines = £8,000,000

   Therefore cost per turbine = £8,000,000 / 10,000 = £800.00

 (ii)  Unavoidable fixed production cost = £3,000,000 − £1,950,000 = £1,050,000

   Therefore unavoidable fixed production cost per turbine for 10,000 units = £1,050,000 / 10,000 = £105.00

 (iii)  Avoidable production cost per turbine for 10,000 units = £800 − £105 = £695.00

(b) (i)  Full production cost per turbine based upon production of 14,000 turbines = £10,000,000

   Therefore cost per turbine = £10,000,000 / 14,000 = £714.29

 (ii)  Unavoidable fixed production cost = £3,000,000 − £1,950,000 = £1,050,000

   Therefore unavoidable fixed production cost per turbine for 14,000 units = £1,050,000 / 14,000 = £75.00

 (iii)  Avoidable production cost per turbine for 14000 units = £714.29 − £75.00 = £639.29

# Task 9

**Lifecycle costs of renting the machine:**

|  | £ |
|---|---:|
| Rental (£50,000 × 12 months × 10 years) | 6,000,000 |
| Maintenance (£50,000 × 10 years) | 500,000 |
| Decommissioning | 100,000 |
| Total | 6,600,000 |

**Lifecycle costs of buying the machine:**

|  | £ |
|---|---:|
| Purchase | 3,000,000 |
| Maintenance (£50,000 × 10 years) | 500,000 |
| Decommissioning | 100,000 |
| Scrap value | (900,000) |
| Total | 2,700,000 |

# Task 10

(a) **To:**         Finance Director

**Subject:**    Differences in key performance indicators

**From:**       Accounting Technician

**Date:**       18 June 20X7

(i) **Gross profit margin**

The gross profit margin for scenario 1 is 35% but falls to 10% for scenario 2. There are two causes for this difference. The selling price has been reduced by 50% (from £10 to £5) which will have reduced the margin. The reduction in the selling price has, however, increased the volume produced and sold which has reduced the fixed overhead per unit which will have increased the margin. However, the effect of the decreased selling price in reducing the margin has outweighed the beneficial effect of the fixed overheads.

(ii) **Operating profit margin**

The operating profit margin for scenario 1 is 20.5% and this falls to a loss under scenario 2. The reduction in gross profit margin has fed down to the operating profit margin and the selling and distribution costs have increased due to the higher sales volume.

(iii) **Direct materials**

The direct materials cost as a percentage of turnover has increased from 25% under scenario 1 to 50% under scenario 2. This difference is caused by the 50% reduction in the selling price. Every unit that is sold under the two scenarios has the same direct material cost (£2.50) but the selling price in scenario 2 is only £5 giving a percentage material cost of 50%, whereas the selling price in scenario 1 is £10 giving a percentage material cost of 25%.

(b)

|  | % |
|---|---|
| Gross profit margin £ $\left(\dfrac{540,000}{1,800,000}\right) \times 100$ | 30.00 |
| Operating profit margin £ $\left(\dfrac{318,000}{1,800,000}\right) \times 100$ | 17.67 |
| Return on net assets £ $\left(\dfrac{318,000}{1,043,000}\right) \times 100$ | 30.49 |

(c) **To:**       Financial Director

**Subject:**   Differences in key performance indicators

**From:**     Accounting Technician

**Date:**     18 June 20X7

(i) **Gross profit margin**

The revised gross profit has increased to 30%. The increase in the gross profit is caused by the reduction in the cost of raw materials per unit.

However, although the reduction in cost per unit increases the gross profit of scenario 2, it is still below the gross profit of scenario 1 because the effect of scenario 2's lower selling price outweighs the advantages of its lower raw materials and fixed cost absorption rate.

(ii) **Operating profit margin**

The revised operating profit for scenario 2 has increased to £318,000 from a loss. The operating profit margin is now improved to 18% which is fed through from the gross margin but this is still less than the 20.5% for scenario 1.

(iii) **Return on net assets**

The revised return on net assets for scenario 2 is 30.5% compared to 25% for scenario 1. The operating profit and net assets have been recalculated, thus giving us a revised figure of 30.5% for scenario 2. The return on net assets has increased by 5.5% due to an increase in operating profit. However, the net assets only increase by a modest amount in scenario 2, which suggests a more efficient use of resources than in scenario 1.

### Recommendations

Based purely on the above three indicators, the decision should be to set the price at £5 as per scenario 2 because the higher return on net assets indicates that the return on investment is (pound for pound) better in scenario 2 and therefore will increase shareholder value. The fact that scenario 1 still has better gross and operating margins is not decisive. These margins do indicate that there are better operating efficiencies in scenario 1 compared to scenario 2. However, the fact that the revised figures for scenario 2 show that it has a significantly larger operating profit than scenario 1 with net assets for the two scenarios being almost the same causes the return on investment in scenario 2 to be better.

# BPP PRACTICE ASSESSMENT 4
# MANAGEMENT ACCOUNTING:
# DECISION AND CONTROL

**Time allowed: 2.5 hours**

# Management Accounting Decision & Control: BPP practice assessment 4

## Task 1

The following information has been calculated for one unit of product, Plate.

Each unit requires 2 litres of material at a cost of £3.50 per litre.

Each unit requires 0.5 hours of grade A labour at £15 per hour, and 0.25 hours of grade B labour at £10 per hour.

Fixed production overheads are £100,000 and budgeted output is 20,000 units.

**Complete the standard cost card:**

| Standard cost card for per unit of Plate | |
|---|---|
| | £ |
| Direct materials | |
| Direct labour – grade A | |
| Direct labour – grade B | |
| Fixed overhead | |
| Total standard cost per unit | |

........................................................................................

## Task 2

The standard direct materials cost for a business's product is:

3 kg @ £15 per kg = £45.00

During the last month production was 2,600 units of the product and the actual materials cost was £149,910 for 7,890 kg. The market price of the materials unexpectedly increased by 20% for the whole month.

**Complete the following sentences:**

The total materials price variance is £ [            ] adverse/favourable.

The non-controllable element of the materials price variance that has been caused by the price increase is £ [            ] adverse/favourable.

The controllable element of the materials price variance caused by other factors is

£ [            ] adverse/favourable.

........................................................................................

## Task 3

A business makes one product. Fixed overheads are absorbed on the basis of machine hours. The standard cost card shows that fixed overheads are to be absorbed on the basis of 3 machine hours per unit at a rate of £6 per hour. The budgeted level of production is 10,000 units.

The actual results for the period were that fixed overheads were £192,000, actual machine hours were 29,000 and the actual units produced were 9,500.

(a) **The fixed overhead expenditure variance is:**

£12,000 Favourable

£12,000 Adverse

£18,000 Adverse

£21,000 Adverse

(b) **The fixed overhead volume variance is:**

£9,000 Adverse

£9,000 Favourable

£6,000 Adverse

£3,000 Adverse

(c) **The fixed overhead efficiency variance is:**

£3,000 Adverse

£6,000 Adverse

£6,000 Favourable

£9,000 Favourable

(d) **The fixed overhead capacity variance is:**

£3,000 Adverse

£6,000 Adverse

£6,000 Favourable

£21,000 Adverse

## Task 4

The following budgetary control report has been provided

|  | Budget |  | Actual |  |
|---|---|---|---|---|
| Units | 1,100 |  | 1,240 |  |
| Material | 5,280 litres | £14,784 | 5,800 litres | £17,100 |
| Labour | 2,750 hours | £23,375 | 3,280 hours | £27,060 |
| Fixed overheads |  | £4,400 |  | £4,650 |
| Total cost |  | £42,559 |  | £48,810 |

The following variances have been calculated:

| Fixed overhead expenditure | £250 |
|---|---|
| Direct materials price | £860 A |
| Direct materials usage | £426 |
| Direct labour rate | £820 |
| Direct labour efficiency | £1,530 A |
| Fixed overhead volume | £560 F |

### Complete the operating statement:

|  | £ | £ | £ |
|---|---|---|---|
| **Budgeted/Standard cost for actual production** |  |  |  |
| **Variances** | **Favourable** | **Adverse** |  |
| Direct materials price |  |  |  |
| Direct materials usage |  |  |  |
| Direct labour rate |  |  |  |
| Direct labour efficiency |  |  |  |
| Fixed overhead expenditure |  |  |  |
| Fixed overhead volume |  |  |  |
| Total variance |  |  |  |
| Actual cost of actual production |  |  |  |

## Task 5

A company has the following historic information about the cost of material.

|  | May 20X9 | June 20X9 | July 20X9 |
| --- | --- | --- | --- |
|  | £ | £ | £ |
| Total cost | £50,000 | £52,000 | £55,000 |
| Total quantity purchased | 5,000 kg | 5,100 kg | 5,300 kg |

(a)  **The cost index for July 20X9 based on May 20X9 being the base period of 100 is:**

100

90.9

103.8

96.3

(b)  In August 20X9, the cost index is 110 (where May 20X9 is the base period of 100).

**If the total cost is £60,500, the number of kg purchased is:**

6,050 kg

6,655 kg

5,500 kg

5,600 kg

## Task 6

Rix Limited manufactures one standard product. Rix Limited operates a standard costing system.

Data from the budget and the standard product cost for the last month are given below.

1    Budgeted and standard cost data:

Budgeted sales and production for the month 10,500 units

Standard cost for each unit of product:

| Direct material: | A | 4 kilograms @ £2.50 per kilogram |
| --- | --- | --- |
|  | B | 6 kilograms @ £1 per kilogram |
| Labour: |  | 0.5 hours @ £16 per hour |

Fixed production overhead is absorbed @ 300% of direct wages.

2    Actual data for last month:

Production and sales were 11,000 units sold at standard price.

Direct materials consumed:

A 45,000 kilograms, costing £108,000

B 62,000 kilograms, costing £68,200

Direct wages incurred 5,250 hours and cost £94,500.

Fixed production overhead incurred £250,000.

**Prepare a report to the finance director, which includes an operating statement reconciling the standard absorption cost of actual production to actual costs for last months, and explain what the fixed overhead variances reveal about last month's production, and the success of the manager responsible for overhead costs.**

### Report

**To:** A Finance Director

**From:** An Accountant

**Date:** 14 April 20X2

**Subject:** Last month's variances

I enclose (in the appendix) an operating statement reconciling the standard cost of actual production last month to the actual cost.

### Fixed overhead variances

## Appendix

| Reconciliation statement – previous month | | | |
|---|---|---|---|
| | £ | £ | £ |
| **Standard absorption cost of actual production** | | | |
| | (F) | (A) | |
| **Variances** | | | |
| Material A price | | | |
| Material A usage | | | |
| Material B price | | | |
| Material B usage | | | |
| Labour rate | | | |
| Labour efficiency | | | |
| Fixed overhead expenditure | | | |
| Fixed overhead efficiency | | | |
| Fixed overhead capacity | | | |
| | | | |
| **Actual absorption cost of actual production** | | | |

## Task 7

Given below are production and sales figures for a manufacturing organisation for the last three months:

|  | January | February | March |
| --- | --- | --- | --- |
| Production costs | £552,300 | £568,500 | £629,500 |
| Production wages | £104,800 | £98,300 | £110,800 |
| Output in units | 8,540 | 8,670 | 9,320 |
| Hours worked | 8,635 | 7,820 | 9,280 |
| Budgeted output | 8,500 | 8,200 | 9,500 |
| Sales revenue | £916,000 | £923,000 | £965,000 |
| Number of employees | 55 | 55 | 58 |

Production costs are made up of the materials for production and the bought in services required in the month. It is estimated that each unit takes 1.1 hours to produce.

**Complete the table to calculate the performance indicators for each of the last three months. Give your answers to the TWO decimal places:**

|  | January | February | March |
| --- | --- | --- | --- |
| Productivity per labour hour |  |  |  |
| Efficiency ratio |  |  |  |
| Capacity ratio |  |  |  |
| Activity ratio |  |  |  |
| Value added per employee |  |  |  |

....................................................................................................

## Task 8

A company makes three products with the following standard cost information, and predicted maximum sales demand.

The material available in the coming period is 8,000 kg

The labour hours available in the coming period are 2,000 hours.

|  | Product | | |
|---|---|---|---|
|  | A | B | C |
| Direct materials @ £3 per kg | £9 | £6 | £12 |
| Direct labour @ £12 per hour | £6 | £12 | £18 |
| Selling price | £20 | £30 | £40 |
| Maximum sales demand | 1,000 units | 800 units | 600 units |

**Complete the table to determine the production plan which will maximise contribution.**

| Product | Units |
|---|---|
|  |  |
|  |  |
|  |  |

## Task 9

(a)   The costs of the maintenance department of a manufacturing business are estimated to be £102,000 for the following quarter. During that period it is estimated that there will be 50 maintenance visits on site. Product X will require 10 maintenance visits during the quarter and Product Y 40 maintenance visits.

**Complete the table below using activity based costing to show how much maintenance overhead will be absorbed into Product X and Product Y.**

|  | £ |
|---|---|
| Overhead included in Product X |  |
| Overhead included in Product Y |  |

(b)   A manufacturer, operating in a competitive market, can sell its product at £35 per unit. It wishes to make a profit margin of 40%. Each unit of product requires 1 hour of labour at £6/hour and incurs other overheads at a rate of £7/labour hour. The product requires 4kg of material per unit.

**What is the maximum that the manufacturer can afford to pay for each kg of material?**

**Maximum £ per kg** [              ]

## Task 10

A company makes and sells a single product. The forecast statement of profit or loss (income statement) and statement of financial position are shown below.

The forecast is based on an assumed sales price of £8 per unit, and anticipated demand of 500,000 units.

| | £000 |
|---|---|
| **Budgeted statement of profit or loss (income statement)** | |
| Revenue | 4,000 |
| Cost of production | |
| Direct materials | 1,500 |
| Direct labour | 500 |
| Fixed production overheads | 800 |
| Total cost of sales | 2,800 |
| **Gross profit** | **1,200** |
| Fixed selling and distribution costs | 85 |
| Fixed administration costs | 210 |
| **Operating profit** | **905** |
| | |
| **Budgeted statement of financial position** | |
| **Non-current assets** | |
| Machinery | 1,600 |
| **Current assets** | |
| Inventory of raw materials | 280 |
| Receivables | 800 |
| **Current liabilities** | |
| Payables | (150) |
| | |
| **Net current assets** | **930** |
| | |
| Long-term loans | 500 |
| | |
| **Net assets** | **2,030** |
| | |
| Represented by: | |
| Share capital and reserves | 2,030 |
| **Net assets** | **2,030** |

### Draft a report to the finance director which

(a) Includes calculations of the performance indicators listed below. Give your answers to the nearest whole number.

  (i)   Gross profit margin
  (ii)  Operating profit margin
  (iii) Direct materials cost per unit
  (iv)  Receivables' collection period in days

(b) Advises on the following scenarios:

    (i)    The gross profit margin for the industry is 35%. Advise the finance director, what the selling price would have to be if demand and costs stay the same, in order to achieve this margin.

    (ii)   The operating profit margin for the industry is 25%. If it is not possible to change the selling price, demand or most costs, but it may be possible to reduce fixed administration costs, what would the percentage reduction in fixed administration costs have to be, in order to achieve a gross profit margin of 25%?

    (iii)  The average receivables' payment period in the industry is 65 days. If sales are unchanged, advise the finance director by how much (in £) the year-end receivables would have to change, to achieve the industry average payment period.

**To:**        Finance Director

**Subject:**   Key performance indicators

**From:**      Accounting Technician

**Date:**      26 October 20X2

**Gross profit margin – selling price to achieve industry margin**




**Operating profit margin – percentage reduction in administration costs**




**Receivables' collection period – change to achieve industry average**

## Appendix

| | £ |
|---|---|
| Gross profit margin | |
| Operating profit margin | |
| Direct materials cost per unit | |
| Receivables' collection period in days | |

# BPP PRACTICE ASSESSMENT 4
# MANAGEMENT ACCOUNTING:
# DECISION AND CONTROL

ANSWERS

# Management Accounting Decision & Control: BPP practice assessment 4

## Task 1

| Standard cost card for per unit of Plate | |
| --- | --- |
| | £ |
| Direct materials (2 × £3.50) | 7.00 |
| Direct labour – grade A (0.5 × £15) | 7.50 |
| Direct labour – grade B (0.25 × £10) | 2.50 |
| Fixed overhead (£100,000/20,000) | 5.00 |
| Total standard cost per unit | 22.00 |

## Task 2

The total materials price variance is £31,560 Adverse.

The non-controllable element of the materials price variance that has been caused by the price increase is £23,670 Adverse.

The controllable element of the materials price variance caused by other factors is £7,890 Adverse.

**Workings**

Total materials price variance

| | £ |
| --- | --- |
| 7,890 should have cost (× £15) | 118,350 |
| But did cost | 149,910 |
| | 31,560 (A) |

Non-controllable variance caused by price increase

| | £ |
| --- | --- |
| Standard cost for actual quantity 7,890 × £15 | 118,350 |
| Adjusted cost for actual quantity 7,890 × £18* | 142,020 |
| | 23,670 (A) |

*Adjusted price is 120% of £15 = £18

Controllable variance caused by other factors

|  | £ |
|---|---|
| Adjusted cost for actual quantity 7,890 × £18 | 142,020 |
| Actual cost | 149,910 |
|  | 7,890 (A) |

## Task 3

(a)  £12,000 Adverse
(b)  £9,000 Adverse
(c)  £3,000 Adverse
(d)  £6,000 Adverse

**Workings**

Fixed overhead expenditure variance

|  | £ |
|---|---|
| Budgeted fixed overhead 10,000 units × 3 hours × £6 | 180,000 |
| Actual fixed overhead | 192,000 |
| Expenditure variance | 12,000 (A) |

Fixed overhead volume variance

|  | £ |
|---|---|
| Standard hours for actual production @ standard OAR 9,500 units × 3 hours × £6 | 171,000 |
| Standard hours for budgeted production @ standard OAR 10,000 units × 3 hours × £6 | 180,000 |
| Volume variance | 9,000 (A) |

Fixed overhead efficiency variance

|  | £ |
|---|---|
| Standard hours for actual production @ standard OAR 9,500 × 3 hours × £6 | 171,000 |
| Actual hours @ standard OAR 29,000 × £6 | 174,000 |
| Efficiency variance | 3,000 (A) |

*Fixed overhead capacity variance*

| | £ |
|---|---:|
| Actual hours @ standard OAR 29,000 × £6 | 174,000 |
| Budgeted hours @ standard OAR 10,000 × 3 × £6 | 180,000 |
| Capacity variance | 6,000 (A) |

## Task 4

| | £ | £ | £ |
|---|---|---|---|
| Budgeted/Standard cost for actual production | | | 47,976 |
| Variances | Favourable | Adverse | |
| Direct materials price | | 860 | |
| Direct materials usage | 426 | | |
| Direct labour rate | 820 | | |
| Direct labour efficiency | | 1,530 | |
| Fixed overhead expenditure | | 250 | |
| Fixed overhead volume | 560 | | |
| Total variance | 1,806 F | 2,640 A | 834 A |
| Actual cost of actual production | | | 48,810 |

### Workings

Standard cost of actual production.

Budgeted cost per unit = £42,559/1,100 = £38.69 per unit

Budgeted cost of 1,240 units = £38.69 × 1,240 = £47,976

Fixed overhead expenditure variance – actual overheads larger than budgeted, therefore expenditure variance is adverse.

Direct materials usage variance – budgeted usage = 5,280/1,100 = 4.8 litres/unit

Actual usage = 5,800/1,240 =4.68 litres/unit ie lower usage than budgeted so favourable.

Labour rate variance – budgeted rate = £23,375/2,750 = £8.50 per hour

Actual rate = £27,060/3,280 = £8.25 per hour ie lower rate than budgeted, so favourable.

# Task 5

(a) The cost index for July 20X9 based on May 20X9 being the base period of 100 is:

103.8

**Workings**

Cost per kg for May = £50,000/5,000kg = £10 per kg

Cost per kg for July = £55,000/5,300kg = £10.38 per kg

Therefore July's index = £10.38/£10 × 100 = 103.8

(b) In August 20X9, the cost index is 110 (where May 20X9 is the base period of 100). If the total cost is £60,500, the number of kg purchased is 5,500 kg.

**Workings**

Cost per kg in May is £10 per kg

So cost in August = £10/100 × 110 = £11 per kg

Therefore, number of kg purchased = £60,500/£11 = 5,500 kg.

# Task 6

**Report**

**To:** A Finance Director

**From:** An Accountant

**Date:** 14 April 20X2

**Subject:** Last month's variances

I enclose (in the appendix) an operating statement reconciling the standard cost of actual production last month to the actual cost.

**Fixed overhead variances**

The total fixed overhead variance is a favourable variance £14,000. £14,000 more fixed overheads were absorbed than were actually incurred.

Only £2,000 of this favourable variance is due to the actual fixed overheads being lower than the budgeted fixed overheads (this difference is the fixed overhead expenditure variance). Therefore, a manager responsible for incurring fixed overheads, can only be credited with a saving of £2,000.

The remaining £12,000 variance is caused by the volume of units produced being greater than expected. The volume was greater entirely because of increased efficiency of labour – more units (11,000) were produced in the labour hours available (5,520) than were expected (10,500).

None of the favourable variance was due to the company having greater capacity than expected (nil capacity variance) as the actual hours worked were equal to those budgeted.

## Appendix

### Reconciliation statement for last month

|  | £ | £ | £ |
|---|---|---|---|
| Budgeted cost (W) |  |  | 528,000 |
| **Cost variances** | F | A |  |
| Material A price | 4,500 |  |  |
| Material A usage |  | 2,500 |  |
| Material B price |  | 6,200 |  |
| Material B usage | 4,000 |  |  |
| Direct wages rate |  | 10,500 |  |
| Direct wages efficiency | 4,000 |  |  |
| Fixed overhead expenditure | 2,000 |  |  |
| Fixed overhead efficiency | 12,000 |  |  |
| Fixed overhead capacity | 0 |  |  |
|  | 26,500 | 19,200 | 7,300 F |
| Actual cost (£108,000 + £68,200 + £94,500 + £250,000) |  |  | 520,700 |

## Workings

### Standard absorption cost per unit

|  |  |  | £ | £ |
|---|---|---|---|---|
| Direct material A | 4 kg | @ | 2.50 | 10.00 |
| Direct material B | 6 kg | @ | 1.00 | 6.00 |
| Labour | 0.5 hrs | @ | 16.00 | 8.00 |
| Fixed overhead | 300% of direct labour |  |  | 24.00 |
| Total standard cost |  |  |  | 48.00 |

Therefore, standard cost for actual production = 11,000 × £48 = £528,000

## Cost variances

### Material A price variance

|  | £ |
|---|---|
| 45,000 should have cost (× £2.50) | 112,500 |
| But did cost | 108,000 |
|  | 4,500 Fav |

### Material A usage variance

|  |  |
|---|---|
| 11,000 should have used (× 4 kg) | 44,000 |
| But did use | 45,000 |
|  | 1,000 Adv |
| × standard rate of £2.50 | × £2.50 |
|  | 2,500 Adv |

### Material B price variance

|  | £ |
|---|---|
| 62,000 should have cost (× £1) | 62,000 |
| But did cost | 68,200 |
|  | 6,200 Adv |

### Material B usage variance

|  |  |
|---|---|
| 11,000 should have used (× 6 kg) | 66,000 |
| But did use | 62,000 |
|  | 4,000 Fav |
| × standard rate | × £1 |
|  | 4,000 Fav |

### Labour rate variance

|  | £ |
|---|---|
| 5,250 hours should have cost (× £16) | 84,000 |
| But did cost | 94,500 |
|  | 10,500 Adv |

## Labour efficiency variance

| | |
|---|---:|
| 11,000 should have taken (× 0.5) | 5,500 |
| But did take | 5,250 |
| | 250 |
| × standard rate | × £16 |
| | 4,000 Fav |

## Fixed overhead expenditure variance

| | £ |
|---|---:|
| Budgeted fixed overhead (£24 × 10,500) | 252,000 |
| Actual fixed overhead | 250,000 |
| | 2,000 Fav |

## Fixed overhead efficiency variance

| | |
|---|---:|
| Standard hours for actual production at standard absorption rate | |
| 11,000 × 0.5 × £48* | 264,000 |
| Actual hours at standard absorption rate | |
| 5,250 × £48 | 252,000 |
| | 12,000 Fav |

*£24 per unit is absorbed, or £24/0.5 = £48 per labour hour

## Fixed overhead capacity variance

| | |
|---|---:|
| Actual hours at standard absorption rate | |
| 5,250 × £48 | 252,000 |
| Budgeted hours at standard absorption rate | |
| 10,500 × 0.5 × £48 | 252,000 |
| | 0 |

# Task 7

|  | January | February | March |
|---|---|---|---|
| Productivity per labour hour | 0.99 units | 1.11 units | 1.00 units |
| Efficiency ratio | 108.78% | 121.96% | 110.47% |
| Capacity ratio | 92.35% | 86.69% | 88.80% |
| Activity ratio | 100.47% | 105.73% | 98.11% |
| Value added per employee | £6,613.00 | £6,445.00 | £5,784.00 |

## Workings

|  |  | January | February | March |
|---|---|---|---|---|
| (i) | Productivity per labour hour | $\dfrac{8,540}{8,635}$ | $\dfrac{8,670}{7,820}$ | $\dfrac{9,320}{9,280}$ |
|  |  | 0.99 units per hour | 1.11 units per hour | 1.00 unit per hour |
| (ii) | Efficiency ratio | $\dfrac{8,540 \times 1.1}{8,635}$ | $\dfrac{8,670 \times 1.1}{7,820}$ | $\dfrac{9,320 \times 1.1}{9,280}$ |
|  |  | 108.78% | 121.96% | 110.47% |
| (iii) | Capacity ratio | $\dfrac{8,635}{8,500 \times 1.1}$ | $\dfrac{7,820}{8,200 \times 1.1}$ | $\dfrac{9,280}{9,500 \times 1.1}$ |
|  |  | 92.35% | 86.69% | 88.80% |
| (iv) | Activity ratio | $\dfrac{8,540}{8,500}$ | $\dfrac{8,670}{8,200}$ | $\dfrac{9,320}{9,500}$ |
|  |  | 100.47% | 105.73% | 98.11% |

|  |  | £ | £ | £ |
|---|---|---|---|---|
| (v) | Value added per employee |  |  |  |
|  | Sales | 916,000 | 923,000 | 965,000 |
|  | Production costs | (552,300) | (568,500) | (629,500) |
|  | Value added | 363,700 | 354,500 | 335,500 |
|  | Value added per employee | £6,613 | £6,445 | £5,784 |

## Task 8

| Product | Units |
|---------|-------|
| A | 1,000 |
| B | 800 |
| C | 466 |

### Workings

1 **Determine the limiting factor**

Material usage per unit of each product:

A £9/£3 = 3 kg per unit
B £6/£3 = 2 kg per unit
C £12/£3 = 4 kg per unit

So maximum sales demand would use:

A 3 kg × 1,000 = 3,000 kg
B 2 kg × 800 = 1,600 kg
C 4 kg × 600 = 2,400 kg

Therefore total materials usage for this demand = 3,000 + 1,600 + 2,400 = 7,000 kg

8,000 kg are available so material is not the limiting factor

Labour hours per unit of each product:

A £6/£12 = 0.5 hours per unit
B £12/£12 = 1 hour per unit
C £18/£12 = 1.5 hours per unit

So maximum sales demand would require:

A 0.5 × 1,000 = 500 hours
B 1 × 800 = 800 hours
C 1.5 × 600 = 900 hours

Therefore, total labour hours for this demand = 500 + 800 + 900 = 2,200 hours
Only 2,000 hours are available so labour hours is a limiting factor.

2 **Contribution per limiting factor:**

A (£20 – £9 – £6)/0.5 = £10 per labour hour
B (£30 – £12 – £6)/1 = £12 per labour hour
C (£40 – £12 – £18)/1.5 = £6.67 per labour hour

Therefore, rank B, A and then C.

3 **Production to maximise contribution**

B 800 units use 800 hours
A 1,000 units use 500 hours, so 1,300 hours used so far
C Remaining 2,000 – 1,300 = 700 hours can be used for product C. Makes 700/1.5 = 466 units.

## Task 9

(a)

| Overhead included in Product X | £20,400 |
|---|---|
| Overhead included in Product Y | £81,600 |

**Workings**

| Maintenance cost per visit = | | £102,000/50 | = | £2,040 |
|---|---|---|---|---|
| Product X | = 10 × £2,040 | = | £20,400 | |
| Product Y | = 40 × £2,040 | = | £81,600 | |

(b)  Maximum £ per kg = £2.00

|  | £ |
|---|---|
| Selling price | 35.00 |
| 40% margin | 14.00 |
| Target cost | 21.00 |
| Less | |
| Labour       1 hr @ £6/hr | (6.00) |
| Overheads   1 hr @ £7/hr | (7.00) |
| Available for 4kg material | 8.00 |
| Maximum price per kg | £2.00 |

## Task 10

(a)

| Gross profit margin | 30% |
|---|---|
| Operating profit margin | 23% |
| Direct materials cost per unit | £3 per unit |
| Receivables' collection period in days | 73 days |

**Workings**

Gross profit = $\dfrac{£1,200,000}{£4,000,000} \times 100 = 30\%$

Operating profit margin = $\dfrac{£905,000}{£4,000,000} \times 100 = 23\%$

Direct materials cost per unit = $\dfrac{£1,500,000}{500,000} = £3$ per unit

Receivables' collection period in days = $\dfrac{£800,000}{£4,000,000} \times 365 = 73$ days

(b) **To:**              Finance Director

    **Subject:**      Key performance indicators

    **From:**        Accounting Technician

    **Date:**         26 October 20X2

(i) **Gross profit margin – selling price to achieve industry margin**

The current gross profit margin is 30% but the industry margin is 35%. Therefore, for the same level of costs, the sales price would have to increase to £8.62 per unit.

(ii) **Operating profit margin – percentage reduction in administration costs**

For an operating profit margin of 25% when the only cost/revenue that can change is administration costs, these would have to decrease by 45.24%

(iii) **Receivables' collection period – change to achieve industry average**

Receivables would have to reduce by £87,671 to achieve the industry average of receivables' days of 65, for this level of revenue.

**Workings**

(i) Gross profit margin of 35%

Cost of sales = £2,800,000

Revenue would have to be £2,800,000/65% = £4,307,692

Sales price per unit would have to be £4,307,692/500,000 = £8.62

(ii) Operating profit margin of 25%

Operating profit/revenue = 25%

Revenue would be unchanged, so operating profit would be 25% × £4,000,000 = £1,000,000 ie an increase of £95,000.

Therefore, fixed administration overheads would have to decrease by £95,000.

Percentage reduction in fixed administration overheads = £95,000/£210,000 = 45.24%

(iii) Industry receivables' days are 65 days

Revenue × 65/365 = receivables

£4,000,000 × 65/365 = £712,329

Reduction in receivables = £800,000 – £712,329 = £87,671

**Notes**

**Notes**